100 THINGS
FLAMES FANS
SHOULD KNOW & DO
BEFORE THEY DIE

George Johnson

TRIUMPH
BOOKS

Library of Congress Cataloging-in-Publication Data

Names: Johnson, George, 1957– author.
Title: 100 things Flames fans should know & do before they die / George Johnson.
Other titles: One hundred things Flames fans should know and do before they die
Description: Chicago, Illinois : Triumph Books LLC, [2017]
Identifiers: LCCN 2017019817 | ISBN 9781629372280
Subjects: LCSH: Calgary Flames (Hockey team)—Miscellanea. | Calgary Flames (Hockey team)—History. | Hockey—Alberta—History—Miscellanea. | National Hockey League—Miscellanea.
Classification: LCC GV848.C25 J64 2017 | DDC 796.962/64097123—dc23 LC record available at https://lccn.loc.gov/2017019817

This book is available in quantity at special discounts for your group or organization. For further information, contact:

Triumph Books LLC
814 North Franklin Street
Chicago, Illinois 60610
(312) 337-0747
www.triumphbooks.com

Printed in U.S.A.
ISBN: 978-1-62937-228-0
Design by Patricia Frey
All photos courtesy of AP Images

For Flames fans

Contents

Foreword

When I was I living in Russell, Manitoba, I remember we played against Sheldon and Troy Kennedy in this tournament, and the winning team got tickets to a Winnipeg Jets game. And it just happened to be that famous game between Colorado and Winnipeg—whoever lost got the lower pick in the draft. We won our game, and I managed to have enough money to buy a program at the old Winnipeg Arena. So I had my program, and I ran down to where the Rockies were coming off the ice and I got Lanny McDonald's autograph. I was 12 years old.

Eleven years later we were both carrying the Stanley Cup around the Montreal Forum. And at my first training camp, who was I sitting next to in the main locker room? Lanny. So, looking back, that game when I was a kid might've been some foreshadowing of my future relationship with him.

Being in Calgary when I started out was essential for my development. To have the type of teammates I had at the time made all the difference in the world. Nobody thought I'd play one game in the National Hockey League, so I'll be forever grateful. Scout Ian McKenzie saw something in me no one else did. And the rest is history.

In that first camp, I needed to make the organization believe I could be a full-time NHL player. I knew that wasn't going to be easy. I remember one day playing against Otts (Joel Otto), in one of the scrimmages, and him trying to beat the crap out of me. I remember Jim Peplinski giving me one of his well-placed elbows. But I left that training camp and went back to Moose Jaw with a lot more belief that I could actually do it.

I'll never forget playing a game that camp against the Canadian Olympic team, looking to my left, and there was John Tonelli—I'd grown up a huge Islanders fan, when they were winning all those Cups—and looking to my right and there was Lanny McDonald—and Lanny's…well, *Lanny*. An iconic figure. And I'm thinking, *This is so cool!*

In Calgary, not only were you expected to be a great hockey player, you were expected to be a citizen of Calgary, involved in the community, to give back to the charities. That's one thing that sets Calgary apart from any other community I've been around: the degree of giving back. With the team, that came right from the top—from Harley Hotchkiss, Doc and B.J. Seaman. They set the tone, set the standards.

I'm a Western Canadian kid. I love Calgary. I still live in the city. I love the people in the city. I've transitioned into another part of my life, but the lessons I learned while I was playing, while I was a Calgary Flame, haven't changed. The people in the city really take care of us, and that's really cool, too.

Calgary lives and dies with the team. So it's nice to see the old Saddledome alive again and people excited about the team again. They're definitely moving in the right direction. With guys such as Johnny Gaudreau and Sean Monahan and T.J. Brodie and Sam Bennett, they've got a good core of players who are going to be around a long time.

It's a great organization. I played in other organizations, but I'll always consider myself a Calgary Flame. Of course. I can't remember how many rounds went by in the draft. Twenty? And they gave me a chance when no one else would. For that, I'll forever be loyal, forever be grateful. I have a flaming *C* tattooed on my heart.

—Theoren Fleury
February 5, 2016

1 May 25, 1989

All these years later, Lanny McDonald still hasn't sat down in front of his flat-screen TV and watched Game 6 from start to finish. Oh, he's often seen highlights. Snippets. Bits and pieces.

The images never change: His younger self, peeling away, arms outstretched, after cashing a diagonal Joe Nieuwendyk pass beyond Montreal netminder Patrick Roy at 4:24 of the second period to establish a 2–1 Calgary Flames lead. The indomitable Doug Gilmour slotting into an empty Montreal net—Roy at the end of the Habs bench—at 18:57 of the third to seal the deal. The gutted but gracious crowd at the fabled old Montreal Forum staying put to salute the only invaders ever to lift the big silver chalice on their hallowed ice. McDonald's own hands wrapped around the Stanley Cup, at the center of the commemorative keepsake on-ice photo, flanked by GM Cliff Fletcher and Nieuwendyk, goaltender Mike Vernon popping up just behind him.

"I could probably play the majority of the game, shift by shift, if I just closed my eyes," the emotional fulcrum of the Calgary Flames' only Stanley Cup–winning march said more than a quarter century later.

They'd done it. Broken the reign of the dynastic Edmonton Oilers, their northern tormentors for so long. Exorcised the demons. After battling through a near loss in round one versus Vancouver, followed by a sweep of the L.A. Kings, the Flames had ousted the Chicago Blackhawks in five games to reach the Finals against hockey's most storied, revered franchise, the Montreal Canadiens. The Canadiens had Roy, Chris Chelios at his snarly

1

best, the sleek Mats Naslund up front, and Pat Burns behind the bench.

It had been a difficult season for McDonald, the Flames' most beloved icon, as a new era dawned in Calgary. The man with the mustache had been shuffled in and out of the lineup during 82 games and then through the playoffs. He'd sat out Game 5's 3–2 Flames win that had put the Campbell Conference champions one night away from the ultimate prize: the Stanley Cup. Given the opponent, the venue, and the stakes, these Flames needed that certain something only Lanny McDonald's presence in the lineup could provide.

"[Assistant coach] Doug Risebrough called me into the trainers' room," recalled McDonald. "He didn't even say it in those words—'You're in the lineup.' All he said was, 'Do you know where you've got to be in all situations?' That was his way of telling me.

"I'll never forget, I'm looking over [Risebrough's] shoulder and there's Bearcat [trainer Jim Murray] kinda peeking around the corner—[Risebrough had] kicked him out of the room—and he let out a whoop, then goes into the room to tell the rest of the players. And I heard a little bit of a cheer. So it was pretty cool."

In a series so evenly matched, the karma of a 16-year unfulfilled quest by one of the modern game's classiest players proved to be the difference. "We kept saying in the dressing room, 'Let's win this for Lanny,'" said Vernon amidst the celebrations that night.

Echoed head coach Terry Crisp: "He is the kind of leader words cannot describe. We hoped that by putting him back in, we'd get a lift for this team, not only emotionally in the dressing room but physically on the ice. And that's what we got."

Game 6 followed the tight style of its five predecessors—none decided by more than two goals. Checking winger Colin Patterson opened scoring, the only goal of the first period. After the nefarious Claude Lemieux equalized early in the second stanza, McDonald broke out with Nieuwendyk and fleet Swedish left winger Hakan Loob. There was less chance of legendary Dunn's famous deli taking Montreal smoked meat off the menu than the old pro McDonald missing the net on that chance.

Because of the emotional resonance of that goal, people still assume it was the game winner. Sorry. Officially, that went to Gilmour, who swatted his first of the game and 10th of the playoffs out of the air at 11:02 of the third during a power play for a 3–1 Calgary advantage. Habs defenseman Rick Green, of all people, pulled one back before Gilmour hit the empty net.

"Storybook?" said McDonald—who would announce his retirement later that summer—in the cramped visiting quarters at the Forum. "I don't know if it's storybook or not. But it certainly is a hell of a way to write the final chapter. This is the most powerful feeling ever in hockey."

Asked about how it felt to finally lift Lord Stanley's chalice, he said, "You know, there isn't an awful lot to it. It's nice to hold. It's the nicest feeling in the world. You feel like you could carry it forever. And I think I will." In the imaginations of Calgarians, and Flames fans everyone, he always has.

The city of oil and stampeding has enjoyed its share of sporting highlights over the years—an Olympic Games in 1988, seven Grey Cup championships in the Canadian Football League—but May 25, 1989, remains special, apart, unique.

For Crisp, a two-time Cup champion as a player in Philadelphia, there was a special kind of satisfaction. He'd taken the best assemblage of talent and won with it. "That's why I admire Scotty Bowman so much," explained Crisp. "Yeah, he had thoroughbreds, but I'll tell ya, as a coach it's often harder to coach thoroughbreds than Mennonite plow horses. It's easy to get the Mennonite plow horses up and working. When you have thoroughbreds, they all want to be first to the starting gate. They all want to be on the power play. They all want the ice time.

"Try keeping them happy. They're all good, but you can't put 'em all on the ice at once. Hell, the hockey, the *X*s and *O*s, is easy. It's the people management. When do you tap a guy, when do you pull him in, when do you turn him loose?"

The players would eventually disperse, torn apart by a shifting economic landscape in the NHL and the passage of time, but together they forged an exceptional season, a tremendous playoff run that bonds them together even now.

As a member of the ultraexclusive Triple Gold Club—reserved for those who've won a Stanley Cup, a World Championship, and an Olympic gold medal—right winger Hakan Loob is uniquely qualified to judge which carries the most luster. "Oh," replied the silky Swede without hesitation a few years back. "The Stanley Cup. Not even close. Take out a knife or a pistol…I'll never change my mind about that. It's special.

"Ask guys who have never won it. They'd pay, lie, cheat, or steal—whatever they had to—to lift it. Cut off their arm. People visit the Hockey Hall of Fame, and you see these kids and their dads just staring at it. It's the Stanley Cup. It's magic."

2 The Move North

They arrived from the deep American South. From the land of Peachtree Street, soft summer breezes rustling through resplendent azaleas, and wonderful gabled mansions fronted by towering columns. From Scarlett and Rhett and "Frankly my dear, I don't give a damn" land.

The Atlanta Flames were born in 1971, along with the New York Islanders, in response to the threat posed by the fledgling

World Hockey Association. Their competitive history could, at best, be considered checkered, qualifying for the playoffs in six of their eight seasons but never advancing past the first round, and winning only two games during that stretch.

Hockey at their home, the Omni, certainly had its moments. It had the Rebel, a superfan outfitted in Confederate garb, charging up and down the aisles waving a Confederate flag. It had the Painted Lady, a busty miss who'd squeeze into low-cut dresses, paint a flaming *A* across her ample bosom, and primp behind the opposition net during warm-ups. For a while it had the legendary Bernie "Boom Boom" Geoffrion—flamboyant, outspoken—as coach ("His voice," wrote one Atlanta sportswriter, was "like rich, thick French onion soup").

There were individual player highlights: two Calder Trophy winners in Eric Vail (1974–75) and Willi Plett (1975–76), a Lady Byng Memorial Trophy recipient in Bob MacMillan (1978–79), and a 50-goal scorer in Guy Chouinard (1978–79).

Hockey as a sport was as foreign to Atlanta as swimsuits to Alaska, but over their existence the Flames did develop a hard-core group of fans. The problem was that group wasn't nearly large enough, often enough. Attendance peaked in the team's second year, averaging 14,161 fans per game. But that number quickly began to erode. Relocation rumors surfaced as early as 1976, with players and local politicians buying season tickets to help stanch the bleeding.

"First," reminisced winger Tom Lysiak a decade after the move north (which eventually happened in 1980), "you'd get your Falcons and Braves season tickets. Then basketball. So we were fourth. If you had enough money and enough time, there we were."

In retrospect, general manager Cliff Fletcher felt three key factors worked against the team's viability: the location of the Omni, the size of the Omni, and a lack of revenue from a local TV deal. The absence of luxury suites in the area, becoming a huge

5

money earner for teams housed in newer buildings, also didn't help. Neither did the lack of postseason success. "There was no urgency to be a winner," said Al MacNeil, the final coach in Atlanta Flames history.

In what would turn out to be their swan-song season in Atlanta, the team averaged only 10,024 fans per game. Owner Tom Cousins, rumored to have lost $12 million over the eight years of the franchise's existence, announced his intention to sell. In stepped two prominent Calgary businessmen, Doc and B. J. Seaman. They quickly enlisted another friend, Harley Hotchkiss. Working closely with Alberta premier Peter Lougheed and the provincial government, they began their quest. At the time, Calgary had its sights set on hosting the 1988 Winter Olympics. To do that, a new, state-of-the-art arena had to be built.

All the stars seemed to be in alignment. Then in stepped Vancouver-based wheeler-dealer Nelson Skalbania. Skalbania flew his daughter down to Atlanta and, using an up-front deal involving cash, scooped the Flames out from under the noses of the Calgary group for $16 million. Within a week after bringing a pair of business associates—Normie Kwong and Norm Green—on board, Skalbania, without the necessary cash to move forward properly and looking for quick payday, sold 49 percent of the team to the Calgary group. By July of the next year, the Calgary business consortium had it all.

Originally the ownership breakdown went this way: Hotchkiss, the Seaman brothers, Green, and ski hill operator Ralph Scurfield owned 18 percent apiece, and Kwong, a former Canadian Football League star, owned 10 percent. A solid, dedicated foundation. The Flames—as the Calgary Flames—were off and running.

For the players from Atlanta, forced to uproot, the relocation had to be jarring. What did they miss about Atlanta? "Well," reasoned rugged winger Plett, "the weather is nice [in Atlanta]. No silly snow to mess with."

"There was a lot of grumbling initially," recalled defenseman Paul Reinhart. "But I remember Alan Eagleson calling me and saying, 'Paul, give it a chance. This will be the best move you've ever made.'" Turns out, Eagleson was right. About this, at any rate.

Reinhart, like many of the Atlanta Flames, traveled to Calgary to begin the new chapter but would be gone when the team finally hit pay dirt.

For the franchise, though, the shift was a positive boon from the get-go. They were immediately accepted and adored by the Calgary community, playing in front of sellout crowds in first the tiny Corral and then the sumptuous Olympic Saddledome.

When the Flames finally lifted the Stanley Cup nine years after clearing out of the Deep South, the old-timers from Atlanta were watching. "Kinda like my ex-wife winning the lottery," is how center Curt Bennett, who retired the year the franchise moved, described the feeling. "Excited, but…"

3 The Corral: First Home

It held only 8,700 souls. Each seat for each game cost $25. Such was the clamor to attend, standing-room-only places were all of 18 inches apart. The first year, 10,000 full- and part-time season tickets were sold. If ever a place epitomized the old supply-and-demand rule, the Calgary (now Stampede) Corral was it.

In 1980 the NHL arrived in southern Alberta with the Calgary Flames, and with it the chance to see Wayne Gretzky, Mike Bossy, Denis Potvin, Marcel Dionne, and the rest of the league's glittering stars playing for visiting teams. The outcry for tickets, predictably, was noisy and far-reaching.

When the Corral opened three decades earlier, in 1950, at the then-staggering cost of $1.25 million to replace the old Victoria Arena and house the Calgary Stampeders Pacific Coast League pro hockey club, it instantly became the largest arena west of Toronto. A litany of famous entertainers and acts—Duke Ellington, Bill Haley and the Comets, Fats Domino, Louis Armstrong—performed there over the years. By the time the Flames relocated from Atlanta and got around to tenancy, though, the onetime showpiece seemed outdated, cramped, a relic removed from another, distant time.

The Corral had already once been deemed insufficient by the NHL, in 1977, forcing the World Hockey Association Calgary Cowboys to fold rather than try to become part of the WHA-NHL merger that welcomed Winnipeg, Hartford, and Quebec City into the established circuit. But the International Olympic Committee had thrown Calgary and its NHL dreams a lifeline. Soon to be seen going up across the street from the Corral, on the Stampede Grounds—its shadow growing ever larger—was the Olympic Saddledome, a $97.7 million state-of-the-art arena tied to the city's successful bid for the 1988 Winter Olympic Games.

If in 1983 the Saddledome arrived with all the attending bells and whistles, its predecessor—the Corral—still possessed a unique, quirky charm. "It was barely adequate," remembered coach Al MacNeil. "The psychological thing was that everything was too small except the boards, which were four or five inches higher than any other building in the league.

"We had a big team. The other club looked at us and said, 'Well, we're going to get killed in here!' It kinda took the edge off their interest in playing that night."

Inside the cozy, claustrophobic—visiting teams might use the term *oppressive*—confines of the Corral, the Flames flourished. Over three seasons housed there, they compiled a rather impressive 66–28–26 record, including an amazing first-year record of 25–5–10.

"It was like a gladiator pit," recalled right winger Lanny McDonald, who scored many of his single-season franchise-record 66 goals there during the 1982–83 season, the year before the team move to the Saddledome. "You'd walk out from the dressing room right through the crowd, it seemed, and onto the ice. Just an amazing place to play. There was such a great atmosphere in that old barn."

The benches were small, narrow and, believe it or not, tiered. The boards, again, were higher than NHL standard. So high, joked winger Jim Peplinski, "Theoren Fleury never would've made the NHL playing in that building. He might've killed himself jumping from the bench onto the ice."

The Flames players of that era remember the experience fondly. Peplinski recalls signing so many autographs for one fan named Danny that the young man presented him with a bottle of English Leather cologne as a thank-you gift.

"Our dressing room was on the other side of the lobby, so at the end of every period and the beginning of every period, we'd have to walk through the crowd," recalled defenseman Bob Murdoch. "They had cardboard down on the floor so we didn't wreck the edges of our skates.

"If you played a horseshit game, fans were yelling and screaming at you. You go out for the warm-up, you come back. You go out for the first period, you come back. You're walking the gauntlet six times at night. And there was no hiding. Everybody had access to you while they were buying their hot dogs and popcorn."

Trainer Bearcat Murray's room had nothing more than a chair and training table. The Flames dressing room was Spartan, the size of a water closet. ("Just big enough," recalled Peplinski, "for Bobby MacMillan to have a smoke.") Four showers, one toilet, two urinals.

"Those boards," sighed Murray. "Rigid, about shoulder height. Guys that got hammered into those boards, it was like pushing them into a cement wall. Which it was, because the seats behind it were cement, right up against the boards. They had no give. Today, you can see boards rattling all the way down, one end to the other. I can remember there were a lot of injuries, mostly shoulder injuries, from that."

Yet the players of that era enjoyed their brief tenure there immensely. "There's a photo outside the dressing room we used to use," said Peplinski. "It's still there, of the 30th birthday party for the Corral. A bunch of us are in it, and I distinctly remember Guy Chouinard singing that day—'Happy birthday to you, happy birthday to you, happy birthday dear Co-raaaaaaaal.' And then he turns to me and says: 'What am I doing?'"

The Saddledome (above) saw plenty of action over the years, but it never held the same mystique as the Corral.

The opening of the Saddledome was understandably met with much fanfare. It allowed 19,000 people to watch in person the team that had become a city's passion. Those 18-inch standing-room-only spots were a thing of the past.

In March 2016 the Calgary Stampede announced that plans to sacrifice the 66-year-old facility were being drawn up in a half-billion-dollar expansion at Stampede Park that would double the size of the nearby BMO Center.

A lot of memories are stored in that old barn. "When we left for the Saddledome, it was time," recalled winger Jamie Hislop. "But I did enjoy the years at the Corral, for sure. It was such a huge advantage for us. Darker than any NHL building. Small, the fans—and they were loud—right on top of you. High boards so the ice surface seemed small. I'm sure teams coming in there took a first look and said to themselves, 'What is this?'"

4 Beating Philly

There were easier places to venture into to wage a winner-take-all showdown back in the day. The Black Hole of Calcutta, for instance. Or the Marquis de Sade's personal playroom.

"Going into the Spectrum back then," mused Jim Peplinski, "was like that moment in *Gladiator*, remember, where the guys are walking into the Colosseum and a few of them are peeing their pants? You get the picture. It was an intimidating place to play, to put it mildly."

That's where Game 7 of the Calgary Flames–Philadelphia Flyers second-round playoff series of 1981 would be contested. Not that the love affair between the first-season Flames and their new city hadn't already taken root, of course, but a series triumph against the big, bad Flyers would amp up the relationship to a whole different octave.

"We had a very, very good team at that time," said Calgary's key defenseman of the era, Paul Reinhart. "They were in their heyday—Clarke, Barber, Leach, Kenny Linseman, the Rat. Not the Broad Street Bullies of old, I suppose, but pretty darn close.

"People forget, though, that we were the biggest team in the league that year—Willi Plett, Guy Chouinard, Eric Vail, Pep, Kenny Houston, Phil Russell—and were physically able to stand up to the Flyers.

"Beyond all the crap, and it had its share of that, that was an intense, intense series with an awful lot of great hockey."

The Flames had never won a playoff series during their years in Atlanta but began their Canadian account by sweeping aside Chicago in the minimum three games in the spring of 1981.

Then it was on to the waiting Flyers, which was a vastly different proposition. Sure, Calgary had gone 2–2 against the two-time Stanley Cup champions during the seasonal series and trailed them by only five points (97 to 92) in the Patrick Division standings during the regular campaign. Still, this was a Philly team that had reached the Finals the year before while piecing together a record 35-game unbeaten streak. So when the upstart Flames were thumped 4–0 in the opener, all seemed to be on course with the world. But they stormed back for 5–4, 2–1, and 5–4 wins to jump out to a 3–1 series lead.

"Then we got overconfident, if you can believe it," laughed Peplinski. "I think we were reasonably satisfied after beating Chicago. Not sure we expected to beat Philadelphia, especially with four games at the Spectrum.

"But after we were up 3–1 we got really quite cocky. It's amazing how after only six days you can go from 'Let's not embarrass ourselves' to 'We've got this in the bag.'"

The favored Flyers rebounded for 9–4 and 3–2 wins to send the slugfest the distance. And back to their pit of doom.

"There was a part of that series the guys playing today would never understand," recalled Reinhart. "And that was the schedule. We played back-to-back, travel day, back-to-back, travel day. Four games in five nights. In the playoffs. And we flew commercial.

"The exception was Game 7, when we had a charter going to Philly. But even with a charter, I think we had to stop along the way."

Game 7 loomed. The Flyers were reinstalled as a heavy favorite to move on to the semifinals. "Bruce Hood refereed that night," recalled Peplinski. "He called, if memory serves me correctly, three elbowing penalties on Paul Holmgren. I couldn't believe that a referee would go into the Spectrum in Philadelphia at that time, in 1981, and call three penalties like that in such an important game. To have that kind of courage…I said to myself, 'Bruce Hood, you have a pass from me for the rest of my life.' I just thought, *What an example of integrity and courage.*"

The Flyers' poor discipline and Calgary's power play proved the difference. The Flyers were tagged for too many men just 1:26 into the first period, and Plett deflected a Chouinard pass behind Philly goalie Rick St. Croix to stake the visitors to a shocking lead. Five minutes later, with Holmgren incarcerated, Ken Houston doubled the lead on a two-on-one pass from Chouinard.

Kevin LaVallee hit for Calgary's third power play goal of the night before Bill Barber briefly pulled the hosts back into it. But a third-period Bob MacMillan tip-in sealed the deal.

The Flames would go on to lose the next round in six games to Minnesota, a regret that lingers to this day with many of that edition. "Minnesota was, I don't know how to say it, a 'different' kind of series," said Reinhart. "When you play a seven-game series against the Flyers, and four them are in the Spectrum, you can't help but be a little tired, mentally as much as physically."

But in beating Philadelphia, the first-year Calgary Flames had set the bar higher than ever before and won over a city. "That series, that entire playoff, established an elevated degree of confidence in almost every player," said Reinhart. "Including me.

"It was also a bit of a defining moment for the organization. That playoff performance, just winning the first series, let alone second, changed the mentality and the history of that franchise and helped bring us into the present, helped separate us from the Atlanta days."

5 Something...Missing

Nurtured in the most regal, the most historic, the most ambitious of environments, Al MacNeil was in for a shock when he packed up and moved to the Deep South. "I mean," said the last coach of the Atlanta incarnation of the Flames and the first coach of Calgary's, "I [came] out of a Montreal Canadiens setup where Sam Pollock, two days after we'd win another Cup, he'd be the most unhappy guy in the world because he's already looking ahead, wondering how he's going to compete next year.

"He was happy with the achievement, Sam. But he never celebrated. He was forever looking ahead, never satisfied. There was a restlessness in him, a standard there, in Montreal, that never wavered.

"You couldn't translate that sort of culture into a club that had come out of a non-hockey environment like Atlanta. It was a stretch to think everybody was going to buy in on it."

After a 524-game NHL career as a rock-solid defenseman, Al MacNeil coached the Montreal Voyageurs for the 1969–70 season before being hired by the Montreal Canadiens as an assistant to Claude Ruel. He became the head coach after Ruel resigned during the 1970–71 season and went on to coach the Canadiens to the Stanley Cup that season. After being demoted to coaching the Canadiens' American Hockey League affiliate, the Nova Scotia Voyageurs, he led the team to three Calder Cup Championships in six years. Later he briefly returned to the Habs as director of player personnel and helped the team collect two more titles, in 1978 and 1979.

Coaching remained in his blood. Hooking up with an old friend, Atlanta GM Cliff Fletcher, MacNeil left the Canadiens cocoon to replace Fred Creighton behind the Flames bench in the summer of 1979.

MacNeil said, "I'd already lived in Houston, playing for Montreal's farm club. I thought Atlanta was a good spot to land. I liked the weather. Who wouldn't? I also liked the club. A big club. Skill. Toughness. I thought there was a lot of potential. But the lifestyle down there really legislated against really competing. When you come out of an operation like Montreal, all drive all the time, then to go down to a laid-back, laconic environment, well, they never exactly achieved the level they should've. There was just something…missing."

In his only Atlanta season, the Flames accumulated 83 points during the regular season before tumbling in the first round of the playoffs to the NY Rangers in four games. With attendance dipping (down to an average of 10,024 in 1978–79) and losses mounting (a reported $12 million over the previous eight seasons), owner Tom Cousins began to listen to offers to move the franchise.

"When I went down [to Atlanta]," said MacNeil, "I certainly didn't realize the club would be leaving. Then, geez, lo and behold, he up and sells to [Nelson] Skalbania, under the noses of Harley [Hotchkiss] and Doc [Seaman] and those guys, who were legitimately in it to bring the club to Calgary. Slipped the club right out from underneath them, brought the club here, and then sold them 49 percent. Eventually, of course, they bought him out."

The inaugural season in Calgary would solidify the team in the public consciousness. "That first year," MacNeil admitted, "all the stars lined up together." The Magic Man, Kent Nilsson, dazzled, piling up 131 points, a club record. Big Willi Plett scored 38 goals, Guy Chouinard 31. Their home rink, the claustrophobic Corral, proved to be a fortress.

Playoffs were even sweeter. After dusting Chicago in the minimum three games, the Flames upset Philadelphia over seven to reach the conference final. "We were so elated to get even that far," said MacNeil, "when we got around to playing Minny there was no push there. We didn't even show." The Flames were ousted in six by the North Stars.

In Nilsson, they possessed a superstar. They had good goaltending in Pat Riggin and Reggie Lemelin. For that era, they had size to spare in Plett (6'3", 205 pounds), Eric "Big Train" Vail (6'1", 220 pounds), Jim Peplinski (6'3", 210 pounds), Phil Russell (6'2", 200 pounds), and Brad Marsh (6'3", 220 pounds). But as MacNeil said, something was…missing.

"Eric Vail," he said reflectively, "was probably as gifted a left winger as ever laced on skates. But he had an average career instead of being a superstar. The result is, the club he's on never wins the big prize. There's a lot of guys like that. A ton of guys like that. He had everything. Size. Could skate. He could handle himself. Great touch. You'd just drool, the way he could skate down the side and shoot. But…

"Willi Plett was a really good hockey player. A feared guy in the league, genuinely tough. Bobby MacMillan. [Paul] Reinhart. [Guy] Chouinard. So you look at it, piece by piece, and you're thinking, *We've really got something here.* But if your core group isn't totally committed, completely invested, then all the rest of them go along too."

That was the beginning of the reimagining of the Flames, and the gradual dismantling of the team that had pulled up stakes and moved north. "Cliff had to change things," he continued. "There just wasn't enough commitment. When you come to the realization you can get this high with what you've got, but no higher, that's when decisions are made. It took a while. But we got there."

6 The Magic Man

His gifts were singular. Beyond analysis. There was an almost ethereal effortlessness about it all. Watch the old, slightly grainy tapes, and even in a game that seems so distant from today's, the power of No. 14—Kent Nilsson—to astound remains undiminished.

He was christened the Magic Man. And that fit, except that magic, at its root, is about deception and deceit. Nilsson's audaciousness was as pure as the water in a mountain stream. He was hockey's Peter Pan, the incorrigible man-boy who never grew up.

Pre–Mario Lemieux, Wayne Gretzky once called him the most talented player he'd seen ("Nice of him," said Nilsson, "but not true"). But along with the talent came the curse. Nothing was ever good enough. People always expected more. No matter what Nilsson did, so many seemed somehow disappointed. His quick wit and fun-loving attitude were put down by many as nothing more than a lack of caring.

The numbers, though, looking back, are pretty darn good. In 345 games as a Calgary Flame, Kent Nilsson registered 469 points. Throw in his one year in Atlanta, 93 points in 80 starts, and that's a mighty impressive haul for a franchise.

When the Atlanta Flames chose Nilsson in the draft from Winnipeg as part of the WHA merger with the NHL, Jets general manager John Ferguson told Calgary counterpart Cliff Fletcher that the Swede was the purest natural talent he'd ever seen. High praise, indeed, from Fergie, a guy who'd been around the likes of Jean Beliveau, Yvan Cournoyer, Guy Lafleur, and the great Montreal Canadiens stars. Ferguson warned Fletcher, "He'll also drive you absolutely nuts!"

That first year after the team relocated from Georgia ranks as arguably the finest by any player in Flames history. Nilsson's eye-popping numbers—49 goals, 82 assists, 131 points—are off-the-dial stunning.

To illustrate just how truly dominant he was that season, next on the Calgary scoring charts was Guy Chouinard, a whopping 48 points in arrears. Wayne Gretzky—surprise!—won the 1980–81 Art Ross Trophy, with 164 points. L.A. Kings Hall of Fame centerman Marcel Dionne placed second at 135. Then came Nilsson. Mighty heady company.

"How good was Kent Nilsson that year?" asked Al MacNeil, coach of the Flames at the time. "Well, he got hurt the next season, missed about 35 games, and we all got fired!

"To be honest, he just leaves me tongue-tied. I'm stumped as to how to explain the guy. He was one of the purest athletes ever. I mean, if this guy took up golf seriously, he would've been on the PGA Tour. If he'd put his mind to tennis, he'd have played at Wimbledon. But with such gifts comes a curse. A lot of guys it comes that easy to never need to develop their competitive juices. You were never sure how much of Kent Nilsson you were getting. That year [1980–81], I think we saw as much as he was willing to let any of us in on."

Nilsson's right winger that year, Willi Plett, said he felt almost guilty about it all; it was like taking candy from a baby. Being out on the ice with Nilsson was something akin to winning the lottery

80 times in six months. "We used to have what we'd call Yay-ers," Plett once reminisced. "Kent would tell me, 'Willi, you just go to the side of the net, I'll do the rest, deke the goalie, get you the puck, and then you just put your hands in the air and go 'Yay!' okay?' I scored 38 goals that year. Half of 'em must have been Yay-ers."

No one knew it at the time, but the Kent Nilsson era was drawing to a close in Calgary. He was always the quickest way to an argument around town during that era. Black or white, you either loved him or loathed him—there was no gray area involved.

His champions—quite rightly—doted on the innate skill. His detractors had a standing joke about his nickname—they called him the Magic Man because, without fail, he'd disappear every year come playoff time, when things got tough.

Eventually, in the eyes of the organization, Nilsson's inconsistency overrode his bouts of gasp-inducing brilliance. So Fletcher, the Silver Fox, hatched a trade with Minnesota GM Lou Nanne and flipped the Magic Man to the North Stars for a draft pick the Flames would turn into a guy whose name no one could spell for a while—Joe Nieuwendyk. The headline on one Calgary newspaper: Nanne Gets Our Goat.

Nilsson spent a year and a half in Bloomington before moving on to help the Edmonton Oilers win the 1987 Stanley Cup. His legacy, though, is as a Calgary Flame, when his comet-like brilliance shone brightest.

Winger Jim Peplinski, who had a front-row seat to the years of the magic show, is one of those who believes people should judge his friend on the very real achievements, and not dwell on the perceived failures. "What you got with Kent," he said, in summation, "is what you saw. And when he was 'on'…God, there was nothing finer."

7 Badger Bob

The notebooks, the nose tugging, those trips to the sauna, and the golf course and mountain-climbing analogies have passed into legend, where they belong. As has the catch phrase that—when delivered by Bob Johnson—became an almost anthemic hymn to a sport: "It's a great day for hockey!"

When "Badger" Bob Johnson arrived in Calgary to coach the Flames in 1982, he was already a whistle-toting legend stateside, having piloted the University of Wisconsin to seven NCAA Championship tournaments, winning three titles, not to mention coaching the US entries at the 1976 Winter Olympic Games and the 1981 Canada Cup.

Nobody around the NHL had ever seen the likes of him. He was so overflowing with quirks, idiosyncrasies, fresh ideas, and rampant—almost uncontainable—enthusiasm that he seemed like some kind of Nutty Professor. He talked in quick, staccato bursts and made more facial contortions on the bench than you'd see in a Jerry Lewis comedy. "He didn't just have a love for the game," said tough guy Tim Hunter, "he had a lust for the game."

Unsurprisingly, Johnson's all-time favorite movie was *The Natural*, the Robert Redford baseball yarn. Badger absolutely adored the payoff-pitch part where Roy Hobbs (Redford) smacks the ball to the deepest part of the park on a 3–2 pitch to win the game, blood seeping through his jersey.

Occasionally he'd stand up on the team bus, dig his heels into an imaginary batter's box, and swing for the fences. He reveled in the drama of it, the sentimentality of it, the sports mythology of it. It was bigger than life. Then again, so was he.

No deficit was ever too great. No hurdle too high. No opponent too formidable (not even, in his mind, those Edmonton powerhouses that featured Wayne Gretzky, Mark Messier, Paul Coffey, and Grant Fuhr).

One thing Bob Johnson achieved in Calgary: he made players better. He mentored young players to improve their skill sets. He convinced veterans to think differently. "Badger," recalled longtime Flames executive Al MacNeil, "always worked with guys after practice. And he really used to push Al MacInnis hard, wanted him to get better. After he'd worked with him a while this one day, he turned his attention to someone else. Al, bent over and gasping for air by now, skates slowly over to the bench and sits down. Exhausted.

"Badger's busy with another guy until he glances over and just happens to see MacInnis taking that breather on the bench.

"He forgets all about what he's doing and makes a beeline for him, waving his arms and yelling, 'Allan! Allan! Get up, son! You gotta love it!'"

Former defenseman Paul Baxter loved the morning Badger arrived at work claiming he'd undergone "10 temperature changes" before 10:30:

1. Badger hopped out of bed and went outside to grab the morning paper. One temperature change.
2. He came back in the house. Two.
3–4. He had a shower, during which he switched the water from hot to cold.
5. He got out of the shower, shaved, got dressed, and readied for the rink. Five.
6. He got in the car and turned on the heater. Six.
7. He got out of the car. Seven.
8. He went into the rink. Eight.
9. He jumped in the sauna to think. Nine.
10. He got out of the sauna.

"That's 10...temperature changes before 10:30!" Badger crowed.

Even during Badger's most trying days down at the Saddledome, wading through a franchise-worst 11-game losing streak dating from December 14, 1985, through January 7, 1986, he remained almost insanely upbeat. The last game of the streak was an embarrassing 9–1 pummeling by Hartford at home. In the coaches' room afterward, he seemed undeterred. "I'm sick and tired," he began, chiding the assembled media mongrels, "of you guys writing about our so-called slump!" (The Flames, by the way, would make their first visit to the Stanley Cup Finals five months later.)

In Calgary, his watershed moment can undoubtedly be traced back to April 30, 1986, as his prohibitive underdogs briefly derailed the Oilers bullet train, winning Game 7 of an epic seven-game Smythe Division final 3–2 at Northlands Coliseum on Steve Smith's own goal off netminder Grant Fuhr's left leg. The monster, after so long, had been slain.

From there, he guided the Flames past St. Louis in another seven-game marathon and into that improbable 1986 Stanley Cup Finals against the Montreal Canadiens, eventually losing in five.

Following a first-round playoff ouster by Winnipeg the next spring, he moved on to a spot with US Hockey, then over to the Pittsburgh Penguins. Joining forces with, among others, Mario Lemieux, Rick Tocchet, Ron Francis, Paul Coffey, Larry Murphy, Tom Barrasso, and Scotty Bowman, Badger finally achieved his one remaining hockey dream: a Stanley Cup title. Tragically, he wouldn't have long to savor it.

A few short months later came the diagnosis: brain cancer. If anyone could be described as the patron saint of long odds, his friends and admirers hoped, it was Bob Johnson. If anyone could beat this, it was him.

When the first tumor was detected, muckraking defenseman Neil Sheehy sat down and penned a note of encouragement to his former coach. "When I wrote," said Sheehy, now a player agent, "I told him he not only influenced my career, he influenced my life. How many times do I find myself spouting a Badgerism? How many times do you?" Often. Still. To this day.

Bob Johnson passed away on November 26, 1991, two months after attending an emotional preseason game in Denver between the two NHL teams he had coached, Calgary and Pittsburgh. He'd undergone radiation treatment at a hospital in his home of Colorado Springs, and had done the hourlong drive to the game in an ambulance. But he wouldn't miss the chance to see his people again—hockey people.

Reached at his home in Farjestad, Sweden, former Flames right winger Hakan Loob had not heard the news of Johnson's death, owing to the eight-hour time difference. Loob's spontaneous reaction spoke for all who knew Badger Bob or loved the game, who believed implicitly in the truth of his "It's a great day for hockey" catch phrase nearly as much as he did: "Oh, God. No."

Like Oil and Water

Kent Nilsson, the supremely talented, maddeningly inconsistent game changer. Bob Johnson, the hockey-consumed, college-trained coach determined to make everyone on his roster better. They mixed like oil and water, Sean Penn and the paparazzi, tightrope walking and gale-force winds. Respect was mutual and genuine, but coexisting often proved difficult.

The two franchise icons spent three uneasy seasons together in Calgary, operating on vastly different wavelengths. To Johnson, Nilsson represented the ultimate test of his coaching mettle. Turns out Badger never did figure out the Magic Man. Then again, no one did. Not really. But the dynamic between the two men made for some memorable stories.

Once, strolling out of the old Pacific Coliseum in Vancouver, a rookie Flames beat writer caught up to Badger Bob on the way to the bus following a preseason morning skate. "Wanna know why coaches go gray prematurely?" Johnson asked the young scribbler. "Wanna know why they get ulcers? Go crazy?" The grass-green kid nodded dumbly. Johnson jerked his head over a shoulder, where maybe 30 feet behind walked a whistling Nilsson, happy as a lark, as always.

Kent Nilsson's life-to-the-fullest outlook was natural and irresistible. Always full of mischief, ready for fun, it was literally impossible not to like the man, regardless of how exasperating the dips in his play often were.

This is someone who, when asked the reason for a poor World Championship showing by Team Sweden, replied, straight-faced: "Too many Swedes." Who, after piling up four points against Vancouver during a first period, was exhorted by Johnson during the information to keep going and eclipse the NHL record for points in a game. "No, Coach," was the reply. "Then you'll expect me to do it every night."

On a day when Nilsson was fighting the flu, Badger Bob suggested he go off and lie down in a corner to try and recuperate for the upcoming game. "Coach," was the rejoinder, "you know Swedes don't go in corners."

The only difference between Wayne Gretzky and Nilsson, Johnson always maintained, was strictly in attitude, in appetite. Having piled up five points in the final minute of a 5–0 game, No. 99—Gretzky—would be clamoring to be back on the ice, ravenously in search of that sixth point; Nilsson, in identical circumstances, would already be showered and changed.

During a frustrating losing stretch, the Flames headed into Buffalo, into the claustrophobic bandbox that was the old Aud, in dire need of a win to transform fading fortunes. Given the bumper-car constrictions of the building, Nilsson did not often shine in Buffalo. In desperation, though, Badger Bob went directly to his enigmatic talisman to try and light a fire, because if anyone could drag the Flames out of their rut, it was Kent Nilsson. "Kent," he implored, "we need you tonight. You're the greatest player in the game. You can do this, Kent."

His enigmatic star could only reply: "Oh, Coach, you know I always play bad in Buffalo. The ice is so small, I'm always getting hit…"

"No, no, Kent," protested Johnson. "You *can* do this. I believe in you, Kent."

The story goes, in the first couple shifts, Nilsson was setting the dark, dank old barn alight. But by the end of the second period, Johnson had screwed him to the end of the bench. After yet another loss, as the Flames prepared to depart, Nilsson approached his boss. If Badger Bob was expecting an apology, he wound up disappointed. "See, Coach, I told you I always play bad in Buffalo," Nilsson said.

One Johnson-Nilsson yarn, though, towers above the rest: Early one morning at the Saddledome, Badger—in retrospect, far ahead of the curve in terms of innovative ideas—had conscripted a fitness expert to show up and lead his players in a series of pre-practice stretching exercises.

"Okay," the effervescent, perennially upbeat Johnson announced to his sleepy, decidedly disinterested crew, "we're going to do something today that's new, something that's going to make us better."

They all stared at him.

"You all know the lion, the king of the beasts, the lord of the jungle?" began Badger, warming to his task. "He gets what he wants, takes what he wants, is the ruler of his domain." By then, to illustrate his point, he had begun to stretch exaggeratedly, thrusting his arms in the air, straining, twisting, writhing for emphasis. "And what," he continued, "does the lion, the king of the beasts, the lord of the jungle, the ruler of his domain, do the first thing he gets up in the morning?"

From the back of the room came Nilsson's voice, unmistakable out of silence: "He licks his balls."

The stuff of legend.

9 The Silver Fox

Looking back, Lanny McDonald may have been the consensus man of the people, Jarome Iginla the franchise's greatest-ever player, and Al MacInnis its finest defenseman. Doug Gilmour represented the indomitable, and Kent Nilsson the sublime. Tim Hunter kept the peace, Miikka Kiprusoff and Mike Vernon held the fort. But in terms of influence on the finished product, no one compared to the architect: Cliff Fletcher. Trader Cliff, they called him, the Silver Fox. He is the single-most-important person in Calgary Flames franchise history.

"Maybe," Cliff Fletcher mused a quarter century after his, and the organization's, lone Stanley Cup–winning assault, "we didn't have that one superstar. Maybe we didn't have a Gretzky or a Lemieux. People can say that, and I guess it'd be true." A small smile of satisfaction crossed his face as he added, "But we had, top to bottom, a pretty damned good hockey team."

That championship year, 1988–89, saw a 117-point team. A team Fletcher had spent half a decade blueprinting and building and tinkering with to complete.

During Fletcher's shrewd managerial stewardship, the Flames franchise was justifiably regarded as the Rolls-Royce of the NHL at the time. He was the undisputed chauffeur, mechanic, and showroom salesman all wrapped up into one well-appointed package.

Cutting his teeth in the business in the most regal of settings, a 21-year-old Cliff Fletcher joined the Montreal Canadiens as a scout in 1956. A decade later he moved to the expansion St. Louis Blues and fast-tracked up to assistant GM. In 1972, with expansion dawning again, after a season running a CHL team on his own, he felt ready, packed up again, and relocated south, to Atlanta.

Eight years later, Fletcher followed the Flames to Calgary from Georgia, and charted course for NHL supremacy. "You can take all the other stuff, all the other people, that contributed to the success of that club," lauded Fletcher's longtime right-hand man, Al MacNeil, "and put Cliff in another category altogether. He was the design mechanism. His knack for making the right deal? Unequalled.

"I mean, Cliff had a great background in the game. He worked with 'em all. With [Sam] Pollock, Scotty [Bowman], and Ronnie Caron.

"He took the team over from scratch in Atlanta, and all the mistakes you have to make, he got 'em out of his system, so by the time he got to Calgary, this franchise [had] a pretty good god-damned executive."

Fletcher understood instinctively that the target lay up north, in the Oilers, the machine Glen Sather had forged. So step by step, brick by brick, he built a team to tame the beast. It took time. It took experimentation. It took a lot of heartache. But it happened. He thought outside the box and hired "Badger" Bob Johnson out of Wisconsin to coach. In 1986 he added old Oilers killer John Tonelli from the New York Islanders and sniper Joey Mullen out of St. Louis to the mix and trumped Gretzky and Co. in a Smythe Division final series they still talk about in hushed, reverential tones along the Bow River. The Flames reached the Stanley Cup Finals that year, losing to Montreal in five games. The beast had been slain, but the ultimate prize still lay unclaimed.

The culmination of Fletcher's vision, of course, arrived on May 25, 1989. "The night we won the Cup," he recalled, "it wasn't just about that game or that series or that playoff run. It was about building something, all the sleepless nights trying to catch the Oilers, finding ways to improve. It was the culmination of something we started when the team first moved up from Atlanta."

What Fletcher achieved was significant. That Cup-winning team was the sum of his ambition, his ideas, his foresight. The Flames appeared dynastic, without flaw. But they'd be beaten by old nemesis Gretzky, modeling L.A. Kings black-and-silver now, the next spring, and the Oilers the year after that.

Fletcher's wheeling and dealing remains legendary. Among others, he brought Doug Gilmour, Joe Mullen, Brad McCrimmon, and Rob Ramage to Calgary; drafted Hakan Loob, Theo Fleury, Gary Roberts, Joe Nieuwendyk, Gary Suter, and Mike Vernon; signed free agents no one had ever heard of who played vital roles in the Cup-winning run: Joel Otto, Colin Patterson, Jamie Macoun. He pioneered scouting US colleges and coaxed Russians over to the NHL, first Sergei Pryakhin and then the marvelous Sergei Makarov. And he got everybody rings.

The day Fletcher walked away from the franchise he'd overseen for nearly two decades—May 16, 1991, following a seven-game playoff ouster by those dastardly Edmonton Oilers—Trader Cliff strode to the microphone at the Saddledome, as he had so often in the past to announce a major swap, adjusted his notes, and peered up from the familiar half-spectacles he used for reading. "I have," he announced, waiting for a mild ripple of laughter to die down, "one *minor* announcement to make." Nothing could have been less minor.

"What I am," he said that day, "is stale. Really stale. I turned 55, and I thought to myself, *I need a career change. I need to get the old juices flowing again.* I've been here 19½ years. I figured if I waited much longer to make a change, it'd be too late. I need some enthusiasm. A challenge."

He'd get all that and more in Toronto. The years passed, but neither he nor his old organization reached those dizzying 1989 heights again. It made sense, in retrospect. They were the sum of each other, he and the Flames. "He can leave this team," said MacNeil, "but his stamp is on it forever."

10 The 50-Goal Swede

The most goals Peter Forsberg ever put up in a season was 30. Mats Sundin? Try 47, in his early years as a Quebec Nordique. Mats Naslund never hit the magic number of 50. Nor have either of the Sedin twins, Daniel or Henrik. Mats Naslund? Sorry. Markus Naslund or Henrik Zetterberg? Nope and nope. Kent Nilsson, the mercurial Magic Man, blazed to 49 back during his wildly audacious 131-point 1980–81 campaign, the Flames' first in Calgary following their relocation from Atlanta.

But 50 goals—the consensus watershed for stardom—over the length of an NHL campaign? Only one Swedish-born player can lay claim to that distinction: Hakan Loob. And it occurred 29 years ago.

Selected in the ninth round at the 1980 draft on a late flier, the 181st pick overall arrived at Calgary International Airport to pursue the NHL dream three years later, and at season's close he was selected to the NHL All-Rookie Team, posting 55 points. The next year, in an expanded role, he finished tied for the Flames' lead in goals at 37 with his Swedish sidekick, the irrepressible Nilsson.

By 1988 Loob could consider himself a bona fide star, a 50-goal scorer, who was selected first-team NHL All-Star on right wing. And he was far, far from the outdated old stereotype of a weak Swede. He was small, true, but tungsten tough, Shetland pony strong. And wonderfully gifted.

Among Flames faithful, Hakan Loob remains mostly a connoisseur's pick. In rating the franchise's all-time best players, he lacks the tenure of a Jarome Iginla, an Al MacInnis, or a Joe Nieuwendyk; Lanny McDonald's luxurious upper-lip thicket or populist appeal; the can't-take-your-eyes-off-him fire of Fleury; the career numbers of Gary Roberts; or the tide-turning tenacity of Doug Gilmour.

Yet those who were around back in the day knew exactly what Loob meant, and what they missed when he left. "He just had such a great amount of skill," lauded Joe Nieuwendyk, thoughts drifting back to his Calder Trophy–winning season. "He could do things none of the rest of us could.

"The luckiest thing that happened to me was getting put on Hakan Loob's line my first full year in Calgary. He helped me so much, starting my career the right way…. He could put pucks into areas, make plays nobody else would dream of."

In the wake of the team's 1989 Stanley Cup triumph, Loob made a family choice. He decided to head back to Sweden so his two children, Henrik and Niclas, could grow up in their homeland. He was giving up his dream and a goodly amount of money for something he felt was right. The day of his departure, as the Flames cleaned out their locker stalls down at the Saddledome, Loob seemed far from melancholy. "I come in here today and some guy had already pulled out the screws," he joked when collecting his nameplate from his locker and saying good-bye. "My name was just hanging there, crooked. I thought, *At least wait until I'm gone.*"

In no time at all, the Flames regretted his choice, even if he didn't. "Everyone could understand why he went back to Sweden when he did, but we missed him, no doubt about that," admitted Nieuwendyk decades later. "He wasn't the quiet Swede you always hear about. Loober said things when they needed saying. He had bite to his game when required.

"You can't lose veteran leaders like Loober and Lanny and Rammer, the way we did, and not have it affect you. We suffered as a result."

Besides being a heckuva right winger, Hakan Loob was nothing if not a man of his word. Al Coates remembered picking up the newest Flame at the airport to begin his North American adventure in the fall of 1983. "He said on the ride in," recalled Coates, "and I'll never forget this, he said: 'I'll play here five or six years, and then I'm going home.' He felt that it was important to play here but also for his family to be home. And I'm thinking, *Well, he'll change his mind.* Well, he played six and then he went back to Sweden. We won the Cup, and it ended perfectly for him, but I have no doubt that he would've gone back no matter what. That's the kind of person he is."

Upon returning to Sweden, Loob continued to excel at a playing level, both domestically and internationally, then moved into management with Farjestad (a professional Swedish ice hockey team) and enjoyed more success as GM and then president. He retired from the business end of the game following the 2016–17 season.

"How good was Loober?" asked Flames backup goalie of the day Rick Wamsley. "How do you define 'good'? He was a good player on a team full of good players. He could produce. Great vision. Went into the tough areas. Smart. Could make plays. And, as I said, produce. What else is there?"

Given the playoff frustrations that began in the springtime following Loob's departure, Flames fans were left to ask themselves *What if...?* Those sorts of questions aren't Loob's style, though.

When asked, Loob continues to politely repeat that he's never regretted his decision to forsake the NHL at 28, at the peak of his powers. Not really. "Maybe there were times over the years when I wondered if I would've scored 50 goals again, or 100 points, or won another Stanley Cup or two," he once conceded. "But at the time I came home, no, I never thought about it. I had too much to do.

"I was treated here in Sweden like a superstar. People couldn't have been nicer to me. And my family came first.

"I guess there was the odd time thinking back, wondering, *What kind of contract could I have signed?* Twenty-eight years old, Stanley Cup, 50 goals, 100 points, blah, blah, blah… That's human nature. But I've always said money has never been the major issue with me. I knew I was coming back to a situation, to a league, where people weren't throwing money around all over the place, driving the greatest cars, owning huge houses. You realize pretty quick you don't need that much money. If I'd gone for the wallet, I never, ever would've signed for Farjestad. So do I regret it? No. I did the right thing."

That depends on which side of the ocean you're on.

11 "It's Eva, Dahling…"

In the early 1980s the Calgary Flames were stuck out in New Jersey awaiting a game against the Devils, the bright lights of Manhattan beckoning in the distance. So a plan was hatched to take in the Tony Award–winning musical *Dreamgirls* at the Imperial Theatre. Max Offenberger, the team's sports psychologist at the time, laughed, "I wanted to get these guys some culture."

"These guys," that group, consisted of defenseman Paul Baxter, the always-ready-for-fun Kent Nilsson, newly recruited Hakan Loob, and Bruce Eakin of the Saskatoon Blades (to this day Offenberger can't for the life of him remember what Eakin was doing there, or why he would have been tagging along).

Offenberger continued, "So I'm able to get tickets. We find a cab. It's pouring rain. Pouring. We're going through the Holland Tunnel, and traffic's backed up. So [we're] 15 minutes late for the show. Go up to the wicket and they tell us we can't go in until intermission because the show's started. So [the guys are] like, 'Where should we go now, Maxie?'"

Max chose Elaine's for dinner. The legendary now-closed restaurant on 1703 Second Avenue in Manhattan was then a trendy hub for writers and artists of New York, most famously Woody Allen.

Offenberger continued, "We get a table. A little chichi, you know? White tablecloths, French waiters—'What would you like, monsieur?' And [Baxter] was, shall we say, in the party atmosphere already.

"All of a sudden, who comes in with her whole family but Joan Rivers. They're sitting next to us. Maybe eight people. Baxie, of course, leans over to me and says, 'Maxie, who is that?' 'It's Joan Rivers, the comedienne.' 'Joan Rivers! I've got to meet her.' I said, 'Baxie, I don't think that'd be appropriate. She's with her whole family.'

"So Kent pipes up: 'Why don't you send her over a drink?' So Baxie's got to get a waiter. He calls the waiter over: 'Garçon! Garçon!'

"'Maybe we should buy her a bottle of wine,' [Baxter said].

"So Kent immediately pipes up: 'Don't be a cheapskate. Let's see that list.' This was—what?—1984. A couple bottles there for $85, which would be like $300 now. He says: 'Here! Send her over some real wine.'

"So he does.

"Then Baxie goes over to the table and introduces himself to everyone. 'Hi. Paul Baxter, Calgary Flames.' 'Hi. Paul Baxter, Calgary Flames.' 'Hi. Paul…'

"All of a sudden, a woman walks in. I remember it distinctly—in a black leather pantsuit and a white ermine [cloak]. White-blond hair. Picture this coming into the dining room. What an entrance.

"Paul jabs me in the ribs: 'Max, who is that?' I said, 'I think it's Zsa Zsa Gabor.'

"'You've got introduce me.' I said, 'Paul, I don't know her. I just know her from television and movies.'

"So he jumps up, walks to the front; he jumps in front of her and her husband—or whoever it is—puts out his hand, and says, 'Zsa Zsa! Paul Baxter. Calgary Flames.'

"She jumps back—I think she was a little startled—looks him over, up and down, and says, 'It's Eva, dahling. And vat ees a Calgary Flame?'

"By [then] Kent [was] laughing so hard he [had] slid underneath the table."

12 Lanny

Other stars have passed through the Calgary Flames firmament—a whole constellation of them, in fact: Kent Nilsson, Joe Nieuwendyk, Al MacInnis, Doug Gilmour, Gary Roberts, Gary Suter, Jarome Iginla, Miikka Kiprusoff, Sergei Makarov, and many more. Among them, though, Lanny McDonald remains special, apart. The man with the mustache.

Even back in the day, he somehow made it hip to be square. The ultimate family guy. The ultimate charity guy. The ultimate teammate. The ultimate competitor. The big star who never lost his small-town values, as if he'd been plucked off a Norman Rockwell canvas and made human.

"He's a stubborn Westerner," was how former Flames assistant coach Bob Murdoch once described McDonald. "A competitor. An old warrior. He had the courage of his convictions. One thing I don't think many people realize is how tough an old bird he is. I've never seen him back down from anyone or anything. He never picked his spots."

Or as onetime teammate and longtime adversary Tiger Williams added, respectfully: "I've seen a lot of stars—guys who've had smoke blown up their asses their whole career—spout the regular cliches [but] when times get tough say, 'I've had enough of this BS,' and get the hell out. Not McDonald."

He always, in a sense, belonged here. He hailed from Hanna, Alberta, which is 218 kilometers, or 135 miles, outside Calgary. He spent his early days as a junior star in Medicine Hat, three hours to the east down the Trans-Canada Highway. But before he landed in Calgary, he had to travel east to conquer Toronto as a Maple Leaf, then endure the losing and instability of life with the Colorado Rockies.

The trade that eventually brought Lanny McDonald home, after two seasons in Denver, was finalized on November 25, 1981, with the Rockies on a bus heading to Winnipeg Arena in a snowstorm. The man from Calgary who pulled the trigger, Cliff Fletcher, had only glimpsed the impact the new arrival would bring, and those on the other side knew exactly what they were losing. Goaltender Chico Resch was among them.

"When Lanny left the Rockies, to be honest with you, some of my hockey dreams died," admitted Resch. "With all due respect to the other guys on that team, when they traded him...well, with Lanny there I always felt like something good might happen." He had that effect on people. Still does.

Instantly, the change of scenery, being back in a hockey market, a competitive environment, revitalized the former Toronto Maple Leafs' first-round (fourth overall) pick. At the time, the Flames had the on-again/off-again wizardry of Kent Nilsson, Paul Reinhart on defense, and Mel Bridgman and Guy Chouinard up front. What the team lacked was a centerpiece, an emotional core, a talismanic figure to knit the separate parts together. Those types of players, those types of people, are rare.

In the 55 games as a Flame following the trade that first season, McDonald scored 34 goals. The next year, he scaled the heights with a team-record 66 that continues to stand and has never seriously been approached. A connection between populace and player was forged back then that endures to this day.

As the years passed, the organization inched ever closer to greatness. The Flames reached one Stanley Cup Finals, in 1986, losing to the Canadiens. McDonald scored his 500th goal, notched his 1,000[th] point, and played in his 1,000[th] game. Only one item—conspicuously—was missing from his list of achievements: a Stanley Cup. And then the spring of 1989 arrived.

When Terry Crisp inserted McDonald into the lineup for Game 6 of the 1989 Finals, he'd played only two of the first five games. But he hadn't made himself a distraction to that point. There was too much at stake. "Being angry," he said at the time, "is for little kids."

And everyone remembers how it all ended: that goal, his first of the playoffs, to give Calgary a 2–1 lead. The Stanley Cup he had long dreamt of, claimed on hallowed ice, in the place he'd scored his first-ever NHL goal. Left winger Gary Roberts recalled his Whitby, Ontario, buddy Joe Nieuwendyk tearing up on the ice at the Forum that night when McDonald held the Cup aloft. The man with the mustache had that effect on people.

"It's funny," McDonald said in reflection, "but something I vividly remember is just sitting in the dressing room and feeling

McDonald, seen here playing the 2016 NHL Centennial Classic Alumni Game, will forever be hockey royalty.

this sense of…peace. The place is still going crazy, and Nieuwy and Robs and Jiri Hrdina are asking me: 'Lanny, aren't you excited?' And I told them: 'I am excited. Really excited. Inside.'

"There was just a peacefulness to it that was almost overwhelming. After 16 years, to finally get what you've been after, to be a Stanley Cup champion.

"I tried to tell those kids, warn the young guys, you know, that it won't be like this every year. That team had a bond. We were there for each other. We just refused to let anyone get offside. If it was the coaching staff, or something happened…we were going to see it through, together. That doesn't happen every year you play."

So with the perfect ending already written, McDonald made the hardest call. He later admitted he'd come to grips with the decision months before. McDonald's retirement soiree was held on August 28, 1989, at his sprawling home out in Springbank, just west of the city, nearly three months to the day after he'd held the Cup aloft at the Montreal Forum.

He revealed another offer from an unnamed organization to continue on with a 16-year playing career but couldn't see himself finishing his career in any other uniform than the one he wore on his greatest of nights. "I've had the opportunity of a lifetime," said the icon, brushing away tears. "To play for the Calgary Flames. I'm lucky."

Truth be told, they were the lucky ones.

13 The Shot

The legend was born, appropriately, on the western bank of the Mississippi River. In the old, echoing, cavernous, and long-ago-demolished St. Louis Arena.

"I was maybe five feet outside the blueline," reminisced Al MacInnis years later. "The rink's not that bright in St. Louis, so [Mike] Liut must have had a hard time picking the puck up. But the shot still took off like a golf ball."

Intercepting an errant pass, the Flames' young defenseman took two strides and then…leaned into the shot. The puck, exploding up and in on Mike Liut out of the hazy darkness, conked him right on the mask. Stunned, he lurched, then toppled. To heighten the drama just a tad, the puck somehow dropped into the net.

Later, the Blues franchise goaltender muttered the now-famous quote: "There's hard, then there's MacInnis hard."

(Ironically enough, as memorable as that howitzer remains in people's imaginations, MacInnis feels another of his shots, against Philadelphia Flyers goaltender Pelle Lindbergh in the more brightly lit Saddledome, was even faster. "That puck," he recalled with delight, "was in and out of the net, and I swear he never even saw it. Probably never knew I'd even shot it. It was just a rumor to him.")

What made Al MacInnis special, though, what puts him at the very summit of any greatest-ever-Flames compilation, wasn't how hard he shot a puck but rather how hard he worked to execute that shot.

He might've had to move on, to leave for St. Louis, in order to collect his long-overdue Norris Trophy, but the acceleration in his all-around game made during the dozen seasons in his first NHL home is inarguably what laid the groundwork for a Hall of Fame career.

During the formative years, arriving as 1981's 15th overall choice out of OHL Kitchener (the Rangers), there were the inevitable detractors. With the Rangers, MacInnis had tied Bobby Orr's single-season goal record for defensemen at 38, helped capture the 1982 Memorial Cup, and won the Max Kaminsky Trophy that honors the loop's top defenseman.

Impressive résumé. Still, the jibes, the perceived and actual flaws, were all anyone seemed to concentrate on: can't play defense, skates on his ankles, knees won't hold up. Even that shot, the .32 caliber slug he'd begun developing as a kid shooting puck against a piece of plywood back on the family farm in Port Hood, Nova Scotia, was thrown back derisively in his face. Nothing but a one-trick pony.

One newspaper headline proved particularly irksome: THE FLAMES PICKED ANOTHER FIRST-ROUND FLOP. "When I read that article," said MacInnis, "I promised myself there was no way it was going to happen to me." Just goes to show.

"I remember some people saying Gretzky would never amount to anything too," mused former Flames cocaptain Jim Peplinski. "Sometimes people are just...wrong.

"I think what Al did a lot sooner than anybody else is that he figured out what it meant to be a pro. He just went about his business, every day. You know, putting the grain of sand in the bucket every day, and pretty soon the bucket's full. But if you miss one day here, take a day off there...

"More than anything else he had a discipline and a professionalism about him. He put sand in that bucket every day." Pretty soon, the bucket was full to overflowing.

In retrospect, 1986–87 can be considered his breakout season: 76 points, a plus-20, a team-high 262 shots on goal, a berth on the NHL's second All-Star team and his first All-Star Game appearance. More important, Coach Bob Johnson was deploying him in every conceivable situation.

From then on, MacInnis seemed to pick up speed faster than one of his trademark slappers from the point. His zenith, of course, came during the Stanley Cup–winning postseason of 1989. His 31 points topped the playoff charts, and he became the first defenseman to do so, setting a record by scoring at least one per game over 17 straight games. Naturally he won the Conn Smythe Trophy as playoff MVP.

"The feeling you get winning it...the feeling you get holding it...God, you just never want to be second-best again," MacInnis said in exultation. "From that moment, you just can't imagine sitting in front of the TV in May, watching. It's something you can never get enough of."

While MacInnis continued to excel, the Flames began a frustrating habit of disappointing in the springtime. In the 1990–91 campaign, MacInnis became one of five players at his position to ever reach the 100-point plateau, piling up 103, including 75 assists.

A year later, after five seasons of not advancing past the first round of the postseason, MacInnis was coming up on the end of his contract, a restricted free agent. The Flames offered him $2.5 million a year. The Blues countered with $3.5 per year for four years on an offer sheet. MacInnis wanted a change, and the organization balked at the numbers. Eventually the two teams worked out a deal that dispatched D-man Phil Housley and two second-round picks to Calgary in exchange for Calgary's all-time franchise scoring leader and a three-time Norris Trophy finalist.

He went on to play nine more distinguished seasons in St. Louis, eclipsed the 1,000-point plateau, and at long last, in 1999, won a Norris before retiring on September 9, 2005, and moving into management with the Blues.

Still, the ties to Calgary remained strong. On February 27, 2012, MacInnis was celebrated back at the Scotiabank Saddledome as the first honoree in the organization's Forever a Flame program.

"Calgary," he said as the big day approached, "is where I reached a dream that every kid who ever pulls on a pair of skates aspires to. I had 13 great years there, 803 games. Made lifetime friendships. Met fantastic people, coaches, people that cared about me, like Cliff Fletcher and Al MacNeil. Had so many great, great teammates, unforgettable memories."

Retired a Blue, maybe, but Forever a Flame. In the spring of 2017, during its centenary year, the league recognized him as one of its 100 greatest all-time players.

14 The Kid from the Kitchen

Joe Mullen reportedly cried the night the St. Louis Blues dealt him north. That pining for the American Midwest cleared up quickly, though. "I had the best years of my career in Calgary," he reflected years later. "I won my first Stanley Cup there. And the guys on the team...what a cast of characters. Pep. The Beast. And Patter. Nat. Killer.... Not only were those my best years, they were the most fun, too. That first Cup stays with you, no matter how many you win."

It might be difficult for anyone to wrap their head around, but a guy standing 5'9" and weighing 180 pounds, a two-time Lady Byng Memorial Trophy winner, could arguably, fairly, be described as the toughest player in franchise history. Mullen was one stubborn, spunky hombre—as durable as the shell on an old sea turtle and as lethal as a puff adder.

Too often toughness is mistakenly measured by mayhem incited, fights won and lost, and accumulated penalty minutes. Well, toughness can also be measured in resiliency, in a stubborn refusal to quit. The cruiserweight from Hell's Kitchen, New York City, simply refused to back down, to be intimidated, standing resolutely in the greasy areas, taking a pounding to score goals, during the anything-goes days of hatchet-handed defensemen given free reign to protect their assets.

His first coach in Calgary, "Badger" Bob Johnson, once described Mullen as one of those inflatable vinyl punching bags everyone had as a kid at one time or another. Give the thing a bop, and—*boooooooing!*—it just pops right back up.

The deal that brought Mullen north looks absurdly one-sided today: Mullen, a proven 40-goal man, along with two stay-at-home defensemen—Terry Johnson and Rik Wilson—heading north, wingers Eddy Beers and Gino Cavallini, along with blueliner Charlie Bourgeois, packing up for Missouri.

His arrival proved to be the first of two key components GM Cliff Fletcher would add during the course of the 1985–86 season, later acquiring proven Oilers killer John Tonelli from the Islanders.

Quickly adapting to unfamiliar surroundings, Mullen concluded the final two and a half months of the season by piling up 38 points in 29 games in his debut turn as a Flame. During the playoffs, he proved even more lethal, scoring a dozen times as Calgary ended its Oilers subservience in a touchstone seven-game Smythe Division finale and advanced to its first Stanley Cup Finals.

Two seasons later, Mullen, nothing if not consistent, topped Calgary's regular-season scoring charts with 47 goals and 87 points, but the Presidents' Trophy–winning Flames were embarrassingly swept aside with the minimum amount of fuss by the archrival Oilers in the second round of the playoffs.

Then came the arrival of 1988–89. No coincidence that Joe Mullen's finest-ever season dovetailed into Calgary's. That year he established personal highs with 51 goals and 110 points (a full 25 more than runner-up Hakan Loob), while being slapped with only 16 penalty minutes. The 117-point Flames claimed their second Presidents' Trophy and—more vitally—their first, and to date only, Stanley Cup. Mullen poached 16 goals over the course of 22 postseason games, although the Conn Smythe was ultimately lifted by defenseman Al MacInnis.

It seemed to the hockey world that Fletcher had plotted a dynastic blueprint, perhaps lacking that one authentic superstar but one that was overflowing with good to great players who would keep the Flames on top for years to come. However, that was not to be. The reigning Cup champs were eliminated by the Gretzky-fueled L.A. Kings in six games in round one of 1990, and immediate changes were in the offing.

Mullen's regular-season point total had dipped by 41, down to 69. The man who'd brought him aboard, Fletcher, left for a new challenge, to attempt to resurrect the Toronto Maples Leafs. Coach Terry Crisp was jettisoned.

The Flames were convinced that, at 33, they had a declining asset on their hands, that the bounce in Joe Mullen's step had diminished. The Flames then flipped him to the Pittsburgh Penguins on draft day in 1990 in exchange for a second-round pick. That selection turned into defenseman Nicolas Perreault, who never played a game in the National Hockey League.

Mullen went on to win two more Stanley Cups as a Penguin, becoming the league's first US-born player to reach the 500-goal and 1,000-point milestones in the process.

His Flames accomplishments are impressive on their own: 388 points in 345 career regular-season jousts (190G,198A), two Lady Byng Memorial Trophies, an NHL plus-minus leader award, and the franchise's first All-Star team berth on right wing. All in the relatively short space of four and a half seasons.

When the inevitable call to hockey's Hall of Fame arrived in 2000, Joe Mullen's legion of fans with unbreakable ties to his Calgary days led the applause. "Mully," said former teammate Brad McCrimmon in tribute, "spent a career excelling in areas of the ice a lot guys wouldn't visit on threat of death. Great balance on his skates. Great desire. Great teammate. I couldn't be happier for him. A little guy with big talent and a huge heart."

15 The Ol' Potlicker

Jim "Bearcat" Murray sharpened his first skate at age 12, rode as a jockey on the Alberta bush-league racing circuit, and worked as a wildcatter in the oil fields. His dad hung the moniker Potlicker on him during the Depression-era Dirty Thirties because, as family legend goes, little Jim Murray would lick the pot clean after his mom baked a cake. "I really like the expression Bald-Headed Little Potlicker from Okotoks," said Bearcat, "because that really explains what I am."

Dissatisfied with a job in the oil patch, young Jim Murray began his training career on a whim with the old Western Major Junior League's Calgary Centennials, way back when. He could not, in his wildest dreams, have imagined where that shot in the dark would eventually lead him.

Down through the years he has morphed into a provincial icon as a self-taught healer tending to the wounds of the big team in town, from the World Hockey Association Calgary Cowboys and then, for 16 memorable seasons, the NHL Flames. *Beloved* wouldn't be too strong an adjective to ascribe to how people feel about Jim Murray.

In short order Bearcat became as instantly recognizable as any of the famous names put in his care. That bushy mustache is quite possibly as famous around southern Alberta as Lanny McDonald's. And like McDonald, Murray has those innate, populist people skills that draw people to him.

A familiar sight whenever the Flames ventured out on the road was the Ol' Potlicker on his roller skates, doing laps around the concourses of the rink in whatever city the team was playing, in order to keep in shape.

Bearcat stories, it seems, rush down like a faucet that cannot be turned off. What other pro sports trainer can possibly have once inspired a fan club? And in a rival city, no less. Well, the Bearcat Murray Fan Club was born in the late 1980s the night a group of hockey fans in Boston were watching a game in which Bearcat leapt off the bench and into the stands at Edmonton's Northlands Coliseum to rescue his son, Calgary assistant trainer Al Murray.

Defenseman Gary Suter's stick had been knocked into the stands, pinched by an Oilers fan, and stuffed under a seat for safe-keeping. Al Murray—nicknamed Alley Cat, naturally—went off in pursuit of the stolen stick but quickly disappeared in the sea of fans. That's when a father's instinct took over and Ol' Potlicker, ever up for a good fracas, joined the fray. "I saw a couple of guys wrestling with Allan," he explained, needlessly, "so I couldn't just stand there." In the ensuing chaos, Bearcat wound up ripping ligaments in his right ankle on the stone steps while giving chase.

"The camera followed me out to the ambulance while the game was going on. I could see the red light on [the camera] so I knew [it was recording], so I started blowing kisses and stuff," he recalled. "These guys watching in Boston loved it. They said, 'That's our man!'"

Fan club T-shirts and stationery were produced. Whenever the Flames would visit Beantown, the group would meet at the Penalty Box Pub and then head off to the old Garden, wearing bald caps and fake mustaches to honor their hero.

Another of the legendary Bearcat moments concerns the night he hopped on the ice during a Kings-Flames game to attend to an (apparently) stricken netminder, Mike Vernon, during a 1989 playoff game. While he was out there, the Flames scored a goal. Pandemonium ensued. L.A. captain Wayne Gretzky howled in protest that Calgary actually had an extra man on the ice.

"Bernie Nicholls punched me," Vernon explained later. "So I dropped, looking to draw a penalty. I'm lying there wondering when might be a good time to sit up, and all of a sudden there's Bearcat kneeling over top of me. 'Vernie, Vernie, are you hurt?' I told him, 'No, Bear, I'm fine.' And he looked worried, more worried than I'd ever seen him. Scared, almost. 'No, no, Vernie, are you hurt?'

"We'd just scored a goal with him on the ice, and Gretzky was going ballistic. I think Bear thought I'd better be hurt or he might lose his job."

Not much chance of that. By then, Bearcat Murray had become a staple, an irreplaceable part of the fabric of the organization. He and equipment manager Bobby Stewart were the Doug Gilmour–Joe Mullen of the traveling staff.

Bearcat now has a place in the Hockey Hall of Fame, the Alberta Sports Hall of Fame, the Flames' Alumni Hall of Fame, and the Okotoks Hall of Fame, and has been honored by the Native Calgarian Society.

He still gets stopped on the street by people he's never seen before who consider him a feel-good part of their growing-up years. And he's immensely grateful, if somewhat mystified, by the enduring adulation.

"When you think of me, just this little potlicker from Okotoks, and everything that's happened," he said, with a soft shake of the head, "well…that's a story even I'd have a hard time believing."

16 The Great White Shark

George Pelawa was known as the Great White Shark. Or the Ice Box. "You can't teach size," was a credo Calgary Flames general manager Cliff Fletcher repeated often, and one he built his team by. In George Pelawa, he believed he'd hit the mother lode.

The kid was just 18, stood 6'4", and weighed 245 pounds. He was an All-Star linebacker in high school, and quick enough despite his size to have clocked the 100-yard dash in 11 seconds. His final year of high school hockey for the Bemidji High School Thunderbirds, Pelawa had piled up 29 goals and 55 points in 26 games. A man, quite literally, among boys.

The only sport Pelawa admitted to struggling with was swimming. He knew he'd never be Mark Spitz. "I can't float," Pelawa told reporters the day the Calgary Flames drafted him 16th overall at the fabled Montreal Forum in the summer of 1986. "I've got heavy bones, and I keep sinking.

"I play all sports, but sometimes I just like to sit in front of the TV and eat." (This last sentence led one GM to quip: "Only two things can keep Pelawa out of the NHL: a knife and fork.")

His nickname the Great White Shark was attached by a coach. "Because I didn't skate so good," explained Pelawa, "I had to go in circles sometimes, and he said I looked like a shark circling around."

But could the raw-boned farm kid take a bite out of the NHL? The Pelawa selection, particularly early in the first round, raised more than a few eyebrows. Minnesota North Stars GM Lou Nanne, for one, felt the selection was a waste of a pick. Others, however, saw the vast potential in the big farm kid. Count Scotty Bowman of the Buffalo Sabres, a pretty shrewd cookie, amongst the latter group. "For a team that can afford to wait," adjudged Bowman, "he might be a very good one. He's a project."

A project that, sadly, never came to fruition. For on the night of August 30, 1986, on a poorly lit stretch of rural Minnesota highway, George Pelawa was tragically killed in a two-car collision.

After committing to play that winter at the University of North Dakota, with a bright future spreading out before him, Pelawa returned home after setting up shop in his dorm room. On August 30, he and his brother Joe were returning from a night out when their car broke down. After picking up another car, with Joe driving, the two were returning to the stalled vehicle when they were struck by a car around 2:00 AM.

Neither Pelawa, his brother, nor the driver of the second vehicle, Henry Vold, were wearing seat belts at the time of the crash. Joe Pelawa and Vold were taken to the hospital with extensive injuries. George Pelawa died at the scene of the accident of a torn vena cava vein, one of the two large veins that bring blood to the heart. Both drivers were found to be intoxicated.

The news understandably rocked the Flames organization. "It's scary, that's what it is," said a shaken Coach "Badger" Bob Johnson, reached at his home in Colorado Springs. "Shocking. Eighteen years old and with potential that everybody would love to have, and suddenly, *bango*, it's over."

Bryan Grand, Pelawa's high school coach the three previous years, predicted his star would've been "a factor player" at the pro level after a year or two of prepping in college.

Beltrami County sheriff Orielle Norland said that while alcohol was involved, Pelawa himself had not been drinking. "People who saw him an hour earlier before the accident said he was eating chips and drinking pop," Norland said.

The tragedy was keenly felt in the small resort town of Bemidji, Minnesota, Norland reflecting that only three months earlier the entire populace had been in on the excitement leading up to the draft. "Everybody followed it here, day to day. And when he went to Calgary, that was great. Joel Otto is such a nice fellow, and the people there have treated him so well."

Unsurprisingly, Otto had become something of a hero to Pelawa. Both big men, Otto was proof that it was possible to come out of Bemidji and reach the NHL. The two, in fact, had skated together that summer at a hockey camp in St. Paul, Minnesota. "It's a shock," said Otto. "He had so much talent. Loads of it. It was just going to take some maturing, and he was starting to get that sorted out. George was a great kid. Any death is a tragedy, but at 18 you haven't had time to experience a lot of things. That's a real shame."

In Pelawa's honor, the Flames organization established a scholarship in his name at Bemidji High School. When the organization's commitment ran out after 20 years, in 2007, Pelawa's parents, Frank and Winnie, quietly kept it going, paying $1,000 out of their own pockets. Three years later, Pelawa's friends from Bemidji rallied behind the fund, and the Flames recommitted financially.

17 Hometown Hero

Hometown hero. Now there's a job title that leaves little to no room for error. People who grew up with you (or think they did) or know you (or think they do) tend to put a claim on you, demand the most of you, cast you in a different, more intrusive light. Mike Vernon: Born and raised in Calgary. Played junior in Calgary. Won a Stanley Cup for Calgary.

Explaining the inherent pitfall of the position, Vernon himself once said: "You've got to have a pretty thick skin to play goal."

Thick as an African rhino to play goal in the city where you were born.

Selected 56th overall in the 1981 NHL Entry Draft, he back-stopped the Portland Winterhawks to a Memorial Cup two years later. Vernon's big break professionally arrived when the Flames summoned him from their minor league affiliate in Colorado to play against Soviet club team Dynamo Moscow in the 1986 Super Series. Starter Reggie Lemelin was rested, and backup Marc D'Amour was saddled with an injury. Vernon was outstanding in beating the Russian side 4–3. That certainly got everyone's attention.

Then, stuck in the mire of a club-record 11-game losing streak and looking for a magic elixir to somehow pull them out of it and salvage playoff aspirations, Calgary management summoned him again. Immediately he helped end the slide by shading the Vancouver Canucks 5–4 in OT. From then on, the job was his.

That year, against all logic, Calgary upset the reigning champion Edmonton Oilers and burrowed through to reach the Stanley Cup Finals before bowing in five games to the Montreal Canadiens. Mike Vernon, hometown hero, had reached undisputed No. 1 status.

He and his Flames undoubtedly underwent growing pains together. They won a Presidents' Trophy in 1988 but were bulldozed in four straight by Wayne Gretzky and the Edmonton Oilers in Round 2.

Then 1988–89 arrived, and with it Vernon's defining moment. His save against Vancouver's Stan Smyl in OT of Game 7 of the opening round at the Saddledome remains a touchstone moment for a generation. Smyl dug in off the right wing and unleashed a wrist shot labeled for the short side. Vernon flashed leather, Brooks Robinson at the hot corner–style, to save Calgary's season ("Maybe that's why I'm still so popular in Calgary," Smyl later joked. "To this day, I can walk down the streets there, and people high-five me").

The Flames won in OT on a goal that deflected in off the right skate of towering centerman Joel Otto and moved on to fulfill their destiny. Without Vernon, that never would have happened.

"Holy smokes!" whistled Blues VP of hockey operations Al MacInnis from his office in St. Louis years later. "Talk about pressure. How'd you like to be a guy in your hometown, where you

Mike Vernon leaps to make a save against the Columbus Blue Jackets in 2002.

grew up playing your whole life, and have everyone's Stanley Cup hopes riding on you? I can't imagine.

"The saves that he made in round one were amazing. You look back, and goddamn it, you don't really pay too much attention to it at the time, but he wasn't a very big goalie, either. Then to think of the career he had and what he meant to us during those playoffs…

"Those three saves he made in Game 7 against Vancouver that could've ended it, off [Petri] Skriko, [Tony] Tanti, and [Stan] Smyl, I believe I still get nervous thinking about them now, 25 years later."

"Save your breath," chided right winger Hakan Loob in the aftermath of Game 7 against the Canucks. "I know the question. Mike Vernon can't do it in the playoffs, right? He chokes, right? Okay, so who saved our ass in OT? Vernie gave us the chance to win. Without him, we're finished. Done. That reputation—one he's never deserved—rub it out. Now."

Still, even a Stanley Cup victory that year—against the Canadiens, no less, and in Montreal—failed to bring respite from the scrutiny. He remained the hometown hero, a target. "If someone's got something to say," Vernon complained of overly verbal Saddledome patrons only a year after claiming hockey's ultimate prize, "say it to *me*. It's kind of sad when my dad can't come to a game anymore. My mom comes sometimes, but she wears headphones, so all she's listening to is Peter Maher. My brothers show up, somebody gets a few beers in him and says different things. I don't think people even realize what they say, either. It's the emotion of the game, or whatever, but they get on a different wavelength. Hey, I'm my biggest critic. They think they are, but they're not."

Vernon was eventually dealt to Detroit in exchange for defenseman Steve Chiasson in order to make way for top draft pick Trevor Kidd to tend goal. After a return stint he held in his possession franchise records for games played (526), wins (262), minutes played (29,649), playoff games by a goalie (81), playoff wins (43), and minutes (4,773). And he held them until a silent Finn named Miikka Kiprusoff took the scene by storm. Surely a contribution to be celebrated, not scorned.

Anyway, Vernon wound up enjoying the last laugh. The Trevor Kidd experiment didn't pan out for Calgary, while Vernon went on to claim a second Stanley Cup ring and won the Conn Smythe Trophy in the spring of 1977.

Time has a way of healing old wounds, of sharpening perspective. In 2007 Mike Vernon's No. 30 was raised to the rafters at the Saddledome, making him only the second Flame to be so honored after Lanny McDonald and his signature No. 9.

"People have been very supportive since we came back to Calgary," he said of the softening of Calgarians' stance on him. "I'll be out, a dad will introduce me to his son and say, 'That's Mike Vernon. He won a Stanley Cup with the Flames.' That's really nice."

Not to mention long, long overdue.

18 The "So-Called Slump"

Nearly three decades later, it remains unequaled in franchise annals: the Slump. Or if you're buying Coach "Badger" Bob Johnson's now-legendary take on the matter, the "so-called slump."

From December 14, 1985 (a 4–3 setback in Vancouver that gave no hint of the pain ahead), through January 7 (a 9–1 desecration at home by the Hartford Whalers), the Calgary Flames lost a staggering 11 games on the trot. Seven of those by a goal.

No matter the margin of defeat, be it close or clocked, during the drop of doom the Flames tumbled from eight games above .500 (17–8–3) to two below and in danger of missing out on the playoffs altogether.

The saving grace through the slide? Johnson. While those around him were running around as if they'd only just listened to Orson Welles' *War of the Worlds* radio broadcast, convinced Martians had invaded earth, Badger remained relentlessly, defiantly optimistic. "I thought he was absolutely crazy at the time," recalled winger Perry Berezan, "but looking back on it, Badger being so positive was the difference between pulling ourselves out of that slump and it continuing. I can't imagine a coach, anywhere, being as upbeat through a losing streak that long."

The first loss, at the old Pacific Coliseum in Vancouver, was met with a shrug and marked the opener of a five-game road swing. The troubles escalated quickly from there. Losses by identical scores of 4–3 in Pittsburgh and Hartford were compounded by a 5–2 beating by the Blues in St. Louis and another narrow defeat, 5–4 in OT at Chicago. The Flames staggered home in full swoon and were shaded again, this time 6–5 by the Philadelphia Flyers.

How did the players attempt to cope with the compounding misery? "Try to smile once in a while," replied Berezan. "No matter how bad things get, it can't be a funeral march every day."

Oh, yes it could. A 6–3 loss at Minnesota on New Year's Eve didn't have anyone singing "Auld Lang Syne," and in short order, they were beaten twice by the Edmonton Oilers, 4–3 and 6–3, then subdued 6–5 at the Saddledome by the Montreal Canadiens. If the first 10 losses could have been largely chalked up to some degree of bad luck, the 9–1 pistol-whipping by the Whalers on January 7 represented a nadir.

In the wake of such an embarrassment, Badger was staggeringly upbeat—even for Mr. Positivism himself. "I'm tired," he admonished the assembled media in his office, "of reading about our so-called slump!"

"I vividly remember visiting the coaches' room after the last loss of that streak," recalled Flames GM Cliff Fletcher, 24 years after the fact, and every bit as amazed as he was that night, "and honest to God, if I'd been parachuted off a spaceship into that room, listening to Badger Bob, I wouldn't have known who the hell won or lost that game."

The Flames finally ended the agony two nights later, on January 9 at Pacific Coliseum in Vancouver, where the slide had begun 26 days earlier. Jim Peplinski scored 13 seconds into OT to drop the Canucks 5–4.

The catalyst for the season-changing, streak-busting win was a 22-year-old goaltender summoned from the AHL Moncton Golden Flames, whose only other NHL appearance had been in a 4–3 exhibition victory over touring Dynamo Moscow on December 29. His name? Mike Vernon. "I guess," reasoned Vernon after stopping 32 Canucks shots, "they thought they'd throw a kid in there and see if he could bounce things around."

In short order the local boy supplanted Reggie Lemelin as No. 1 between the Calgary pipes, and the Flames went on a 16–6–4 tear and wound up 40–31–9, good enough for second in the Smythe Division.

In retrospect, surviving such a test of resolve might've served to toughen their collective hide. "I remember we beat the Russians during that streak, after the eighth loss, I believe, and everybody's thinking, *Wow! I'm glad that's over!*" recalled Doug Risebrough, a gap-toothed, heart-on-his-sleeve cocaptain at the time. "Then we lost again. And again. And again. When it got to six, we couldn't believe it. Then seven. Then eight…

"If you'd said it'd reach 11, I'd have laughed or called you a liar. But that's how it happens. It's almost as if you're powerless to stem the tide.

"And actually, we weren't playing any differently when we lost all those games to when we ended the streak and started winning again. Just a bounce here or there."

Those bounces do tend to even out, and a few months later the Flames would be beneficiaries of the most famous bounce of all, involving Grant Fuhr's left leg 5:14 into the third period of Game 7 of the Smythe Division Finals, against the advertised-as-unbeatable Oilers.

19 The Best Deadline-Day Deal

That familiar stretch of hallway between the dressing rooms at event level of the old Nassau County Coliseum had witnessed its share of unforgettable moments through the years. On the morning of the trade deadline in 1986, it added another.

There's a hum, a buzz, an air of suspended belief as the whispered workings of a major deal begin percolating at an NHL rink on trade deadline morning, especially in the old days before cable sports channels began speculating and analyzing potential deals into minutiae.

On this day, a seismic swap happened right there, in full view, on-site. It turned out to be the most affecting deadline-day deal in Calgary Flames history.

"I was in shock," John Tonelli recalled years later. "I didn't see it coming at all. In hindsight, maybe the signs were there and I just wasn't paying attention. I remember that morning, being in the back room, the stick room, getting my sticks ready for the game that night. I was by myself. Bill [Torrey] walked in and quietly shut the door. I knew. Right then, I knew. I said one word: 'Where?' He said, 'Calgary.' And I walked out."

He headed down that familiar hall, maybe 150 feet or so, to his new team, ending a partnership that had touched the heights. It hardly seemed possible: Tonelli, the Tasmanian Devil, indispensible component of the Islanders' four-years-running Stanley Cup dynasty, gone. He seemed as much a part of the New York experience as Rockefeller Center, the Empire State Building, or a piled-high pastrami sandwich at the Stage or Carnegie Delis. Why, he'd been named MVP of the Canada Cup only two years earlier.

Along with Trots and Boss and Jethro and Butchie with the battered helmet and Battlin' Billy, Tonelli had become synonymous with glory on Long Island. All elbows and angles and industry. The guy who put the puck on Bob Nystrom's stick for one of the most famous overtime, Stanley Cup–clinching goals in recent memory.

Someone once described the inimitable Tonelli style as a "skating epileptic fit." Careening into a corner with him was what strolling into the teeth of a farm combine must feel like.

The Flames had parted with youth—21-year-old winger Rich Kromm and 25-year-old defenseman Steve Konroyd—to take dead aim at the titans from the north: the Edmonton Oilers. Tonelli would prove to be a vital component in that battle.

John Tonelli seemed set to be an Islander for life. But the ingredients for change were there, in plain sight for all to see. Refusing to attend training camp the previous summer, he missed 22 days until his contract was renegotiated, creating a rift between organization and star. His offensive contributions—20 goals, 61 points—were down. At 28, given his frenetic playing style, the Islanders felt he'd lost a little off the old fastball, and high heat was the only way John Tonelli ever knew how to pitch.

The surreal feel to the morning was unique. Gear for the three involved simply had to be moved down the hallway. Winger Perry Berezan reckoned Tonelli must've downed "14 cups of coffee" that night, waiting to play. Somehow he, Kromm, and Konroyd slipped into unfamiliar garb, stared across the ice at old comrades, and stumbled through the game, understandably in a bit of a blur. Tonelli's old team spanked his new one 8–4.

"I don't know how I had the courage to do it," he admitted. But the deal was done. Life moved on.

To the *Montreal Gazette*, Islanders bow-tied dynasty builder Bill Torrey admitted dealing the immensely popular Tonelli was "one of the most unpopular decisions [he'd] ever had to make.

"But remember, too, that our last Stanley Cup was in '83. It's now '86.... We've stayed a long time with basic personnel of those [championship] teams but haven't been playing nearly as well defensively as they did."

Cliff Fletcher had acquired Tonelli for a specific purpose, and that task lay ahead. In round one of the playoffs that spring, the Flames eliminated the Winnipeg Jets in three straight games, Tonelli slipping a pass across to Lanny McDonald 8:25 into OT, two-on-one, to send Calgary through to the Smythe Division finale. "As soon as I saw the two guys breaking out," admitted Jets GM John Ferguson, "I was on my way downstairs. I knew it was in."

Up next, the Oilers. The seven games that followed—and eventually saw the Flames emerge victorious over the hated Oilers—are etched in the imaginations of Flames fans everywhere. Calgary's title bid would be thwarted at the final hurdle by the Montreal Canadiens, of course. But no one could argue that John Tonelli hadn't done his bit—unflinching industry, unbridled achievement, 16 points through 22 playoff dates, and a hand in slaying the hated Oilers.

"I call John the Bearded Rototiller [a rotary-blade machine for tilling soil]," Calgary cocaptain Lanny McDonald told the *Los Angeles Times*. "He's made a tremendous amount of difference. What more can you say about him? He plays like an out-of-control Rototiller. He's put [the team] all together with his enthusiasm.

He's got four Stanley Cup rings and he's shown all of us what it takes to get there."

"It's one of my great hockey memories, going to that final in '86," Tonelli later reminisced. "We had an awful lot of talent on that team. A great bunch of guys. Everything you need. Maybe it didn't end the way we wanted, but we had a great run.

"I'll always remember the night we came back to Calgary after winning Game 7 against the Oilers. The thousands and thousands of people at the airport to meet us, so excited. It's something I'll never forget. Those are the moments that stay with you. We'd beaten a great team. We'd beaten the monster."

John Tonelli spent two more seasons in Calgary before moving on to the L.A. Kings.

20 The Most Famous Goal

He was actually standing in front of the bench when it happened. With nowhere to sit. Back to the ice. "From all this noise," recalled Perry Berezan, "to a hush. All over the building. Just dead silence."

The image: Steve Smith on his knees, in agony. Yes, *that* goal. The one breaking a taut 2–2 score line in Game 7 of the 1986 Smythe Division Finals at Northlands Coliseum. Arguably the most famous goal in Calgary Flames history. And most infamous in the annals of the Edmonton Oilers.

"Badger," recalled Berezan, "was playing me a lot that night, with [John] Tonelli and Lanny [McDonald]. I was just trying the safe play near the end of a shift. Get across the red line and dump it into the corner, right in front of our bench, turn for a change.

"I think one guy on our bench went, like 'Yeah!' Everybody else was silent, like 'What the hell just happened?' They announced the goal and there still wasn't a lot of screaming. I remember Lanny coming back to the bench, and I asked him, 'What happened?' He just looked kinda confused and said, 'I dunno. We scored.' And I'm like, 'Okay...'"

The time: 5:14 of the third period. Nearly three-quarters of a period remained for the most amazing offensive act in NHL history to tie the game, or maybe win it. And somehow the Edmonton Oilers—the Gretzky-Coffey-Messier-Kurri-Anderson Oilers—failed to find a way through.

That night, the elation, the shedding of so much emotional baggage, of finally getting a little of their own back, remains a touchstone, keepsake moment among Flames fans of a generation: the Oilers' Smith rounding the net, firing a cross-ice pass too tight to the net and the puck bouncing in off the left leg of Edmonton goalie Grant Fuhr. As the last Flame to touch the puck, Berezan received credit for the goal.

"In hindsight," the unwitting hero says now, "the way it went in was probably the best thing that could've happened to us. Because nobody got too excited. We weren't jarred out of that mode of calmness. If, say, Lanny had scored or someone like that, it'd have been huge jubilation, we'd have been all [been] pumped up, then you go, 'Holy crap, we can't screw up...'

"Instead, you just keep moving along, you're given this gift, this goal. They now, all of a sudden, look like a deer in the headlights. For maybe the first time in all the years we'd [been] playing them.

"From then on, Vernie made a ton of great saves, and we held on."

Berezan was only a kid, 21, playing his first full season that year. When the time arrived for the press to be allowed into a jubilant Calgary dressing room, many of the veterans were yelling out interview advice for the young'un as the notepads and microphones and TV cameras descended upon him: "Do not feel sorry for Steve Smith! Do *not!*"

Berezan said, "I'm kinda like, 'Well…I do.' I felt bad for the guy. So I think I just tried to ignore the question.

"For the guys that had been there a while, though, it was pretty raw. I was new to the league so I'm just trying to take it all [in]. For those other guys, this was personal. They'd gone through a lot against the Oilers. This, to them, was the hard part of professional sports—at the end of the day, basically, 'Too bad for you.'"

For the Flames organization, this was more than merely the culmination of a quest or a challenge. It was an obsession, really. "You're trying," said Berezan, "to beat this demon. That year, listening to everyone, including the coaches, it was only about slaying the dragon. The dragon up north. It had nothing to do with anybody else. Whoever else we played, we must've learned something to make us better prepared to slay the dragon. And we had."

When the Flames returned home from the 45-minute charter flight south, the young Berezan got a glimpse of how much it meant not only to his teammates—the McDonalds and Peplinskis and Tonellis and Hunters—but to the entire city of Calgary. "Landing and seeing the hordes, the thousands of people, against that fence at the airport…amazing. What round was this? Second? You'd think we'd won the Stanley Cup that night. High-fiving people over the fence. Everyone cheering. Like rock stars.

"All my years loving the movie *Stripes*, I got to live Bill Murray's scene where he gets out of the plane after beating the Czechs, standing there on the runway and going, 'What? A surprise party, for me?' It was…awesome."

A bus drove the players from the airport tarmac to their cars, where more hordes of fans awaited them. The hero of the hour remembered a few overzealous fans following him in their cars, and he wound up having to lose them on the drive back to his place.

"That," he admitted, "was kind of weird. I don't want people following me home. But that feeling was as cool as it gets.

"Then you're home, you get into bed, just you. After all that had happened that day. Everything's quiet. You're replaying it in [your] head. And you're just thinking, *Boy, the job's not done. We've got another series or two we have to win.*

"You wake up the next day and start it all over again."

21 "Thank You, Flames"

The feeling, remembered defenseman Neil Sheehy, encapsulated every complicated nuance of the word *bittersweet.* As the seconds wound inexorably down on an unparalleled season to that point in franchise history, trailing 4–3 in the game, 3–1 in the penultimate series, the death of a dream inching ever closer, tick by tick of the Saddledome score clock, one final amazing thing happened in a springtime when amazing things had become the norm.

"We had hit just complete exhaustion," recalled Sheehy. "I mean, I couldn't give any more. I know everybody else felt exactly the same. It was all left on the ice. You just felt…limp. You're ready to cry, you're *so* disappointed, got *so* close, you're hurting *so* bad, and then all of a sudden the fans are chanting, 'Thank you, Flames! Thank you, Flames!' It was emotional. It was unexpected. It was… so appreciated."

"You should never hope for an ovation like that, a tribute like that, when you…lose," marveled team catalyst/captain Lanny McDonald. "I remember doing an interview right after the game. We were all just devastated. We'd come so close and just couldn't finish it off. You never know when you're going back.

Then, I mean, the city had a parade for us. How amazing is that? Thousands and thousands of people on the parade route. And we hadn't won the damn thing."

From April 9 through May 24, 1986, Calgarians received an intoxicating taste of first-blush Stanley Cup fever, through four playoffs rounds, one seismic upset, and a closing chapter against a legendary foe. This was the improbable Stanley Cup finale: The 89-point Flames vs. the 87-point Montreal Canadiens.

Oh, Calgary GM Cliff Fletcher had bulked up the team over the course of the year, adding sniper Joey Mullen from St. Louis and an old nemesis of the reigning Cup champion Edmonton Oilers, John Tonelli, off Long Island. But no one seriously expected the Flames to still be playing in May—not with the big oil drop standing resolutely in the middle of the highway, blocking their path.

Yet after brushing aside the Winnipeg Jets 3–0 in a best-of format in round one came the epic 4–3 mega-upset over their northern antagonists. Beforehand, people were lighting candles for the Flames, not picking them to pull off the shocker.

After all, the Oilers' Wayne Gretzky had gone ballistic that year, scoring 215 points, an astounding 74 more than Art Ross Trophy runner-up Mario Lemieux. Paul Coffey racked up 138, one off Bobby Orr's 15-year-old record by a defenseman, finishing third on the points chart. The nimble Grant Fuhr was only the best clutch goalie in the game. Gretzky's right-hand man, Jari Kurri, scored a league-high 68 goals. Just goes to show.

"The guys," reflected assistant coach Bob Murdoch, "just ran out of steam at the end. Simple as that. The problem, in my mind, was that our Stanley Cup was beating the Oilers. We'd put so much effort into that one goal. They were the best team in hockey. Had been our target for such a long time. Everything we'd worked for was channeled into beating them.

"Bob Johnson was amazing in that. He had the seven-point plan that everyone laughed at, but it worked. He was phenomenal, really, in how much thought and effort he put into it. It was perfectly logical, and it helped the guys focus.

"But after that high, after beating the Oilers, reaching the top of that mountain, as Bob always used to say…" The inevitable dip.

Next up were the St. Louis Blues, armed with future Hall of Famer Bernie Federko, future Hall of Famer and future Flame Doug Gilmour, and future Flames coach Brian Sutter. "Once we reached St. Louis," said Murdoch, "rather than beat them in four or five, like we should've, we struggled with it, to find that same intensity and drive. So it took seven games.

"Then we had to go in and play Montreal. The guys were just emotionally, physically, mentally…finished. It was frustrating to watch them trying to play 'cause they were working so hard, trying to do so much, and they just had nothing left. Montreal was really refreshed. They'd won four straight"—shoved aside the New York Rangers in five games in the Eastern Conference final, actually—"and they were rested and waiting."

Calgary jumped out front, pocketing Game 1 at the Saddledome 5–2. But a major turning point occurred two nights later, heading into overtime with a chance to take a 2–0 series lead.

Patrons barely had time to return to their seats from the beer lines before Hab Brian Skrudland had cashed a Mike McPhee two-on-one pass behind goalie Mike Vernon. Nine seconds in. Fastest overtime goal in playoff history.

"Montreal really needed a super effort, and they came up with one," sighed Badger Bob after the loss. "This win should give them a pretty good jump for Tuesday's game." And then some.

From there, Calgary sagged and the Canadiens, powered on by old hands Bob Gainey, Mats Naslund, Larry Robinson and 20-year-old rookie goaltender Patrick Roy (pre-sainthood), reeled off two more wins, 5–3 and 1–0, to take a stranglehold on the series and the Cup.

The Flames were feeling decidedly hard done by. "These guys," snorted assistant coach Pierre Page, "like to cry and complain to get an edge. They really get under your skin. They want everyone to think they're the great skating, freewheeling Flying Frenchmen of old. I've got news for you. They're not. They throw more picks than any team we've played. They run the goalie more than any team, too. I know [Habs coach] Jean Perron. We're friends. But this is a con."

The gas gauge might've been edging toward E on the Flames' dashboard, but they were still capable of drawing on empty reserves.

Facing elimination, down 4–1 midway through the third period on the night of Game 5 and already being fitted for a toe tag, they summoned one last push. Winger Steve Bozek scored his second goal of the night at 16:46 of the third period, and then, with 46 seconds remaining, Mullen sliced the Montreal deficit to one. Out of nowhere, the Canadiens were on their heels and reeling slightly.

It was left to Roy to produce one more stellar save, and cement his Conn Smythe Trophy as playoff MVP, as the home team drove furiously forward in search of a tying goal that would send the game to OT. "The Flames were all around the net," said Roy, "and I had made the first save on Mullen, but the rebound went to [Jamie] Macoun, who was right beside me. I did the splits and got my pad on his shot and then covered the puck with my glove. I was really lucky on that play, but you make your own luck, eh?"

Undeterred, the 19,000 gathered in the Saddledome refused to grieve. Instead, they chose to celebrate. They would wait another three years to enjoy the ultimate prize, but the appreciation for what had just happened, this amazing run by an unheralded team, deserved acknowledgment.

As the players went through the traditional handshake line, the chant of appreciation began to grow in volume. "I can still hear them," said Neil Sheehy, recalling the echoes nearly three decades later. "'Thank you, Flames! Thank you, Flames!' Wow! And then the parade they gave us…phenomenal. And we all thought we loved the city of Calgary before that."

22 That's Suter, Not Sutter

His hockey team had just won a game in a place of worship, the Montreal Forum, that had held nothing but miserly for a long while. Still, Badger would not be appeased. "That," spat Flames coach Bob Johnson on March 15, 1986, "is a hockey tragedy!" The indignation was heartfelt. The cause of his ire? A mispronunciation of the name of his outstanding rookie defenseman following the 5–3 Calgary victory.

"The second star," intoned longtime Habs PA announcer Claude Mouton, "from the Calgary Flames…Gary Sutter!"

"I remember that," laughed Gary Suter, from his northern outpost home in Lac du Flambeau, Wisconsin. "To this day, people still think I was one of the Sutter brothers. And funny thing is, Garry Sutter is the Sutter brother that never played hockey, the oldest one. So that added to the confusion, I guess."

When Gary Suter (no extra *t*) arrived for training camp in the fall of 1985, a ninth-round pick, no one seemed quite sure what to expect. But positive vibes were there from the start. Sharing the U of Wisconsin tie with his coach. Trying to crack a lineup on the lookout for a left-handed defenseman after Kari Eloranta had returned home to play in Finland. And the style of game itself in that era—wide-open, begging for strong-skating defensemen who could move the puck—fit his assets perfectly.

"That whole year," admitted Suter, "was magical for me. I came in hoping to make the team. Had a good camp. Did real well in the fitness testing. Then Badger Bob put me on the power play right away. And [Al] MacInnis and I clicked almost instantly.

"Everything went right. Just being in the league, going into all these new buildings…such an adrenaline rush. It kinda snowballed for me."

"Suter," recalled assistant coach Bob Murdoch, "was a hard guy to get to know. He didn't say very much. But he was a competitor.

"Everybody assumes just because you're young, you're going to get better. There are a lot of guys who've come to play in this town, the first year you think they're going to be world beaters, and pretty soon they're not playing. Suter got better." That freshman season, Suter contributed 68 points, tied for third on the team, alongside Lanny McDonald and Dan Quinn.

"He created," lauded his pal and defense-pair mate Neil Sheehy, "a dimension we didn't have. He could really skate. Hey, [Paul] Reinhart was skilled, but he wasn't a skater. Sutes got the puck and he'd…go.

"I'd say, 'Hey, I've got it covered back here.' He had such great ability, he'd just take it from there. I mean, 68 points for a rookie defenseman was phenomenal."

Suter and Sheehy hit it off on the ice and off. Post-practice, they'd head off to the Golden Arches and engage in epic eating contests. "That," recalled Sheehy, stifling a belch, "was when the McRib sandwiches came in. So we'd have two Big Macs, a couple Quarter Pounders, and then two or three McRib sandwiches. We'd get through those, and I'd spank him on the ice cream."

As the season wore on, the race for the Calder Trophy began to enter the Suter conversation. The overwhelming favorite was Toronto's 34-goal winger Wendel Clark. Clark's closest competitor seemed to be Montreal's 32-goal, 71-point right winger Kjell Dahlin. Suter was the wild card.

Playing out west, where games didn't usually end until after easterners were already in bed, during an age in which media saturation hadn't reached the insane levels of today, certainly didn't help Suter's cause, leading *Calgary Herald* hockey writer Eric Duhatschek to remind fellow Calder Trophy voters not to dismiss the Flames' stellar season out of hand.

At the NHL awards banquet following the playoffs, Suter became the first Flame to win a major award since the franchise shifted north from Atlanta. "It was," says Suter, "a validation of leaving college early. I didn't want to leave and end up being in the minor leagues.

Suter maneuvers past Chicago's Denis Savard in a 1986 regular-season game.

"I remember them putting a Rookie of the Year bonus into my first contract, where I finished in the voting. And I'm thinking, *Yeah, right. That'll never get collected.*"

Gary Suter (no extra *t*) had arrived. By March 1994, when Suter was dealt away to the Chicago Blackhawks in a six-player deal, everyone—well, most everyone—had learned to pronounce his name properly. He had scored 128 goals and 564 points—still good enough for fifth all-time, franchise-wise—in 617 regular-season starts as a Flame.

The greatest regrets of his lengthy Calgary tenure are easy to pinpoint. During the springtime of 1986, a hit from Mark Messier knocked him out 10 games into Calgary's improbable run to the final. Three years later, early on in the Stanley Cup march, Mel Bridgeman of the Canucks broke his jaw on a hit during Game 5 of round one. He sat in the stands on May 25 when the Flames collected the Stanley Cup.

"The injury in '86," he says now, "was tough. I strained knee ligaments. No big deal today, right? If that happened today, I wouldn't have missed more than four or five days. So that was a shame. I had to sit out the rest of the playoffs.

"But at the time, I'm thinking, *This is tough, but I had a great year. There'll be plenty more opportunities.*

"Then in '89, the broken jaw. People kept telling me what a big part of the team I was, but in that situation, when you're not out there on the ice in Montreal when the Cup comes out... You feel like that kid on the sidelines who only gets to watch. You're part of the team but you don't get in to play. A historic moment for the guys, the organization, and you're happy for everyone, but it's just not the same.

"That's something that'll always haunt me, not being healthy for that run and winning the whole deal."

23 Gretzky's Rash

Getting noticed. When you're an undrafted free agent signing out of Harvard University by way of International Falls, Minnesota, wearing, say, No. 71 at training camp…with that high a number, you need to grab people's attention or be lost in the shuffle. But when Wayne Gretzky begins to take notice…

"Best advice I ever had," Neil Sheehy recalled, "came from Badger [Bob Johnson]. He pulls me aside one day, sits me down, and says, 'Sheehy, do you know you're just like an actor in a Broadway play?'

"I'm sitting on the edge of my seat, you know, soaking this all up, getting a pep talk. 'Okay, Coach. All right, Coach, I'm an actor in a Broadway play.'

"He goes: 'You know what happens when actors can't act?'

"I say: 'What, Coach?'

"He goes: 'We bring in new actors! Now get out there and entertain those people!'"

So he did. Not that Gretzky would be giving the show anything approaching a rave review.

In the long, lustrous Battle of Alberta roll call, Neil Sheehy holds a special place of (dis)honor. He was one of those supporting players providing much of the prickly texture of insanity that marked the rivalry at its height (when both Sheehy and Paul Baxter were out there together yammering, Gretzky must've wondered whether he had Dolby Stereo headphones on).

He couldn't shoot the puck like Al MacInnis, skate like Gary Suter, or pull strings like Paul Reinhart. But he did have one undeniably useful talent that set him apart: the very sight of him used to set Gretzky's teeth on edge.

In the third period of Game 5 of the now-famous 1986 series, No. 99 got so PO'd at Sheehy he even took a swing. Gretzky, the advocate of peace and love, used to call Sheehy "gutless" for not dropping his gloves in that instance.

The Oilers considered him a coward, a runner, a poseur, unworthy of their time or their knuckles. Sheehy would then gleefully incite another incident by jabbering at Gretzky, baiting No. 99 mercilessly. In so doing, he gained a profile far beyond his talents, far above someone who played 222 games in Flames colors and collected 47 points (although his 725 penalty minutes do jump out as well).

"When you have that rage—and they had it," says Sheehy, now a successful player agent with I-C-E Hockey based in Minneapolis, "it was so easy to manage. If we were down two or three goals, I knew I had to make something happen. That's the only time I'd fight. If we were ahead, I wasn't fighting anybody.

"I did initially. But then it dawned on me—*Hey, we've got a pretty good power play here. Lanny. Mully. Hakan Loob. MacInnis. Sutes. So why not let [the Oilers] sit in the box?*

"I'd go 'Waaaaayne! Waaaaaayne!' One time, I remember, [Marty] McSorley takes a penalty, [Kevin] McClelland takes a penalty, and Gretzky's furious. He's yelling at me, 'You're a turtle! You're a turtle! Why won't you fight? Why won't you fight?' And I said, 'Wayne, I'm surprised. Aren't you the guy that wants fighting out of the game? And you want me to fight? Which one is it, Wayne? What do you want to do?'

"After the game, he told the writers, 'Neil Sheehy is the single reason fighting should not be banned from the NHL.' I loved it.

"So I'd poke him. I wasn't dirty. I'd never stick him. I'd just kind of stand by him and push him a little bit. Just let him know I was around. And I'd smile. He didn't like me smiling. What he also didn't like was that I didn't have to pay the price. Most guys that went anywhere near him got kicked on by [Dave] Semenko and those guys. But I was antagonizing him and not being made to pay the penalty. That drove him crazy."

Ever the self-promoter, Sheehy lapped up the attention. At one point, he declared himself the onetime heavyweight boxing champion of Harvard. "Harvard," laughed Flames executive Al MacNeil, "doesn't even have a boxing team!" (Turns out it does, numbering author Norman Mailer and former US presidents Teddy Roosevelt and JFK among its alumni.)

"I could take any of those three guys," laughed Sheehy. "Hey, I said we had a boxing club. I didn't say it was a varsity sport. I remember fighting some big football player, a 6'7" guy right out of the *Rocky* movies, a real brawl."

At the height of the Calgary-Edmonton mid-1980s hostility, *Sports Illustrated* arrived to chronicle the ill will. In the ensuing article, Sheehy was labeled the Butcher of Harvard. No man has ever been happier with a nickname. The tagline apparently originated from a sign hung disdainfully inside—where else?—Northlands Coliseum in Edmonton. It read: SHEEHY: THE BUTCHER.

"You know what?" says Sheehy, still delighted by the accolade all these years later. "When I bought my boat one summer, the boat company named the boat the *Butcher*, painted it on the side. I still have the boat. So when I go out on the water, I'm still the Butcher. How great is that?"

24 The Mario All-Star Game

Everyone in hockey had an inkling of the force of nature about to shift the landscape of the league and the game. And typically, Mario Lemieux, even at the precocious age of 19, wound up making his first All-Star Game appearance his own.

The Olympic Saddledome was only two years into its existence when Calgary hosted its first, and only, All-Star event, the 37th edition of the extravaganza. The place, predictably, was stacked to the rafters, 16,825 strong. The teams were lousy with famous names—Wayne Gretzky, Ray Bourque, Marcel Dionne, Michel Goulet, Ron Francis, Grant Fuhr, Pelle Lindbergh, Tom Barrasso.

Representing the Calgary Flames was a pair of defensemen: Al MacInnis, then 21 years old and making his first All-Star appearance, and the more established Paul Reinhart. Mr. Goalie—Glenn Hall—and the then-retired Guy Lafleur were honorary captains, and future Hall of Famer Andy Van Hellemond was the man in charge of the whistle. Canadian astronaut Marc Garneau performed the ceremonial faceoff, using a puck he'd taken into outer space.

Despite all the glitz on display, though, the game itself failed to fizz to life. Anders Hedberg, of the Wales crew and the NY Rangers, spoke for many afterward when he admitted: "Not only did it look slow. It *was* slow."

Added Reinhart glibly: "That wasn't exactly a classic."

Lemieux's sublime skills still managed to save the day, however. Even Gretzky, the game's reigning lord and master, couldn't conjure enough hocus-pocus to upstage the Penguins' teenage savior as Lemieux's two goals—including the game decider at 11:09 of the third period—propelled the Wales Conference elite to a 6–4 victory over the home-standing Campbell Conference.

"The story is born," said Hedberg, with a wink of respect to the Pittsburgh prodigy.

Ron Francis, Hedberg, Tim Kerr of the Philadelphia Flyers, and Washington's Mike Gartner scored the other Wales goals. Ray Bourque of the Bruins chipped in with a then-record four assists. For the Campbells, Dionne, Gretzky, Mirko Frycer, and Randy Carlyle all potted goals. Shots were 36–26 in favor of the Wales Conference.

Bombastic TV pundit Don Cherry had referred to Lemieux as "the biggest floater in the league" earlier in the season (Cherry would, of course, later revise that opinion, along with all of Lemieux's early detractors). The subject was hanging in the thin southern Alberta air. So when Lemieux was presented with the keys to a 1985 Dodge Lancer as game MVP, the first (and still only) time ever for a rookie, the wunderkind smiled and said, "That was for [Cherry]."

"Guys like Mario are the future of this league," said Gretzky, who suffered a few verbal potshots himself while in the early stages of carving out his own legend. "When you're 18 or 19 people want to criticize you. I've been called a lot worse when I was 18 or 19. And my attitude is the same as his—go out and prove them wrong on the ice. That's what Mario did tonight."

In homage to the ongoing Battle of Alberta animosities, Gretzky and Edmonton Oilers boss Glen Sather were booed lustily during introductions prior to the puck drop. The jeering of Gretzky continued each time he touched the puck. While Sather, ever the king of gamesmanship, acted indignant that the rival Flames crowd would dare to subject hockey's greatest impresario to such treatment, Gretzky himself didn't seem too perturbed. "I'd be surprised if they didn't boo," No. 99 laughed later. "I couldn't hear my name when it was announced."

You can wager no one was booing Mario Lemieux. This night, as so many more would in the years to come, belonged to No. 66.

It was a taste, a foreshadowing of things to come. "Hey, Mario," chirped Al Arbour, the Wales coach, seeing Lemieux trotting off, keys to his new ride in hand after the game. "Remember, I get the spare tire!"

25 Joe Who? (Naturally)

More that two decades and 1,200 regular-season games went by. "And that one," acknowledged Joe Nieuwendyk, "might've been the single-most-difficult game I played in my career. That first game back in Calgary. It was so emotional.

"I was booed mercilessly every time I touched the puck. And that was difficult to handle. My buddy Gary [Roberts] was still on the other side, and we took some faceoffs against each other. Just a very tough, tough night. Because so much of me, my heart and my soul, was still in a Flames uniform.

"It was tough, the first while in Dallas. Everything I'd been taught about winning and leadership I'd learned in Calgary. That kind of tie doesn't just disappear overnight. In fact, it never does."

When Cliff Fletcher finally offloaded wildly gifted but enigmatic Swede Kent Nilsson for a second-round draft pick, 27th overall in 1985—which became Joe Nieuwendyk—no one could've imagined the impact the rangy kid from Cornell would make. The Flames had wanted to use the pick on goalie Sean Burke, but Jersey snapped him up three spots earlier.

The lead on one indignant columnist's piece was the now-memorable: "Joe Nieuwendyk for Kent Nilsson? It stinks!" Almost immediately, the Joe Who? tag was born. Calgarians had to wait two years to see exactly what kind of player Cliff Fletcher had dealt the Magic Man away for.

Needless to say, the wait was worth it: mitts as soft as eiderdown or as venomous as a serpent, depending on what was required; that sublime hand-eye coordination honed on the lacrosse floor back home in Whitby, Ontario; tough enough to stand in front of the opposition stronghold and absorb the degree of unrelenting pounding permitted back in the mid-1980s; a swooping stride capable of leaving defenders in its wake.

"The luckiest thing that happened to me was getting put on Hakan Loob's line my first full year," Nieuwendyk admitted. "He helped me so much, starting my career the right way—a big reason why I scored 50. He could put pucks into areas, make plays nobody else would dream of."

The admiration, naturally, was mutual. "Intelligence," Loob replied, when asked to name the young Nieuwendyk's strengths. "Very intelligent hockey player. If you score 32 goals on the power play, mainly in front of the net and down low, people are going to be talking mainly about your hands and your shot, obviously. But I thought he had a touch of European style in him.

"How lucky was I? Here's a rookie, scoring 51 goals, chasing Mike Bossy, one of the best in league history, and I'm playing beside him.

"I've got to admit I'd never heard of the guy, but he was really impressive right away. He knew how to hang onto the puck in the zone, didn't panic or throw it away, was willing to stay there not only for 5 seconds, but for 10 or 15 seconds to create a good scoring chance."

Nieuwendyk's rookie season turned into one for the ages. With 10 games to go on the docket, he'd closed to within three of Bossy's rookie goal-poaching record, scoring his 50th on March 12 against Buffalo, deflecting in a Gary Suter point shot. As the chase narrowed, even Bossy, the Islanders icon, couldn't turn away. "To be honest, it's one of the two [records] that I cherish the most. But I have no control over the situation," admitted Bossy. "All I can do is watch, like you. I don't want anybody in Calgary thinking I'm here on the Island throwing hexes at Joe Nieuwendyk. Because I'm not. I wish him the best."

The Cornell rookie faded down the stretch and finished with 51 (four years later Teemu Selanne would shred the record to bits, scoring 76). There were consolations, however: a spot on the All-Rookie team, a turn at the All-Star Game, and, as the capper, the Calder Trophy.

Turned out 1988–89 proved to be even better. "The whole year was storybook," said Nieuwendyk. "From Lanny getting on a tear that last month to score his 500th goal and 1,000th point, to his big goal in the final game, to winning the Cup. That year, it was a joy to go to the rink."

Nieuwendyk's offensive consistency through his Calgary tenure is what set him apart. Check out the goal totals, by season, in a Flames uniform: 51, 51 45, 45, 22 (when he was limited by injury), 38, 36, 21 (in a lockout-shortened 1994–95 campaign). During his eight seasons, Joe Nieuwendyk graduated from hotshot rookie to dependable contributor to leader to captain and NHLPA rep.

"A dream to coach," lauded his old coach, Terry Crisp. "Nieuwy'd just come into the room, put on his gear, and go out and play. No fuss. No dramatics. You could chew him out, kick his butt. He went out and did the job."

That job netted Joe Who? 616 points in only 577 games, still good for fourth on the franchise's all-time list. The three men above him—Jarome Iginla, Theo Fleury, and Al MacInnis—each played appreciably more games in the flaming C.

When Nieuwendyk forced the Flames' hand and was traded away in 1995, there was much more achievement ahead for him. Two more Cup triumphs, a spot in the Hockey Hall of Fame, and a place on the NHL's top 100 in its centenary celebrations of 2017.

But he has never forgotten the hockey neighborhood he grew up in. "An ideal place to be a young player," he praised. "No question. I think if you asked [Sean] Monahan and [Johnny] Gaudreau and those kids, they'd say the same thing today. I'm sure that hasn't changed.

"Starting with the owners, Harley and Becky [Hotchkiss], the Seamans, Norm Kwong, Sonia [Scurfield]…it was a family atmosphere. People like Lanny and Pep and Timmy Hunter, they embraced me, made me feel so comfortable. Having my buddy Gary [Roberts] there, too. It's a great environment. Great city. I was lucky."

26 Snowstorm in Jersey

January 22, 1987: the 334 game. It was sparsely attended, and it was (and is) unprecedented. Not exactly the way you envision it as a kid lying in bed at night, at home in Scarborough, Ontario, dreaming of the big leagues. In any young goaltender's imagination, NHL debuts are, without fail, dizzyingly successful, 48-stop shutout affairs, ending with a star-making post-win spin as the game's first star.

"The thing for me was the long delay," Doug Dadswell remembered. "I was…uh…pretty anxious, let's say, and here I am sitting for two hours, thinking about everything. On top of that I had the flu. I got called up from Moncton, had been sick for a couple days, and drove up with all the brass. That was high pressure for me. Then I'm sick, the game's delayed, and nobody's in the stands. It was incredible."

A blizzard was relentlessly pummeling the state of New Jersey at the time, 22 inches worth of snow. Roads were virtually impassable. More than 11,000 tickets had reportedly been sold for the Flames-Devils tilt at the old Brendan Byrne Arena. By head count—and there turned out to be plenty of time to check, double-check, and reconfirm—334 hardy souls took in the contest. That 334 crowd count remains the most meager in league history. Welcome to the big time, Doug Dadswell.

"Three hundred and thirty-four?" blurted Flames right winger Lanny McDonald, astonished. "Are you *sure*? Oh my God. I would've thought maybe—maybe—250.

"Well, I knew it was small. The fact that anybody showed up at all still stuns me. You could go to Toronto or Montreal and have more press and fans in to watch the morning skate than we had that night. That great big building looked deserted.

"When we went out for the first warm-up, I don't even think the referees—maybe one—were in the building. I'm pretty sure we didn't finish the game until after midnight."

The major problem was many Devils players hadn't even gotten home from the morning skate by the time the Calgary team bus rolled slowly to the back of the rink, from just across the street, to begin pregame rituals.

There was a rumor of a linesman picking up a New Jersey player on his snowmobile on this way to the arena, and others of Devils GM Max McNab sneakily delaying the start of the game until his best player, Patrik Sundstrom, arrived. The officials wanted to end the suspense and start once Jersey had 14 players in the building, but since this was, after all, worth the customary two points, the Devils apparently held off by hiding players in the team's medical and stick rooms until they had a more representative contingent.

So for the visitors, the wait was long. "I told the guys that baseball players do it all the time during rainouts—sit around and wait to play," said Calgary coach Bob Johnson. "When they had

14 guys, they only wanted us to dress 14! They told me we had an unfair advantage. 'Hey,' I told them, 'that's your problem.' The whole thing was ridiculous."

Calgary assistant coach Bob Murdoch swore there were more arena workers that night than actual, in-the-flesh patrons. The game had been scheduled for the customary 7:30 PM start. There were multiple false starts, a handful of pregame warm-ups. They finally got 'er going at 9:10.

To show their appreciation to the crowd, the Devils PR staff took the names and addresses of each person attending. Those hearty fans would receive a commemorative pin, T-shirt, and tickets to a future game. That night, the super-exclusive 334 Club was born.

The Alberta invaders, however, didn't see much charm in the evening. Compounding the misery of the extended, off-again / on-again wait, the sleepy Flames were eventually singed 7–5, courtesy of a career-high five points from Jersey's Doug Sulliman.

"It was like you were playing a scrimmage," recalled Calgary left winger Colin Patterson. "Somebody would score, and there was no cheering, no booing, no noise…nothing.

"We didn't think we were going to play. And then we ended up getting our ass kicked."

Doug Dadswell would go on to play in only 26 more NHL games, all for the Flames over two seasons, interspersed among minor league stops in Moncton, Indianapolis, Cincinnati, Utica, Salt Lake, and Birmingham before retirement from hockey in 1993.

"[Was it] what I'd dreamed my first NHL game would be like?" Dadswell asked. "Well, no, not really. I'm sure [attendance mark] was the only record I ever broke."

No game—for sheer oddity, anyway—could ever match January 22, 1987. Calgary trainer Jim "Bearcat" Murray offered up a novel reason for the crazy goings-on of that never-to-be-forgotten night. "It was a miracle that we played it," he grumbled. "I always hated it there, in that building, anyway. Not the team, but the arena treated us like a bunch of crap. Forever giving us a hard time. I always said it was because what's-his-name [Jimmy Hoffa] was supposed to be buried under center ice. I said it was his ghost, wrecking things. At least, that was my excuse."

27 He Ain't Nothin' but a Hound Dog

The first suit, concocted in his family basement, was made out of thick sheepskin and sewn together. "Hot?" remembered the designer. "Holy moly, was it ever." He borrowed $1,000 from his mom to offset the total $4,000 cost. The shaggy character—paid $50 for the night—debuted February 16, 1984, at the Olympic Saddledome, in a game that pitted the Calgary Flames against the Pittsburgh Penguins.

"Pre–Mario Lemieux," recalled Grant Kelba, the original man in the suit. "I believe the score was 8–4 Flames, and Doug Risebrough got a hat trick."

These days to fill in the blanks during stoppages in play, there are whales and bears, bald eagles, anthropomorphic ice hogs, ducks, green aliens, and hawks on hand to entertain fans across the 31-stop NHL spectrum. Back then, there was only him. Only a dog. Only Harvey the Hound, the NHL's first mascot.

Kelba parlayed four years as the CFL Stampeders' mascot Ralph the Dog into his gig as Harvey, which dovetailed with the Flames changing addresses from the water-closet-sized Calgary Corral to the brand-new Saddledome.

"Hockey," said Kelba, 17 years removed from his swan song as the Hound, "is so different from football. In football, you've got a sideline, there's a lot of downtime. In hockey, you don't really have any room to work. And back then there were no video replays or anything like that. So as a fan, if you wanted to see the goals, you really had to pay attention.

"But I thought I'd give it a go, do my best. I guess I was as confident, or as cocky, as a 23-year-old kid could be, never thinking it could fail.

"Within the first 10 seconds of my first game as Harvey, [once] the play started, I sat down in the stands, and a guy leans over and whispers in my ear: 'Go to hell.'

"I look back now, and I'm like, 'Geez, what were you thinking?'"

In the years to come, Harvey hijinks became as synonymous with Flames hockey as a Lanny McDonald wrister, a Miikka Kiprusoff theft, or a Johnny Gaudreau shimmy-shake. "The highlights, for me, were the people. The audience. The crowd. The reactions. The interaction I had with them. I never went for the games. I was there doing a job," Kelba said.

During the playoffs in 1989, Harvey ran a small remote-controlled Zamboni over a Canucks sweater between periods of a Calgary-Vancouver first-round tilt. The ploy so enraged the Canucks' big Irishman, president and GM Pat Quinn, that he roared down from the press box and demanded (successfully) that such defaming shenanigans cease and desist.

When L.A. coach Tom Webster was once suspended for throwing a stick on the ice, Harvey greeted the Kings on their next appearance at the Saddledome by strolling the aisles with a stick embedded in his head, wearing a sign stating, I Just Met Tom Webster.

One of the more memorable sights of the Flames trip to Japan to play two regular-season games against San Jose back in the fall of 1998 was Harvey, decked out in full regalia, wedging his way from

Harvey the Hound has been a mainstay of Flames contests since 1984.

a platform onto a commuter train, and no one in the jam-packed car deigning to make so much as eye contact.

On that same junket, he climbed the Olympic-caliber diving board at one end of the converted Tokyo swimming pool hosting the games and did his schtick from 10 meters high.

"It changed a lot," said Kelba. "It all became about marketing. At the end of my stint, it was like, 'Hey, can you not do as much, because we've sold advertising on the Jumbotron?' That's when I knew.

"But the early days were a lot of fun. The Battle of Alberta, boy...I'd be standing by the boards, and [Dave] Semenko, [Wayne] Gretzky, [Mark] Messier, and all those guys would be walking on that rubber mat onto the ice and as they'd be yelling and swearing at me: '*F* you, Harvey.' On and on and on. So I used to blow kisses at them and give them the finger. But I'd do it just out of stick-swinging distance."

Kelba had long since passed the suit along ("I was about to turn 40, and after 4 years as Ralph and 15 as Harvey, I'd spent my entire adult life as a dog") at the time of Harvey's most (in)famous moment—the January 2003 run-in with Edmonton Oilers boss Craig MacTavish. Weary of the Hound's constant taunting and well behind on the scoreboard, MacTavish reached up, ripped the tongue right out of his fuzzy head, and tossed it into the crowd.

Kelba had actually just arrived home after a vacation to Vegas. The next morning his phone was ringing off the hook. "So I turned on the highlights and saw it. Did I ever laugh."

MacTavish, bless him, played along like a trouper. "My daughter," he quipped, "was a little worried. She wondered if I'd go after Barney."

Seems preposterous now, given how beloved the big pooch has become, but the designer and first model reckons it took a full six years for fans to really warm to his creation. "A lot of comments, letters to the editor in the paper at first. Some people said, 'Give it up; we don't need mascots at NHL games.' Don Cherry was, of course, an outspoken critic the whole time. He thought I was turning it into a circus.

"But others said, 'Go on, give it a shot. It's pretty quiet in the building. If there's anything the Flames can do to spice it up a bit, by all means.' So I did. Game by game, inch by inch. And I guess the people in that second group were right. Harvey's still around."

28 "In His Own Little World"

Leave it to Al MacNeil, someone who's forgotten more about hockey than most men with fancy titles in spacious offices will ever know, to spot the unpolished potential underneath the 5'6" of curiosity. "On the surface," admitted the Calgary Flames' assistant GM at the time of Theoren Fleury's rise into the NHL, "you're saying to yourself, 'Why the hell waste a pick on this guy?' Then you see him play, and your head does a 360 on a swivel. He's like Henri Richard. They only brought him into Montreal for a cup of coffee to please his big brother, and he stayed 16 years. You couldn't get the damn puck off him.

"All Fleury's life people have been telling him to get into another line of work, shoot pool or maybe bag groceries. None of the other hotshot little guys give me the jump this kid does. He's special." That he was. Turns out, though, at the absolute beginning, not even as shrewd a judge of hockey horseflesh as Al MacNeil had so much as an inkling.

"When they picked me, Al actually threw his pen across the draft table," laughed Fleury at the recollection, nearly two decades later. "'Geez,' he said, 'not another jockey!' Funny thing is, he wound up being one of my biggest boosters."

Fleury was a pint-sized dynamo of ability and attitude. He was wildly outspoken, wildly entertaining, wildly controversial, wildly ambitious, and wildly talented. Virtually ignored by pro scouts, the Flames chose him 166th overall, in the eighth round of the 1987 draft. Everyone assumed he was around strictly to sell tickets for the team's IHL farm club in Salt Lake. They soon found out otherwise. "How good is he without the puck?" Golden Eagles coach Paul Baxter asked. "I don't know, really. He's always got it."

Theoren Fleury arrived in the big leagues on New Year's Day 1989, for a cup of coffee, like Henri Richard, and stuck around for 11 Calgary seasons, six of those years as the team's leading point producer.

As the stellar names of the Stanley Cup group—Doug Gilmour, Al MacInnis, Joe Nieuwendyk, Mike Vernon, Gary Suter, Gary Roberts, Jim Otto, etc.—all made exits, one by one, Fleury alone remained to soldier on. During the lean, losing years of the mid- to late 1990s, he propped up a fading franchise, twice reaching the 100-point plateau. "I've always had to accept that I was small," Fleury admitted in the fall of 1988, on the cusp of fulfilling his dream. "There was no changing it. I had to dig down deep, real deep, and say, 'Screw the world! There isn't anybody or anything that's going to keep me from reaching my goal.' I've never doubted myself. Sure I'm a cocky little bastard. That's what got me here."

No one back then could've guessed at many of the reasons for the rage in his play, the damage in his soul that in part drove him relentlessly onward. It went far beyond the little-guy syndrome. For much of his NHL career, the drug and alcohol problems, the saga of sexual abuse at the hands of junior coach Graham James, were hidden away, only hinted at, never revealed. His outlet was the game itself. "How can a team like Calgary draft a player as good as Fleury in the [eighth] round?" Wayne Gretzky once wondered out loud.

He took the unique combination of size (lack thereof) and sneer (no shortage) to audacious heights. Not only did he play big, he thought like someone who was 6'2". "Honest to God," blurted Winnipeg Jets defenseman Randy Carlyle, after a run-in with the tiny terror, "he's in his own little world out there."

When the Flames acquired Corey Millen in the deal that saw Joe Nieuwendyk traded for Jarome Iginla, Millen was listed as an inch shorter than Fleury, who quipped, "I could eat an apple off his head." And once, after a 1991 game against the Chicago Blackhawks, 5'8" goaltender Alain Chevrier, tired of being jostled by Fleury the tiny terror, complained, "Bobby McGill said he called *me* a sawed-off runt. I can't figure that one out."

Only Lanny McDonald and Jarome Iginla can claim to have won the hearts of Calgarians, of Flames fans everywhere, to the extent of Theo Fleury. Fleury moments remain among the most indelible in franchise lore. At the very top: his knee slide / arm pump down the ice at Northlands Coliseum after stripping Mark Messier of the puck to score in OT of Game 6 of the Flames' compelling 1991 series against the Oilers, to send the series to the limit.

But as he continued, the Flames struggled and the financial realities of a non–salary cap league began to take a toll. On February 28, 1999, an era ended when Calgary GM Al Coates dealt their most popular, most influential, player to the contending Colorado Avalanche. Fleury exited as the franchise's all-time leading scorer.

The move to Denver didn't work out, nor did subsequent opportunities with the New York Rangers and Chicago Blackhawks. Fleury's personal demons were beginning to manifest themselves in more public ways.

In the fall of 2009, at 41 and six years after his last NHL appearance, Theoren Fleury launched an improbable comeback,

back where it all began. In his first exhibition appearance, he had a deft deke to count the only shootout goal to slay the New York Islanders. Then he got a goal and a helper against the Florida Panthers. The Saddledome once more had the opportunity to rise as one and chant, "Thee-O! Thee-O! Thee-O!"

Ultimately, inevitably, younger legs won the day, but there was lovely symmetry in such an ending. "I get to retire a Calgary Flame," Fleury said the day of his release. "I *had* to retire a Calgary Flame. It's been a long journey. It's time to put down some roots. And there's no better place than here.

"To the fans, what can I say? Please don't be angry. In the last two weeks, I pulled on your heartstrings. I made those of you who were doubters in the beginning believers. We got to say one final good-bye to each other. How many guys get to leave the game to a standing ovation?"

29 Theo Sound Bites

Besides being among the greatest players in franchise history, Theoren Fleury ranked as *the* most quotable. By turns outrageous, engaging, and thoughtful, he brightened many dull days with his comments. "Part of being a hockey player," he's said often, "is entertaining people. You're in the entertainment business, whether you want to admit it or not.

"A guy and his wife and two kids sit in...not the greatest seats, and it costs [the guy] basically one paycheck to take himself and his family to a hockey game. So it was part of our job to be interesting, to be colorful, for the fans. I *got* that part of it."

Even after establishing himself as an NHL star, Fleury still thought and talked like the defiant street urchin of junior days trying to fill the rink in Moose Jaw.

A sampling of his gems:

- "As a kid, I never had anything. Now, geez, it seems I have everything. I remember growing up collecting hockey cards, reading hockey magazines. Now I'm in them."
- On his prairie upbringing: "The winters were tough—long and hard. We didn't have much money; in fact I never owned a brand-new pair of skates until I was in junior. But somewhere, somehow, my dad—he worked for the town—would scrape enough together for me to play in a tournament somewhere. I'll never forget that."
- At his first visit to the fabled Montreal Forum: "You know, this is the one building that looks the same in real life as it does on TV."
- Recalling his favorite Stanley Cup Finals moment (as a spectator) on the flight to Montreal for Game 5 on May 23, 1989: "I remember it vividly. [John Tonelli] passed the puck to [Bob] Nystrom, and he tapped it upstairs on his backhand. We went nuts in my friend's basement. I was the biggest Islanders fan then. The biggest. Tommy Senick! That was the guy's name. Tommy Senick. It was his basement. A year later I was dating his sister."
- After lifting Lord Stanley's mug at the Forum on May 25, 1989: "I remember sleeping on the flight home, the Stanley Cup seat-belted into the chair next to me. I was sleeping on it. The funny thing is I won a World Junior, a Turner Cup, and a Stanley Cup in 18 months. So I'm like, 'Holy cow, is that what my career's going to be like?'"
- With the Flames heading over to the USSR for the fall 1989 Friendship Tour, having captained Canada to a World Junior

gold in Moscow: "McDonald's would be king over there. We had to eat whatever was put in front of us or starve. I don't know what we were eating. German shepherd, maybe."

- Asked about what was sore, after absorbing a lethal Charlie Huddy elbow during the epic 1991 Flames-Oilers playoff series: "Just my teeth. But you don't skate with your teeth."

- On looking for new duds after referee Mark Faucette had ruled his sweater illegal due to the excessive amount of blood on it: "I'm standing on the bench, and a fan throws one of my jerseys down to me. I thought about going out with it on, but it had all these autographs on it. I'm not going out there wearing a sweater with my autograph."

- "What if? What if? I don't know what's going to happen. I can't guarantee anything. Do I look like JoJo [Savard]? I'm no psychic. What does she get for those calls, anyway—$4.99 a minute? If I was a psychic I'd have won seven or eight Lotto 6/49s by now and be retired in Hawaii."

- Taking dead aim at perceived preferential treatment of the Great One in L.A.: "Gary [Bettman] comes over and cuts Wayne's lawn when he's in town, looks after the kids if Janet and Gretz want to go out to a movie."

- Waving his stick at San Jose fans at the Shark Tank, after taking a spin as one of the game's three stars: "I stuck this so far up your ass you'll never get it out."

- Prior to Wayne Gretzky's final Saddledome appearance as a New York Ranger: "Yup, he peed on an awful lot of our parades in here. I mean Gretzky has, what, 2,800 points? There are hundreds of NBA players who don't get that in a career. And they get two points for a basket, sometimes three."

- After No. 99 received a standing ovation, the fans chanting "Gretz-KY! Gretz-KY!" for the first and only time in Calgary, following his swan song game: "With all the pain he's inflicted on the people of Calgary, I couldn't believe they did that."

- After becoming the franchise's all-time leading points producer, on February 20, 1999: "Actually, I'm kind of surprised
  I was able to do this so soon. I've always played with a chip on
  my shoulder. That's what got me here, and that's what's kept
  me here. I just love to play. And I love to score goals. Man, do
  I love to score goals."

- On February 28, 1999, the day of his trade to Colorado: "I had
  to deal with a lot of tough things during my years here, but this
  is one of the toughest. A piece of me will always be a Calgary
  Flame."

- During elation at a jam-packed Fleury household when he was
  selected to Canada's 2002 Olympic team roster: "Good thing I
  made it. Doesn't make much sense to invite all these people to
  a wake."

- Following Canada's gold medal win against the US in Salt
  Lake: "People can't imagine how much that meant to me. I
  was trying to take my life back, and that was such a gesture
  of support, of confidence [from Canada boss Wayne Gretzky,
  in selecting me]. I start[ed] off in hell, and here I am now, in
  heaven. This is the best moment of my life."

- "I remember we were playing in a tournament in Miniota [west
  of Winnipeg], and the winners got tickets to a Jets game. Well, it
  turned out to be the last game of that year. The infamous game
  with Colorado for last place to see who got the top pick. But I
  scrambled down to where the tunnel was, stepping over people,
  and I managed to get Lanny [McDonald's] autograph. Ten years
  later, I'm on the ice celebrating a Stanley Cup with the guy.
  When I told him that story, he just laughed and laughed."

- On retirement: "When you leave the game, it's over. There's
  a void. You're left with a lot of baggage. Aches. Pains.
  Concussions. I'd say the majority of us don't have anything to
  fall back on. It took me six years—six years—to find some kind
  of footing."

- After being released from his wacky but wonderful Flames tryout in 2009, at age 41: "When I left the Saddledome on Friday, I knew this part of my life had come to an end. I knew in my heart it was over. I'd made my peace with it. I needed to do this for me. I remember standing at [former Flames co-owner] Doc Seaman's funeral last year, and one phrase of Doc's really stuck with me: 'Leave it better than you found it.' In the last two weeks, I think I've accomplished that. I have nothing left to prove to myself. Finally."

30 Crispie

The story has been told often, but Terry Crisp still delights in the telling. "To this day," Terry Crisp said, "what sticks in my mind is Tom Watt. After the game. We've won. Well, Tom Watt is just sitting on a little bench with his back up against the wall. He's got one of those championship caps on, with the tag still attached, hanging there. It's on backward.

"The emotion, the adrenaline, is still pumping, of course. He's holding a beer in one hand, crazy look on his face, and he says, 'You know, Crispie, this, right now, blows my mind.' Then he leans back, the beak of the cap up against the wall, and as he pushes his head back the friggin' hat lifts off his head like the lid off a pot. We laughed *so* hard. Like four-year-olds. As if it was the funniest thing in the world ever. Imagine...

"I can still close my eyes and see it. Tom leaning back, the cap lifting up. 'You know, Crispie, this, right now, blows my mind.' Ridiculous, right? But that's what happens when you win a Stanley Cup. It turns you back into a kid."

Among the 16 men who have coached the Flames organization since its relocation from Georgia, Terry Crisp remains singular, unique. "Badger" Bob Johnson is fondly remembered as the optimistic mad genius. Dave King arrived with the vast international pedigree. Darryl Sutter gets deserved kudos as the man who revitalized a flagging franchise. In 2014–15 Bob Hartley collected the lone Jack Adams Award in Flames history for tutorial acumen. But Crisp is the only Flames head coach who can bring out a ring, and who can visit the Hockey Hall of Fame and find his name engraved on the chalice as part of the organization. The guy with the off-the-charts .669 winning percentage. Sure, he inherited a good situation, a group on the precipice of greatness. But the guy in charge of the best team doesn't always win the big bauble.

To start the 1987–88 season, Crisp was promoted after two years in charge of the AHL Moncton Golden Flames. After 400 games in charge, Johnson had exited to become president of the Amateur Hockey Association of the United States. Badger Bob— the eccentric, idiosyncratic mastermind who was far ahead of his time—was no easy act to follow; he was well loved in Calgary and universally respected around the hockey world.

The late Fred Shero, Crisp's mentor during their days together at the Philadelphia Spectrum (Shero as Crisp's coach), backed his protégé from the start, though. In fact, Shero credited his red-headed, pint-sized penalty-killing ace for winning Philly's first of back-to-back Stanley Cups.

"There were a couple minutes left," recalled Shero. "I don't know why, but I lost my mind. Totally lost it. I was sending the wrong players on the ice, trying to be a nice guy, I guess. We were winning so I figured, 'Why not?'"

Crisp wheeled on his boss. "Freddie," he snarled "enough of this horseshit! Stop being such a goddamned nice guy! Not now! This is for the Cup!"

Shero, stunned, gaped at Crisp. "If you think you can do better, Crispie," he shot back sarcastically, "you take over!"

"And I'll be damned if Crispie didn't take over for the last three minutes!" Shero said. "And he put the right players on the ice. So we won the game and the Cup."

Crisp's initial season in charge, Calgary collected its first Presidents' Trophy as overall league regular-season champs, winning 48 games. But after dusting off the L.A. Kings in five games, the Flames were swept aside by Wayne Gretzky and the Edmonton Oilers. It was a crushing but necessary step in the evolution of a championship unit.

As the 1988–89 season dawned, the Flames were once again among the title favorites. The regular season yielded yet another Presidents' Trophy. Led by 51 apiece from Joe Nieuwendyk and Joe Mullen, the offense scored 354 goals as they piled up a franchise-record 54 wins. But playoffs are what mattered. And everyone in Calgary remembers what happened that spring. The idyll, though, would not last long.

When the Flames fell in six games, under controversial circumstances, to Wayne Gretzky and the L.A. Kings a year later in the first round, the braying for change was loud. "I consider myself a damn good coach." Crisp said in defiant defense. "When we won the Cup I never heard anyone say, 'Crisp's a great coach.' Now when we lose, I take all the heat. I guess I don't win Cups, I just lose 'em.

"I never said Terry Crisp was the be-all, end-all. But I've got two Presidents' Trophies, a Stanley Cup, and a .690 winning percentage. Anybody else in the league now done that? Look, I don't want this to sound like bravado. But look at my record. It's there. It's a fact. When I get up in the morning, when I look in the mirror, when I shave, I see exactly what I want to see." After twisting in the wind for 24 days, on May 8, 1990, the ax fell.

More than a quarter century later, Terry Crisp said he's moved beyond bitterness to abject disappointment over the firing. "And [I'm] still a little bit mystified. I've said this many times: When he hired me, Cliff Fletcher told me, 'Your mandate is to win a Cup. Nothing else.' The owners have all the money they'll ever need. They've been to the dance and not gotten the big prize. Well, we got the big prize.

"After we'd lost to L.A., I remember Cliff calling me in the middle of June to come in for a chat. The middle of June, for a coach, is not a good time for a chat with the general manager. And he looks at me, he's smiling, and says, 'Crispie, I think we're making a coaching change.' Then he says, 'No, I know we're making a coaching change. And you're it.' Then we both started to laugh. It seemed so comical but true.

"Yeah, I pushed some guys. Maybe I pushed the wrong guys. Well, in order to make an omelet, you've gotta crack some eggs. Obviously I cracked the wrong eggs. To this day I still can't wrap my brain around why I was fired so quickly."

31 Beast

They affectionately called him Beast. He sported a crew cut and was burly, uncompromising, blunt, and defiantly old-school in an era of nonconformity. He was a rock of dependability at his chosen profession.

Born in Dodsland, Saskatchewan, from farm stock, Brad McCrimmon grew up in nearby Plenty, a small village of fewer than 150 people. The values ingrained in him there at a young age—commitment, hard work—became the basis for his life and his hockey career. What McCrimmon provided every team he joined, and the Flames in particular, was balance and steadiness married to a fierce competitive spirit.

Many a forearm was temporarily deadened for those foolhardy forwards rash enough to take him on and get a step advantage heading toward the net. You simply did not mess with Beast. "Beast was just…solid," Flames backup goaltender Rick Wamsley once summed up. "Stayed within himself. You knew what you were getting. Every day. He was just…Beast. I don't know how to describe it, really.

"He was like that family member that doesn't change, that you can always count on. The one that just makes you feel that everything's all right, we're okay.

"[Coach Terry Crisp] used to say, 'There's too much gray in our game. We need more black and white.' Beast was the black and white."

He'd been Boston's first-round (15th overall) selection out of the Western Hockey League Brandon Wheat Kings in the 1979 NHL Entry Draft. He spent three seasons there before being dealt to the City of Brotherly Love and the Flyers. In Philadelphia, paired with Mark Howe, the young McCrimmon continued to improve. He was largely underrated, except by those he played for, and against.

But his time in Philly was short. In the summer of 1987, Flyers GM Bobby Clarke was plenty miffed at McCrimmon for holding out and heading home over a contract dispute the previous summer, forcing Clarke into signing his evolving defenseman into a stopgap one-year deal. McCrimmon, Clarke decided, had to go.

As fate would have it, one of the Flames' top four on the blueline, Jamie Macoun, had been involved in a car accident, throwing his availability into question. So looking for an insurance policy, Calgary management had designs on both McCrimmon and another prominent pending free agent, Randy Carlyle of the Pittsburgh Penguins.

"I can't remember what the reasoning came down to exactly," confessed longtime Flames executive Al MacNeil, "but after some back and forth we went after McCrimmon. No disrespect to Randy Carlyle, but it was the best decision we ever made." Circumstances being right, a deal was struck. McCrimmon to Calgary in exchange for a third-round pick in the 1988 NHL Entry Draft and a first-rounder in 1989.

"I've said often that getting Doug Gilmour from Toronto was the move that put us over the top," said Calgary GM Cliff Fletcher years afterward, "but the one trade that barely gets a mention anymore but was instrumental in our winning was the acquisition of Brad McCrimmon. He gave us that mean defenseman who could play a lot of minutes, and in any situation."

That year, McCrimmon, on a group prepping for a Stanley Cup, collected the Emery Edge Award for top plus-minus, at plus-48. The next season, he ranked first in that category at his position. Then came the 1988–89 season and the Stanley Cup triumph. Through the 22 playoff games that spring, he collected only three assists. But his presence, his contribution, was immense.

Part of McCrimmon's legacy in the game is the young defensemen he helped groom. In Calgary, he mentored Gary Suter. Among his other "pupils" were Nicklas Lidstrom in Detroit and Chris Pronger in Hartford.

On November 3, 1989, following the Cup triumph, McCrimmon became Calgary's captain, only lasting a year in that position before being offloaded to the Detroit Red Wings. He later had stops at Hartford and Phoenix, concluding his playing career following the 1996–97 season, with a collective plus-444 rating.

Following retirement, he naturally moved to the coaching side of the game, spending time as an assistant with the New York Islanders, back in Calgary, in Atlanta, and finally in Detroit.

His no-frills, take-it-upon-yourself philosophy didn't change. "As a coach, you do what you can from your side of the equation," he said. "Your job is to prepare the team, or certain individuals, as best you can. You're trying to do your part in the suit. But when the puck hits the ice, it's in the hands of the players. At that point, the horse is out of the barn. You've got to step aside and let him run."

What McCrimmon wanted most, though, was to be put in charge of his own NHL team. So in order to demonstrate his abilities as a No. 1 man, he headed over to Russia and the Kontinental Hockey League's Lokomotiv Yaroslavl.

Then came the shocking news of September 7, 2011. Brad McCrimmon and nearly the entire Yaroslavl team had perished in a plane crash just after takeoff en route to a game. He was 52 years old. All of hockey was shaken by the sudden tragedy, but the loss hit home particularly hard in Calgary, where McCrimmon had celebrated his only Stanley Cup triumph.

Former teammate Jim Peplinski ran into a friend at the gas station in Calgary that sad, hollow day. "He asked me, 'Did you hear about Brad?' I told him I had," recalled Peplinski. "And then he said, 'You know, it's funny, but I've never met a Saskatchewan farmer I didn't like.' Beast is in that category."

32 Killer

On a team loaded with front-end talent, he turned out to be the table tipper, the chart topper. The competitive conscience. The adhesive. The indomitable will. "He was the final ingredient of…a pretty good pot of stew," reasoned goaltender Rick Wamsley.

Describe it as you like. The effect was immediate. "Dougie," explained defenseman Ric Nattress, nicely summing up the man and his personal jet propulsion, "probably wouldn't admit it, but he was always out there to prove. To everyone else. To himself. To prove he was good, then great. To prove he wasn't too small. All that stuff drove him. He used it like cars use gas."

Before the controversial ending to his tenure in Calgary and his subsequent rise to Maple Leafs deity, Doug Gilmour was the linch-pin addition that pushed the Flames over the top. The man shrewd enough to add him to the mix, Cliff Fletcher, said so.

As much as Torontonians might like to believe it, Gilmour didn't have to relocate to the Big Smoke to prove his true value. Folks in Calgary were already well aware. He was a star with a blue-collar foundation, capable of checking the opposition's top center to a standstill one night and scoring the winning goal or making that defense-shredding pass the next.

"Dougie," lauded coach Terry Crisp, "had no time for excuses. He had no time for anyone who had a little boo-boo and figured they couldn't play. He was single-minded in his objective, and that was to win hockey games."

Gilmour joined the Flames from the St. Louis blues on September 6, 1988—along with Mark Hunter, Steve Bozek, and defenseman Michael Dark—under a cloud of litigation: a $1 million civil lawsuit filed by the parents of a 14-year-old girl (which was subsequently dropped), claiming sexual misconduct.

The change of locale was welcome, even necessary, but that didn't stop the taunting. "More or less," Gilmour admitted in December of that year, "it's the fans I have to deal with. They're trying to find a weakness, to break you down. I hear something, and I say to myself, 'Don't look at him. Stare straight ahead.' "I grind my teeth and skate by. What am I going to do? They paid their $20, and it's a free world out there."

On the ice, despite the personal upheavals, his play never suffered. In 72 regular-season games, he piled up 85 points. But then, Doug Gilmour's worth went so far beyond any mere statistics.

"Remember when Alberta Boot [Co.] was giving out the pair of boots for a hat trick?" cackled Crisp reflectively. "Well, we were winning late in the season, 6–1 or 7–1, and Killer had two goals. So I said to him, 'Killer, how'd you like a hat trick?' And he said, 'Wouldn't mind.' I said, 'Okay, but I get the boots!'

"So I left him out there the last five minutes of the game. He went through three sets of wingers. But he got his hat trick. And I'm still wearing my snakeskin boots. That Killer…he always delivered."

Never more so than through the spring of 1989. Following a subpar opening series against the Vancouver Canucks, he played—as Nattress described it—"like a man possessed" in the final three rounds, finishing with 22 points in 22 playoff games.

True to form, he saved his best for the penultimate moment: Game 6 against the Canadiens. In Montreal on the night of May 25, 1989, Doug Gilmour swatted a thigh-high puck behind Patrick Roy to count the eventual game-winning goal, and then slotted the puck into an empty net in the closing seconds to ensure a 4–2 win and a championship in that most holy of hockey shrines, the old Montreal Forum.

"As soon as [the game winner] went in, somebody ran [to] me," recalled Gilmour in the spring of 2014. "I think it was [Brian] Skrudland. When I got up, and this is what I remember most, there were three former St. Louis guys right there. Me, Mully, and Rob Ramage. I thought that was pretty fitting.

"I got a picture that night of me kissing the Cup with my dad beside me. You talk about it being 25 years ago. Life changes, and he passed away a year and a half ago. That one's on my phone, and I look at it. Often."

Yes, the stay was brief, but the impact Doug Gilmour exacted in only three and a half seasons in Calgary is indisputable, can never be erased or diminished.

The year following the Cup triumph, Rick Wamsley happened to be shopping for groceries at Safeway and bought a $19.95 video covering the Flames' run to glory. "Every once in a while," he admitted years later, "I'll pop in that old video. And all I know is there's a lot of Doug Gilmour in it."

33 Tim Hunter: Tough Guy

John Brophy, then coach of the Central Hockey League Birmingham Bulls, had a PhD in tough. He practiced, respected, and nurtured toughness. "He said to me one day—'Kid, you're going to make it in the NHL one of either two ways,'" Tim Hunter recalled. "As either the best defenseman in the Central Hockey League. Or the meanest [bleep] in the Central Hockey League.' And he looked at me and said, 'I think No. 2's your choice.'"

In an era of melees and line brawls, they simply didn't make 'em any tougher than Tim Hunter. At 6'2" and tipping the Toledos at slightly more than 200 pounds, he was far from the largest carnivore on the NHL's revolving fight card. Back in the day, every team was in possession of at least one true heavyweight. Fighting then was a tactic, a tool.

During the glory years of the Flames, Tim Hunter was the one keeping the opposition honest and his pals unsullied. "Amazing difference in the game, then to now," he said. "I don't know what you'd call it back then, at times, other than…sheer brutality. Doing whatever it took to win. Then whenever you were down a few goals, let the other team know you were in a hockey game. Some pretty crazy stuff went on."

Selected 54th overall in the 1979 NHL Entry Draft while the Flames were still based in Atlanta, Hunter cited Al MacNeil, who instilled a nonnegotiable caveat to put in the work, and Pierre Page, who pushed the importance of conditioning, as two major early influences in his career. "Those aspects of the game mattered to me because the two things I could control in life were how hard I worked and how fit I was. I thought that gave me an edge, and it turned out to be true."

For anyone, it is no surprise Hunter tops the franchise list in penalty infraction minutes (PIM) at 2,405, nearly 700 more than Gary Roberts. The 375 he accrued during the Stanley Cup season of 1988–89 is the gold—or rather, black-and-blue—standard.

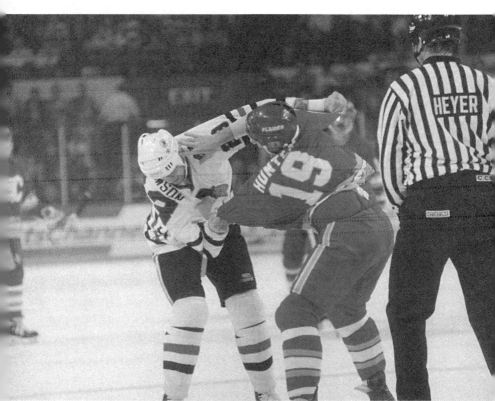

Tim Hunter and Blackhawk Stu Grimson trade punches in 1991.

Hunter fought 'em all during his 14-year career: Dave Semenko. Jim Kyte. Chris Nilan. Glen Cochrane. Kevin McClelland. Pick a significant brawler…any significant brawler.

"Huntsy always had your back. In those days, that was a welcome thing to have," said center Joel Otto, no Hobbit himself at 6'4" and 220 pounds. "I remember one fight he got into with [Marty] McSorley, up in Edmonton. Tim was always one of the best-conditioned guys on the team, but he and Marty fought—it went on forever—and when we got to the dressing room after the period, he was lying on the training table just totally…spent."

Hunter remembered the exhaustion. "I do. I remember asking [trainer] Bearcat [Murray], 'Is there any way you can get me some more oxygen? I can't seem to get enough right now.'

"That was one of the first really long fights I had. Probably, I'd say, just over two minutes. That's a long time to be squared off.

"There was another one with Marty when he was in L.A., after the Gretzky trade. We had a few beauties."

On the first call-up from the minors, Hunter was immediately switched from the blueline to right wing. The first night, the Flames faced Philly; the next night, Boston.

"So I pretty much guessed," he noted ruefully, "that this was going to be my calling.

"I really, really dug in, worked at my craft, watched a lot of video to see how all the best guys fought, trained in the summers with [Calgary heavyweight contender] Willie deWit and Paul Reinhart, Pepper and Riser down at the boxing gym. I figured if I'm going to do this, I'm going to be the best at it. I was always prepared, never afraid of anyone, because I knew I could handle myself."

While he and Semenko are forever intertwined, Hunter's choice for toughest bruiser he ever duked it out with is a Staten Island–born enforcer who would later become a teammate in Calgary: Nick Fotiu.

"Madison Square Garden. Early in my career. I had already fought Don Maloney that night. Thrashed him pretty good, so I'm thinking, *Nick's coming, anytime now.* One of the biggest, toughest guys in the league, right? Never came, never came. Well, there's not even a minute left in the game, faceoff at center ice, and they send out Nick Fotiu, and it's like, 'Ooooooookaaaaaaay.'

"Before the puck's even dropped—he's on left wing, I'm on the right—he spears me on the inside of my left thigh, just below the jewels, and crooks his finger at me: *Let's go. Come to me.*

"I was still young and little bit dumb in terms of being patient. I took one step toward him, he reached out, grabbed me, threw a punch, I ducked at the right time, he hit the top of my head and just blew the helmet off. Clean off. And I'm like, 'Oh…my…God.' He hits me in the face, it's over. Then I did everything I could to just kinda throw a couple of punches, and down we went. I was just thankful he didn't hit me clean, otherwise I was knocked out.… Just the size and strength of the man. How big his hands are."

The night of May 25, 1989, at the Forum, Hunter, Calgary-born, was a healthy scratch, along with another cocaptain, Jim Peplinski, when the Flames claimed the Stanley Cup. In accepting the big, silver chalice, they came onto the ice in sweat gear.

"That," he conceded, "was really hard. I'd already missed one game of that series. Knowing the situation, knowing that it was Lanny [McDonald's] last kick at the can, it was pretty clear that someone was coming out. Riser came into the room and said to Pep and I, 'You guys aren't playing tonight, but I just want you to remember one thing: You're a big part of this, and you always will be. Don't ever forget that.' I was really thankful he said it. It meant a lot.

"They're presenting the Cup, and we've got our sweatpants on. But it doesn't diminish any of it."

After the Calgary part of his career, Hunter went on to play with the Canucks, bookended by brief pit stops in Quebec and San

Jose. "I had a really good experience in Vancouver," he said. "[I was] thrilled to be able to play four and a half seasons there, and to be able to go another Stanley Cup Final [in 1993] was tremendous. "But after 11 seasons in Calgary and 12½ in the organization…for sure, I'll always be a Flame."

34 Paul Bunyan from Bemidji

Joel Otto arrived out of NCAA Division II Bemidji State. Which made perfect sense. Because at 6'4" and 220 pounds, in the mid-1980s he seemed a colossus, every bit as overpowering as the 18-foot-high statue of Paul Bunyan that greets tourists in Bemidji, Minnesota.

He also arrived with literally no fanfare. "The Rangers, Minnesota, and Calgary offered me contracts when I left college," Joel Otto recalled years later. "Minnesota's was a three-way deal— for the NHL, IHL, and AHL. So I thought and thought, and finally my agent at the time, Brian Burke, called and asked me where I wanted to go. I told him Calgary, because I wanted to go somewhere where no one knew me and I knew no one. He said, 'Good, because the Rangers just pulled their offer off the table.' As you can see, I was very much in demand."

At his first camp, he was handed jersey No. 71. "One guy got 72—a defenseman, I think, from Wisconsin," recalled Otto. "He didn't last long. They probably didn't think I would, either." Only 11 seasons, as it turned out.

That original Calgary deal paid him $97,000 if he stuck with the big club, or $27,000 for the year in the minors, along with a $10,000 signing bonus. He spent the season in Moncton, New

Brunswick. "I was a very naive guy then," admitted the big man from Elk River, Minnesota. "I was playing out my life day to day. 'The NHL? Great.' 'Calgary? Great.' 'You're going to give me a contract, pay me money? Great.' Did I have a goal to play in the NHL? No. I just wanted to play hockey. It was fun.

"I got noticed by being big. By running over…"—he searched for a name out of the shadows of the past—"Danny Bolduc. Fighting in training camp. I'd never fought before. I was a college kid. Never fought on the streets before. And all of a sudden I'm fighting on the ice.

"I remember playing my first exhibition game, then going home after I got sent to Moncton. And I'm like, 'Can you believe it? I played in front of 16,000 people!'

"My story is: right place at the right time."

That's a modest oversimplification, of course. For he not only filled a role essential in that era but provided one of the great one-on-one match-ups of a fabled rivalry, a battle that was the whole Edmonton Oilers–Calgary Flames rivalry in microcosm. Joel Otto vs. Mark Messier. Messier, of course, was less a flesh-blood-and-bone man than a force of nature. And it was left to Otto to tame the untamable beast.

Messier and Otto will forever be fused in the imaginations of Alberta hockey fans of a certain generation. Like two ravenous dinosaurs fighting over a kill, their helmet-to-helmet duels in the faceoff circle were worth the price of admission alone.

"I didn't like anybody back then," said Otto. "Messier took liberties with guys. That's why I had no love for anybody that played for the Oilers. You talk about respect in today's game. No. We were trying to hurt people. People were trying to hurt us. Sticks were up. Elbows. You name it. You were fighting for your life out there.

"Messier got me in the league. No question about it. I got an opportunity because Calgary needed a big, physical center to play against him. Knowing what I had to do, I was nervous for

Edmonton games. Because I knew what was going to happen on the ice. It was going to be bedlam.

"For him, he deals with it every game. For me, personally, it was me against him. For him, it was just another guy. He got that kind of attention everywhere."

But Otto, as able a defensive forward as ever played for the franchise, would also score the most vital goal in its history. Late in the first OT period of Game 7, round one of the 1989 playoffs, against the prohibitive underdog Vancouver Canucks, a Jim Peplinski shot glanced in off one of Otto's skates and beyond goalie Kirk McLean. The Flames survived 4–3, both in the game and series. But it had been a near thing. No Otto goal, maybe no Stanley Cup.

"Here's another Joel Otto moment for you," he revealed, self-deprecatingly. "Earlier in the same game, I'm coming down with Brian MacLellan, two-on-one, and I'm squeezing my stick *so* hard that I throw a pass over to Mac and it's gotta be this"—indicating three feet off the ground—"high. He's on the bench afterward, kind of shaking his head, looking at me like, 'What the frick was that?' Then I go the net in overtime and it goes off my skate. What can you say?"

Twice a finalist for the Selke Trophy as the game's top defensive forward, his value went far beyond statistics. Right place at the right time? Maybe. But the good fortune went two ways. Twenty-four years after retiring, and two decades removed from his last game for Calgary, only Jarome Iginla, Robyn Regehr, Al MacInnis, and Theoren Fleury have ever pulled on the flaming *C* more often than Joel Otto.

35 The Toughest Series

Beauty is said to be in the eye of the beholder. "Looked mighty pretty to me," cackled Terry Crisp, with still a dab of nervousness, more than a quarter century later. "Just like [Bryan] Trottier to [Mike] Bossy or [Wayne] Gretzky to [Jari] Kurri. As good as, anyway."

Whatever. However. Whomever. In the eyes of the city, the Jim Peplinski–Joel Otto combination was a sight for sore eyes, balm for a desperate soul, in their darkest hour of need.

The puck that banked off Otto's skate 39 seconds from the first overtime intermission in Game 7 of the opening round of the 1989 first round series against Vancouver stands as arguably the most important goal in franchise lore. A grinding goal, yes. An ugly goal, indubitably. A flukey goal, no question. Whatever. Without it…"I don't even want to imagine," sighed Crisp.

Usually on their way to glory, every Stanley Cup champion is forced at one point or another to face its own mortality. For the 1989 Flames that cold, hard look arrived in round one, arguably the hardest slog of their careers.

The Vancouver Canucks were regarded as nothing more than a blip on the way to bigger, better horizons for the Presidents' Trophy winners early that spring. They had, after all, finished a whopping 43 points in arrears of the Calgary Flames (117 as compared to 74) over the obligatory 82-game campaign in the Smythe Division and were an uninspiring 1–5–2 against them during the season.

Instead of simply being run over, though, the West Coasters set up the largest, most unexpected speed bump in Calgary franchise history. "Everybody's telling you that you should be winning in four or five. Then once you get by the fourth game, and it's tied, you're thinking, *Oh, shit!*" said Crisp. "Then Game 5 comes, and Game 6, and then it's like, *What the hell? We're going to Game 7?* That's when the ol' Adam's apple starts to bob."

The series-clinching Otto goal arrived just in the nick of time. Two superb saves by Flames goalie Mike Vernon, off Vancouver wingers Tony Tanti and Stan Smyl, had already saved Calgary's championship aspirations. The glove snare off Smyl, in particular, remains etched in the minds of partisans for both teams. Without those heroics, of course, the Otto goal never would have happened.

"Yeah, I was in the crease," recalled the big centerman today, "but that wasn't illegal back then. And I didn't kick it.

"What did I feel? Relief. Same thing when we won the Cup. I remember being in the bathroom in Montreal, hunched over, like, 'Ahhhhh, it's over.' It's hard to actually enjoy. You've just put so much into it, you're just totally exhausted. I felt the same way in Game 7 against Vancouver."

"When Otts scored that goal," said Crisp, recalling the celebration, "it was as if a piano had fallen off our back. A whole showroom full of 'em."

The Canucks had certainly been more confident, more unimpressed, and more stubborn than anyone could've imagined. "No one gave Vancouver a second look," recalled Calgary defenseman Ric Nattress. "But they were a lot better than people gave them credit for. We didn't underestimate them, but they got under our skin. When they started to play the way we knew they could, the pressure from the outside world started to creep in on us a little bit.

"I think their attitude was: 'Okay, let's have fun with this, piss 'em off, and maybe we can beat 'em out.' When nobody expects anything of you except yourselves, that's when you can really be dangerous. In '86 when I was with St. Louis, we took Calgary to seven games when no one thought we had a chance. But that series against Vancouver was the most uptight I saw our hockey club in the five years I was there."

The Canucks, spurred on by Coach Bob "Cagey" McCammon, played the underdog role to the hilt, constantly bringing up Calgary's supposed superiority. And vitally, they gained a competitive foothold immediately, ex-Flame Paul Reinhart scoring 2:47 into overtime of Game 1 to silence the 18,307 Saddledome faithful and plant a seed of doubt the size of a manhole cover in the minds of the prohibitive favorites.

Further fueling the idea of crazy destiny, Vancouver was only 2–27–1 in the regular-season campaign when trailing after two periods; Calgary was a near-spotless 45–0–2 when leading after two. Yet Petri Skriko of the Canucks had sent the game into OT, scoring at 8:41 of the third period. An omen? Vancouver must've believed so.

From there, the series shifted to and fro, back and forth. The Flames led two games to one, then they were tied. Calgary surged in front, and the Canucks equalized via a 6–3 win at the old Pacific Coliseum.

Which left Game 7, and literally all the pressure heaped on Crisp and Co. "In that overtime," sighed the coach, "I mean, cripes…Tony Tanti comes around on a wraparound and hits the post. Stan Smyl has the breakaway, and Vernie makes the great glove save everybody remembers. Luck always enters into an overtime, but we dodged a few bullets in that one."

In the end, Calgary survived to fight another day, moving forward to face No. 99 and the L.A. Kings in round two. But it had been close. "They had a lot of players"—Reinhart, Brian Bradley, Steve Bozek, Mel Bridgman, Kevan Guy—"there that had been with us before," said Calgary GM Cliff Fletcher afterward. "And they were on a mission. It was a hell of a tough series."

Reinhart, in particular, played out of his skin. "He was a huge factor," reminisced Nattress. "I'm just speculating, but the chance to knock out the team you thought you'd spend the rest of your career with? That's pretty good motivation."

"The best player on the ice," lauded Crisp. "He was on a single-minded mission to knock us out. And damn near did."

36 Sealed with a Kiss

The moment deserved to be marked by some rash of impetuousness. When Al MacInnis' hockey stick blew a bloody hole in the Chicago Blackhawks' playoff hopes 15:05 into overtime of Game 4, Terry Crisp simply could not help himself. Celebrations were most decidedly in order.

Crisp was so giddy with excitement, so overcome by the magnitude of the shot that had propelled his Calgary Flames to within one win of a Stanley Cup Finals appearance, that he scaled the glass behind the Flames' bench and planted a smooch on Norma MacNeil, the wife of assistant GM Al MacNeil. The smooch, as you'd imagine, received plenty of television time coast-to-coast.

"People still ask me, 'Who was the lady?'" laughed Crisp. "'We know it's not your wife.'

"The funniest thing was, Sheila's sitting right beside Norma. But when Al's shot went in, Norma jumped up. I jumped up. And…

"Now, Norma's a very nice-looking lady—lucky me—but had that lady been the bearded lady from the circus, I still would've kissed her. That's how happy I was.

"What I still can't figure out to this day is: how did I get that high on the glass?"

Crisp wasn't stepping out on his bride, understand. The ramifications of what had just happened had simply overtaken him.

With the Flames up 2–1 in the series, the game tied 1–1, and Hawks defenseman Trent Yawney seated in the penalty box for closing his hand on the puck, MacInnis loaded up his rocket launcher and let fire at Chicago goaltender Alain Chevrier. "I was just trying to get the puck toward the net," admitted the future Hall of Famer. "I really wasn't quite sure it was in until I saw a replay on the TV monitor. The shot was high enough to go over Chevrier's pads and underneath his glove."

If Joel Otto's OT foot-wedge goal in Game 7 of the first round of the Vancouver series allowed the Presidents' Trophy–winning Flames to exhale, the MacInnis blast gave them legitimate reason to believe. "When that goal went in," Crisp said, "I said in my own mind, *That just got us the Cup.*

"I know there's another game to win and another series to win after that game, against a great team like the Canadiens, as it turned out, but that was one of those moments when you just have a… feeling. When it becomes clear in your mind. When you tell yourself, 'Yup, it's ours.'"

Two nights later, back home at the Saddledome, the Flames eliminated Chicago via a 3–1 victory. But MacInnis had, in truth, wrenched the heart out of the Hawks. Worthy of a pucker-up, for sure.

37 Ready to Win

The star-studded lineup, recalled Doug Risebrough, was hockey's equivalent of stumbling onto Oscar's red carpet. A head-table gauntlet of famous faces, unforgettable moments, and legendary deeds. "What I remember most," reflected the ex-Hab and former Flame, comparing Calgary's 1986 and 1989 Cup Finals against the game's most storied franchise, "is that the first time we weren't prepared to win. That was the reality.

"As an example: They used to have a luncheon during the Finals. And the Montreal Canadiens are presenting all their past stars. Henri [Richard] is there, and he's got 11 Cups. [Jean] Beliveau's there, and he's got 9. The Rocket's there. So many others. It can be intimidating.

"I look at our guys, their mouths are all open, and I know they're thinking, *We have no chance.* Because the Canadiens had all this history behind them. That's what history, what tradition, does for you. And the Canadiens play that card really well. The only thing they didn't do was put those guys behind the bench.

"You look at such a deep history of winning, and you wonder how in hell you're ever going to overcome that. That's what's I mean about not being ready to win. We weren't really prepared to say, 'It doesn't matter. Henri Richard's not coming on the ice. Beliveau's not coming on the ice. Guy Lafleur's not coming on the ice. Dickie Moore's not coming on the ice.'

"It's hard to convince yourself that we're playing this edition of the Montreal Canadiens, not those editions, and—know what?—we can beat this edition."

In 1986 Risebrough was in his final season as a gap-toothed, heart-on-his-sleeve indomitable centerman, having won four

Stanley Cups with the Bleu, Blanc, et Rouge. By 1989 he'd retired and graduated to assistant coach on Terry Crisp's staff.

"I kinda felt '86 was a bit my fault, in a way. Not personally, but I'd seen all this before, and you wonder whether you could've done more to make [teammates] understand. What can happen is this: When you get that far, there's a danger of getting caught up being in the Finals. All the attention. All the media. And you lose the focus of actually playing. We went to the receptions, all the functions, and the next thing you know, we're down and we're out." In five games.

During the three years between finals appearances, the Flames had bulked up, adding the likes of Doug Gilmour, Gary Roberts, Brad McCrimmon, Rob Ramage, and Dana Murzyn. But enough vital components from the 1986 entry—Al MacInnis, Joel Otto, Hakan Loob, Lanny McDonald, Mike Vernon, et al—were still around, vividly remembering the sting of failure, and now, every bit as crucially, understanding the drill.

"Losing in '86 really hurt," recalled Risebrough, "because, of course, you never know if you'll get another chance.

"In '89 you could feel we had a better focus on the game. Having been there before, the players knew how to filter stuff out. And if I remember correctly, a lot of the team didn't go to the luncheon/reception this time.

"I know there were players that didn't go because they were hurt. But there were also guys who didn't go because…well…been there, done that, right?

"They didn't need to go through that again. Because when you introduce the Rocket and Henri…it can be pretty impressive, even a second time around.

"I didn't realize the full benefit of it before for the Canadiens until I saw it in '86 as a member of the opposition."

 **Pep**

On most depth charts, Earl Ingarfield Jr. had been slotted into the fourth-line center spot that first training camp at the Stampede Corral in the fall of 1980. Still, head coach Al MacNeil liked the cut of Jim Peplinski's 6'3", 210-pound jib. And GM Cliff Fletcher always placed a premium on size.

"I think that the big moment for Pep came during that [quarterfinals] playoff series against Philadelphia," estimated longtime Flames management man Al Coates. "We had him out there, at center, with Randy Holt and Willi Plett against [Paul] Holmgren's line. And they were a big, big part of why we eventually won."

Before long, Peplinski shifted to the wing, and through nine seasons—along with a brief, nostalgic cameo—he carved out a unique niche. He was strong like a bull. Tough. Willing. And he scored some goals (161 in 711 career games). Peplinski face washes—the raking of the sweaty leather part of a glove palm across the face of an opponent—become the stuff of legend.

What set him apart, though, was his gregariousness, his ability to lift people, to knit them together. Peplinski wore the *C* for a reason. "I never realized at the time that it was business," he admitted now. "One of the reasons I retired at 29 was because I always thought I was playing a game. I thought at some point in time I had to grow up and get a real job.

"Maybe that was of the best misconceptions I had. I wasn't thinking about making money. I was thinking about playing a *game*. When things were going really crummy, I tried to be as happy as I could be. You lose two games in a row back then, and all of a sudden you're looking for a hearse.

"I never thought that was healthy. I thought, *Let's have some fun, make fun of what we're wearing or not wearing.* When things were going really good, we'd won four or five in a row, that's when it's, 'Guys, we're going longer and harder.' Because that's when you can take it.

"In my 10 years, I never thought I was in a business. I had a good friend, an oil and gas lawyer, negotiate my contracts, and it was, 'Whatever you think's fair, Cliff.' Today it's a business. Back then it was a business too, but reflecting, I'm kinda glad I looked at it the way I did."

"He had a good read on the room," praised Coates. "When the salaries were first disclosed, in the *Globe and Mail*, I remember this distinctly: Saturday morning, we were in Quebec City. I walk[ed] into the locker room and some guys were a little sheepish because now the salaries [were] out there, for everybody to look at.

"Pep had an ability to read the tension. Well, I walk in, he says something stupid to me, and then I fire back, and all of a sudden heads come up off the ground, spirits were lifted, there was a return to normalcy. I know he did it on purpose. It was intuitive."

The night of May 25, 1989, Game 6 of the Stanley Cup Finals at the Montreal Forum, both Peplinski and another of the tri-captains, Tim Hunter, were healthy scratches. Peplinski, in his track gear, had to be coaxed out as the Cup was being awarded. "I just didn't see that coming, at all," he said more than a quarter century later. "So my reaction was very frank and short. I look back on that now, and those reactions are completely under my control. I'd handle it differently today.

"So, the sixth game…was it hard? Yeah, at the time. But…so what? We have a friend who's had cerebral palsy ever since he was little and I first met him. He's 35 years old now. That's hard. Not dressing for a game? Don't cry for me, Argentina.

"When I started, I said to my wonderful roommate Bob Murdoch that I was going to play five years, and if I can win a Cup in that time, before that, great. And he said, 'Pep, five years is gonna go in a blink. Ten'll go fast. And your chances of winning a Cup aren't great, so don't base your career on that." So on November 1, 1989, his role diminishing and the business world beckoning, Peplinski announced his retirement at age 29.

A short comeback in the lockout-shortened 1994–95 season, prodded by GM Doug Risebrough, produced six more starts. But things had changed in the interim. "That first game, we were playing Vancouver, I was forechecking and Bret Hedican was hooking me. So I elbowed him. Somewhere later in the shift there's a whistle, and the ref said, 'I've gotta give you a penalty for elbowing.' And I said, 'For what? He was hooking me.' And the ref said, 'Yeah, but you broke his [bleeping] nose!' 'But he was *hooking* me!' And I remember thinking, *But that's what we used to…do.* And I figured I might have to alter my style a bit."

In the final analysis, what set Peplinski apart were those characteristics everyone labels "intangibles": his ability to keep things loose, to instill a communal feeling in a group, never shirking on coming to a teammate's aid.

"I remember toward the end of my career, we were playing Edmonton," recalled Flames defenseman Paul Baxter. "I couldn't tell you why, but I always got stuck with [Kevin] McClelland when something broke out. So some fights start, and I get…guess who? Anyway, Pep is occupied with another guy but sees me and says, 'Hey, Baxie, you've had enough of that guy. Let me have him.' And we *switch*. Now *he's* got McClelland."

Peplinski lit up like the Christmas tree in Rockefeller Center when reminded of the incident. "Yeah," he beamed almost a quarter century later. "It was great. I beat him like a dog, too."

39 A Soviet Legend

How much did Sergei Makarov, already legendary right winger on the Soviet Union / Red Army's fabled KLM Line, mean to the sporting fabric in his homeland? Well, a glimpse could be gleaned shortly after he made the western leap to become a Calgary Flame at age 31. Makarov had joined a new team in Prague for two games to open the 1989 Friendship Tour, the Flames then traveling to the Soviet Union for a series against club teams.

While in Leningrad for a game, the visiting Canadian contingent—players, wives, girlfriends, staff—visited the Hermitage Museum of art. Waving a tiny Canadian flag over the bobbing heads of the throng, their tour guide pointed to a large canvas he'd led them to. "And here," he announced, clearing his throat, "is Rembrandt's famous *The Return of the Prodigal Son*." He smiled and added, "That is like when Mr. Makarov comes back here to play."

A two-time Olympic gold medal winner and seven-time World Championship winner, Makarov and linemates Igor Larionov and Vladimir Krutov—the KLM—were the world's most lethal line, their sublime interplay unmatched anywhere, in any league.

Makarov's way to the North American game had been paved the year before when Sergei Pryakhin, a journeyman winger, served as front man, the first Russian to be negotiated out of the Soviet Union by Flames GM Cliff Fletcher. These days, Russians are plentiful in the NHL. Back then, they were as rare as an Amur leopard.

Having had waters tested, and finding them acceptable, Makarov came next. When Fletcher had selected the slick Soviet 231st overall at the 1983 NHL Entry Draft, there was much head shaking and eye rolling. The chances of prying away any Soviet player, let alone one with the pedigree of a Sergei Makarov, seemed remote, almost laughable.

Makarov arrived in Calgary already a legend. He departed arguably the most controversial player ever to collect the Calder Trophy as the NHL Rookie of the Year. "For my hockey education," he explained of the move, "the only school left was the NHL. During the [1988] Olympic Games"—when the Soviets won gold, in Calgary—"I had doubts about going to [the Flames]. The problem was the Soviet Army.

"I wanted to find the toughest place to play. And that's here. I didn't come for the money."

Makarov's audacious skills were evident from the get-go, even if the seamless collaboration that he, Larionov, and Krutov had perfected over years of trial and error was, understandably, lacking.

One night linemate Gary Roberts attempted to mimic the Soviet superstar's panache and feather a high-risk diagonal pass through two sets of opposition skates to Makarov, waiting impatiently at the back post. "Made it through the first set, then clipped a guy's skate on the way to Sergei," laughed Roberts. "As we're heading back to the bench, Sergei's tapping his stick on the ice, shaking his head. And I'm like, 'Geez, Sergei—sorry, but that's about the best I can do!'"

Warming to his new environment, playing on a line alongside Roberts and center Joe Nieuwendyk, Makarov began to shine. The culmination arrived on February 25, the Flames eviscerating their northern Edmonton rivals 10–4 at the Saddledome. Makarov, unstoppable that evening, established a franchise record for points in a game, seven (two goals, five assists) that stands to this day. When asked what he ascribed the outburst to, the undisputed star of the show played coy, as usual. "Russian secret," he giggled (Makarov always knew more English than he was letting on). "The day before a game you relax in the territory of the enemy. I was up shopping at West Edmonton Mall Saturday."

His age, the wide international experience, sparked the Makarov debate. Should he really be considered for the Calder? This wasn't, after all, an untried, apple-cheeked 18-year-old kid, fresh out of, say, the OHL.

"I'm not crying or anything," complained Chicago Blackhawks coach Mike Keenan, "but theoretically there are only three players in the running—the kids, [Jeremy] Roenick, [Rod] Brind'Amour, and [Mike] Modano. I respect Makarov as a world-class player, but he's not a rookie." Others agreed. Yet the rules—which stated that any first-year player was eligible—technically declared otherwise.

The man himself tried to steer clear of the controversy. "I feel the same way about [the Calder] as I have all season," Makarov protested as the regular season wound down. "It is not my decision. It is the writers'."

Sergei Makarov (far right) brought his formidable talents and Olympic bona fides to Calgary in 1989.

Makarov finished the 82 games scoring 24 goals and 86 points, tops among rookies. And so, naturally, he found himself among the finalists. "The tuxedo is Calgary's problem. Not mine," he joked before flying from Moscow to Toronto for the NHL Awards banquet, to be held at the Metro Toronto Convention Center.

The controversy about his legitimacy, though, continued on unabated. CBC pundit Don Cherry naturally wasn't sitting on the fence on the issue. "How's the vote going on that, anyway?" he asked sarcastically. "Who voted for Makarov? Geez, I can't understand that. Well, it's the easy thing to go for him. Then they can say, 'I'm fair.' What a bunch of BS."

The trip proved worth it. In Toronto, Sergei Makarov added another bauble to his bulging trophy case, becoming the third Calgary Flame to cop the award, following in the footsteps of defenseman Gary Suter and center Joe Nieuwendyk. But the furor did not go unnoticed. His win prompted a change in criteria, to be forever known as the Makarov Rule, whereby only players younger than 26 can qualify for the Calder.

Makarov's on-ice production continued as he contributed 79, 70, and 57 points for the Flames over the next three seasons, but in the summer of 1993 he was offloaded to the San Jose Sharks, where he reconnected with his old pal Larionov.

His second year in the Silicon Valley, Makarov's probing pass set up San Jose teammate Ray Whitney for a deflection goal at 1:54 of double OT that gave the Sharks a 5–4 victory and a 4–3 playoff series victory over the heavily favored Flames. Even adorned in teal, he had one final piece of magic to show the Saddledome faithful that had delighted in his artistry.

In 2016 he was enshrined in the Hockey Hall of Fame.

40 The Friendship Tour

The fabled Luzhniki Sports Palace was full to capacity, 10,000 rubles-paying patrons strong. The mighty Russian Red Army machine at one end, the Stanley Cup champion Calgary Flames at the other. A stirring conclusion to the 1989 Friendship Tour. Reportedly, within Russian borders the game drew the second-highest TV audience ever for a sports event.

For 18 days the Flames and an entourage of 100 strong—management, staff, wives, girlfriends, dads—toured Czechoslovakia and Russia, visiting the Charles Bridge in Prague, Moscow's Red Square, the Hermitage in Leningrad, and other sights. And in between they played some hockey.

Pre-glasnost, the environment was vastly different for a North American traveling party in the fall of 1989. "Let's just say," quipped Calgary defenseman Jamie Macoun, asked about his Russian experience, "it isn't exactly the place you'd want to spend your honeymoon."

Chimed in Gary Suter: "I ate more when I had my jaw wired shut."

In what was billed as a battle between the world's best club teams, a cultural battle as much as an athletic one, Red Army jumped in front 2–0 on goals by Alexei Kasatonov and Igor Chibirev before Paul Ranheim pulled one back for the Flames at 12:31 of the third period.

A furious late Calgary rally wasn't rewarded with the goal that would send the game into overtime. The closest the Flames would come was Joel Otto's deflection of an Al MacInnis point shot that flew inches wide, thumping the boards behind the Soviet net in the game's final minute. So the seals on the bottles of champagne Red Army legend Sergei Makarov had brought for his new teammates to celebrate a historic victory went unbroken.

A disappointing end to a fascinating odyssey that proved, by turns, to be frustrating, exhausting, and ultimately rewarding. "A lot of people said we were in a no-lose situation," declared Macoun of the Red Army duel. "To be honest with you I thought they were in that position. We've been on the road three weeks, living in their hotels, eating their food—you can't exactly run down to the corner and get yourself a grilled cheese sandwich here if you're hungry.

"The game was in their building. If they'd lost, it would have been...I don't want to use the word *embarrassing*; let's just say it wouldn't have looked too good. Even if we play them here in a couple months, the result would be much, much different."

That loss condemned the Flames to finish the tour at 3–3. They lost twice to the Czech national team in Prague (backstopped by Dominik Hasek) by scores of and 4–1 and 4–2—mistakenly believing they'd be playing against two Czech domestic club teams—to open the journey before finding their legs and going 3–1 versus Russian club opposition.

In truth, the NHL kingpins—and the Washington Capitals, who also joined in the tour—were walking into a carefully laid trap. They arrived with no formal training camp, while their European opposition had targeted their visit months before, prepping for the opportunity to dispatch the highly paid, highly publicized NHL stars. "This is September, don't forget. And we don't see this kind of pace until maybe the playoffs," reminded centerman Doug Gilmour.

"Anyone who understands the situation knows it's unfair," chimed in Joe Nieuwendyk.

The first day of travel should've given them a glimpse of what they were in for. Their Air Canada flight was an hour late departing from Calgary, followed by an additional three-hour layover at London's Heathrow International Airport, a 40-minute hassle at customs in Prague over visa squabbles, and an $8,000 tariff for excess baggage weight, due in large part to a plentiful supply of mineral water.

The bedraggled group finally reached the Prague Sports Halle for their first overseas practice on September 6, 1989, at 9:48 PM, and then no one could be found to turn on the lights. "No wonder these Europeans are so good," joked cocaptain Jim Peplinski. "Everybody says they can play blindfolded. I guess so—they practice in the dark."

Welcome to the Friendship Tour.

From there on, it was a whirlwind of Czech cut-glass vases, Russian nesting dolls, and fur-lined caps; sightseeing; dodgy Aeroflot flights; and playing high-tempo, high-pressure tests against excellent opposition while attempting to practice themselves into game shape.

Eighteen days after it began, when the troupe touched down in London for a welcome day off, the players could not have been happier. "The first thing I'm going to do," announced winger Paul Ranheim, "is have a real meal. Then I'm going to go pick up a newspaper I can read. You kind of lose track of the world."

Still, the Friendship Tour turned out to be an event unlike any other in most experiences. "You simply cannot say enough about the people in Czechoslovakia or the Soviet Union," praised Flames boss Terry Crisp. "What they did for us was above and beyond the call of duty. The interpreters, the guides, the hotel staff... unbelievable.

"What will I remember about this tour? Well, that we were 3–3, naturally. But mostly, the warmth of everyone over there."

Everyone arrived home with a favorite funny story to remember the tour by. For Mike Vernon, the chance to meet a hero of his,

Russian legend Vladislav Tretiak, for the first time provided such a moment. "He pointed at my mask and said, 'I use that mask,'" laughed the little goaltender. "So I told him, 'Where do you think I got the idea?'"

41 "Yeah, Baby!"

He provided the soundtrack to a generation. No different from Sinatra or Elvis. As a kid growing up in Campbellton, New Brunswick, Peter Maher dreamt of being the next Danny Gallivan, a fellow Maritimer. Back then, he could not possibly have imagined where those dreams would lead.

Only months before Maher landed his first NHL play-by-play job—with the Toronto Maple Leafs, no less—Gallivan, the great man himself, the voice of the Montreal Canadiens, was keynote speaker at a minor hockey banquet held at a church in Campbellton.

That night Danny Gallivan took the time to praise a local announcer who'd shipped him an audition tape some months before. "During his speech," recalled Maher three decades later, "Danny said, 'You're going to lose somebody in this room very soon, because he's a talented broadcaster. He's got a great future in front of him. He's too good to be here much longer.'

"And then he introduced me. Right out of the blue! I was floored. I was looking around, over my shoulder, to see who he could've been talking about."

Looking back, knowing what Flames fans everywhere know now, there was no one else he possibly could've been talking about. Over 33 seasons at the microphone, three Stanley Cup runs, the historic title-clinching win over the Canadiens on May 25, 1989, at the Montreal Forum, Peter Maher became an honorary member of thousands of southern Alberta families. Calgarians, after all, spent their winters in his company.

One of the stumpers among all Flames trivia questions: Who called the games on radio *before* Peter Maher? Answer: Bart Dailey. For the team's first season, 1980–81, following the franchise relocation from Atlanta. From then on, it was Maher's show.

Players came and went; some retired. Same with coaches and managers. The one constant remained Peter Maher—through good seasons and some awfully lean ones—alongside color analyst sidekicks Doug Barkley, Mike Rogers and, briefly, Peter Loubardias. He never missed a night; he soldiered on through sickness and scratchy pipes and the fatigue 82-game seasons can exact. (He'd fight off vocal ills with a judicious sip of vinegar.)

Among his peers, he is often given the ultimate accolade: a pro's pro. Lauded the longtime voice of the Hartford Whalers / Carolina Hurricanes, Chuck Kaiton: "He's like one of the old-time hockey announcers I used to listen to growing up in Detroit.

"He was one of those guys, when you turned the radio on, the enthusiasm he had for the game blasted right out at you. The excitement in his voice was infectious.

"From the delivery to the style, he didn't sound like anybody else. And that's what I think a lot of the young broadcasters don't get. They don't work on their style. He was his own unique persona. He had charisma. Sounds corny and cliched, I know, but they don't make 'em like that anymore."

His first regular-season game calling the Leafs was in Pittsburgh, at the old Igloo. The first goal scorer was future Flames icon Lanny McDonald (naturally), then in the blue-and-white of Toronto.

Among Maher's treasured memories: the first trip to the Montreal Forum, when the magnitude of where he was, what he was doing, how far he'd come, finally hit home. "Being in the same press box as Danny Gallivan, who was working in the booth right beside me…I thought to myself, *Maybe you have made it after all.*"

The idea for his signature "Yeah, baby!" tagline to celebrate victories (invariably followed by "You can put it in the win column!") was hatched driving home from a game one bitterly cold night, listening to a lyric in a long-forgotten song on the car radio.

One broadcast, Maher sliced open his head in the booth at the Saddledome and called the game with a serviette soaking up the blood. In the first intermission, CFR boss Don Armstrong impishly brought him up a helmet for self-protection.

He called Flames games from Montreal to Moscow, Toronto to Tokyo, Pittsburgh to Prague. In November 2006 Peter Maher was inducted into the Hockey Hall of Fame in Toronto as a media honoree, receiving the Foster Hewitt Memorial Award. Eight years later, the Flames honored him with his own commemorative night, naming the broadcast booth at the Saddledome in his honor.

All of 2,954 games before.

"Why have I lasted so long?" Maher mused back in 2000. "Maybe because I feel—have always felt—it's an honor to do play-by-play on NHL hockey.

"It's still amazing to me, all these years later, that I'm here at all. It doesn't seem so long ago when I was calling Campbellton Tigers games in tiny, cold rinks. This is the best job in the world. I can think of nothing—absolutely nothing—I'd rather do."

When Maher announced his retirement at the end of August 2014, his favorite singer, Rod Stewart, was preparing to make a record 12th appearance at the Scotiabank Saddledome in a couple weeks. "If you happen to be in the crowd when he sings 'Forever Young,' think of me," he told a packed audience by way of the perfect exit line. That voice, at least—the soundtrack of a franchise, hurtling across eras—will never age.

42 The Battle

Goaltender Don Edwards spent only three seasons swept up in the vortex—1982–83 through 1984–85—but he certainly caught the flavor of the thing. "A 10-year saga of bitterness," he called the Battle of Alberta. "It's probably good that the Flames won a Cup, otherwise somebody might've gotten killed.

"From a team standpoint it was wearying to the ego to lose to them all the time. You'd wonder, *What else do we have to do to beat these guys?*

"At times, it was vicious. The hatred in the room…you'd come off after a period wanting to cut some guy's head off."

From the Flames' relocation to Calgary in 1980 onward, the Battle of Alberta held sway, every bit as bitter as Quebec-Montreal or Chicago-Detroit or Rangers-Isles. Starting in the mid-1990s, as the influence of both franchises waned, the battle fizzled into something more along the lines of a skirmish, and a regional one at that. Relevance being a key component of a simmering rivalry.

But back in the day, there was nothing to compare. So much bite and bile to choose from. From Glen Sather's sneer to Bob Johnson's seven-point plan. Hunter vs. Semenko. Peplinski vs. Jackson. From Glenn Anderson's wayward stick to Theoren Fleury's wayward sneer. Paul Baxter and then Neil "the Butcher of Harvard" Sheehy baiting Wayne Gretzky. In Esa Tikkanen's indecipherable Tikk-talk or Messier's might. Grant Fuhr's glove and Mike Vernon's coming-of-age.

There was the darkness of the Oilers' swaggering omnipotence as the Flames struggled to gain some sort of foothold through the early years, followed by a gradual bridging of the gap by Calgary GM Cliff Fletcher's restocking, swinging deals that brought Joe

Mullen, Doug Gilmour, old Oilers killer John Tonelli, and others from the outside into the fray.

"Seems like every time we played Edmonton, I'd be stitching up two, three, four guys," mused longtime Calgary trainer Bearcat Murray. "The doctor they had there was a great guy. Good thing, too. Because a lot of players needed attention during those games. Boy, I must've used hundreds and hundreds of stitches in games against the Oilers."

For all the fame/infamy the Battle enjoys, the provincial rivals have actually collided only five times in the postseason, and those were crammed into a nine-year period:

- **1983 (Second Round):** The Oilers sailed through in five, pummeling the Flames 35–13 in goals for/against.
- **1984 (Second Round):** The Oilers prevailed in the maximum seven, winning the decider 7–4 at Northlands Coliseum. On the dressing room chalkboard after Game 7, Calgary coach Bob Johnson wrote, "Proud of you!!! Hold heads high!!!"

  "I give the Oilers all the credit in the world," whispered pugnacious defenseman Paul Baxter that night. "They stormed us. Our talent is not competitive with theirs. This is difficult to accept."
- **1986 (Second Round):** The Flames turned the tables in seven, the final game decided by Steve Smith's now endlessly replayed "own" goal off Grant Fuhr's left leg at Northlands.

  "People," recalled Calgary's superb checking winger Colin Patterson, "talk about the goal that went in, but to my recollection they still had 15 minutes to tie it up. And they didn't. So we beat them…and they were the best. The champions. Of course it was special.

  "What I remember most is after being in the lineup shaking hands. Paul Coffey said to me, 'Your turn to go get one [a Cup].'"

- **1988 (Second Round):** An emphatic Oilers sweep, after Calgary had claimed its first-ever Presidents' Trophy, no less.

  "We hurt, we bled, and we healed. When you break a bone it's supposed to come back stronger than ever," a shocked Flames coach Terry Crisp said on the feeling of deflation after the series.

- **1991: (First Round):** Edmonton outlasted the Flames over seven memorable games, Esa Tikkanen silencing the Saddledome devotees 6:58 into OT, 5–4 on a wide-angle shot that glanced off the stick of Calgary defenseman Frank Musil.

  "We had such a good feeling when we tied it 4–4," sighed Vernon. "I had such a good feeling. We were rolling, and I made that save off Mess [Mark Messier] early in overtime, and then they get a fluke. It's so disheartening."

For a generation, the moments, playoffs or otherwise, live on in their imagination. The big goals. The brawls. The highs. The lows. Theo Fleury's wild, arm-pumping, rink-length slide after scoring the OT winner in 1988 to send the series the distance. Doug Risebrough hauling Oilers ruffian Marty McSorley's jersey into the penalty box after a scrap, slicing it to ribbons with his skates, and then a defiant Sather, at his most condescending, demanding financial compensation for the tattered garment.

"That," laughed Risebrough later, "was just a guy losing a decision in front of a large group of fans and trying, in some minor way, to get even."

Getting even, getting an edge, getting bragging rights. That was, at its apex, what the Battle of Alberta was all about. Never to be forgotten by those who witnessed the festivities. Or those who lived it firsthand on the ice. McSorley remembered one night, sitting next to Flames defenseman Jamie Macoun up in the press box at the Saddledome. Macoun had been injured in an automobile accident and was trying to get his career back on track. "We talked.

I felt bad for him. And I remember the odd feeling of liking this guy, hoping the pieces would somehow fall back into place for him, then looking down at the ice and seeing all that hate, that bitterness. What a contrast.

"I also remember trying to get down to the locker room from the box. On the way down, I must've had 1,500 offers for fights. Right there. Right then. I mean, these people wanted a piece of my ass, you know. It was the rivalry. These people were living it."

43 Battle Quotes

The Battle of Alberta, in its formative days, was a rivalry to match any in all of sports for dislike, for intensity, for sheer visceral violence. Not only was the hockey (and the shenanigans) great, so were the quotes. A sampling, from the glory years:

- "It was bone-on-bone war. That's the only way to describe it. I couldn't believe some of the things I did. Meanness with my stick. Things like that. Anything to give you an edge." —Calgary center Mike Eaves
- "It's one thing I won't miss. It was getting out of control, bad for the kids. When a 10- or 11-year-old kids starts swearing at the players and his parents are sitting beside him *laughing*... well...something's wrong. That used to happen in both rinks." —Wayne Gretzky, after being dealt to the L.A. Kings
- "I thought he played well, but I didn't like to see him cross-check Jari Kurri on the back of the head. A guy that size has to be careful. Too much of that and somebody might get him." —Glen Sather's warning for Theoren Fleury

- "I thoroughly enjoyed it. They had such great skill players. And [Dave] Semenko. He was the big bully. He affected us. Not too many guys wanted to be on the ice against him. The players would say, 'Ah, it's just another game.' But who were they kidding?" —Flames coach "Badger" Bob Johnson

- "What the hell do you expect? When two big battleships are floating in the same pond, somebody's going to start firing." —Calgary right winger Hakan Loob

- "People do a lot of talking. And newspaper people do most of the talking, not the players." —Flames right winger Lanny McDonald

- "It never seemed to matter who was winning or losing, who won or lost. It was a matter of matchups. When you went into a game and knew it was 99.9 percent certain before they dropped a puck that you were going to have to fight a particular guy, nothing else mattered." —Oilers tough guy Dave Semenko

- "Some of the battles in the Corral were doozies. Pretty scary, blood all over the place. I remember one game, [Dave] Lumley got kicked out and he was headed off the ice. He actually had one foot outside the rink, then all of a sudden he turned around and came roaring back into the fights. It was wild." —Flame Jamie Hislop

- "The Calgary doctor, the staff at the hospital…everyone was great to me. They told me later that I kept insisting I was in Vancouver and it was September." —Oilers defenseman Kevin Lowe after a particularly brutal hit by Calgary's Mark Hunter

- "When we finally beat them in '86, it was the most exciting moment. More exciting than the Stanley Cup, even. At least in my mind. Because of all the games, all the fights, all the times we'd lost to them in the past. And then we come home, and there are 20,000 people at the airport! Other memories aren't so sweet. I remember losing that playoff series to them

[in 1988] and flying back on the plane, crying like a baby, tears just streaming down my cheeks. I was sitting beside Cliff [Fletcher] at the time, and he must've thought I was crazy. But it was just a release of emotion. Playing against Edmonton, the highs seemed higher and the lows lower than any other time."
—Flames trainer Jim "Bearcat" Murray

- "At times, I felt like the city of Calgary and the city of Edmonton created this monster and we were just part of it." —Flame John Tonelli, who came over from the New York Islanders at the 1986 trade deadline
- "Those games consumed your life. One year we played them 17 times." —Oilers defenseman Don Jackson
- "Even though I wasn't playing much when we finally did beat them [in 1986], it's the one memory I hold of the rivalry. All you could think of was, *Those [bleeps]! Finally!* Sather was the kind of obnoxious person…well, he has those eyes, and he'd look at you and you knew he wanted to give it to you. Certain players of theirs carried around that same look. To see those certain cocky guys beaten…well, it got to be personal." —Flames goalie Reggie Lemelin
- "College coach!" —Oilers boss Glen Sather, in full sneer, after counterpart Bob Johnson outfitted a backup goalie in an Edmonton jersey during a practice during the playoffs
- "I was coaching against the Russians when he was still in diapers." —Johnson's rebuttal to Sather's dig
- "Naw, there was never any hate on our side. Why would we hate a team that we beat all the time? Naturally you're going to hate someone who beats you all the time." —Oilers winger Dave Lumley
- "I think the physical stuff mushroomed until it got out of control. It took very little to set it off. And standing in the net, you knew it was going to happen. Almost like turning on

a light switch. I think what was lost in all that was the great hockey played by the two teams." —Oilers goalie Andy Moog

- "I remember [Ken] Linseman speared me once and it hurt so bad, but I wasn't going to let on. You didn't want to give up any kind of edge." —Flames goalie Don Edwards

- "I liked the Edmonton fans. I'd go over to the mall and they'd be on me, in a friendly way. When we finally beat them [in the 1986 playoffs], everybody laughed at our seven-point plan. But it worked! That's something they can never take away from me,

The Battle of Alberta is always a knockdown, drag-out fight.

damn it! I'll cherish that memory, that game, the rest of my life." —Flames coach "Badger" Bob Johnson

- "I'm not saying it's totally wrong, but if somebody's concentrating on me alone, I find it easier to cut off two men and make the easy pass." —Wayne Gretzky, on being assigned a shadow

- "For us to be totally, exclusively aware of Wayne is the wrong concept. I know from experience that in Montreal we played him too much, and other players did a number on us. To be so aware of him can take you away from you completing your job. But let's not fool anybody—you can't just leave him alone; you can't just treat him as an average player. He isn't." —Calgary center Doug Risebrough, one of those shadows

- "How badly was [Mike] Bullard hurt? The ambulance attendant said, 'How do you write up a report? The guy hops off the stretcher and walks into the dressing room.'" —Oilers enforcer Marty McSorley, after Flame Mike Bullard was carried off on a stretcher after a spear during the 1988 playoffs

- "I wouldn't say I cursed his name, exactly…let's just say I didn't fall out of my seat chanting it, either." —Flames goaltending consultant Glenn "Mr. Goalie" Hall, after longtime Flames killer Grant Fuhr wound up playing in Calgary

- "Good thing it wasn't a tie-down or he'd have been inside the bench." —Oilers coach Craig MacTavish after yanking the tongue out of Flames mascot Harvey the Hound's mouth

- "Edmonton-Calgary is a rivalry etched in stone, like New York–New York, Toronto-Chicago, Boston-Montreal." —Oilers goalie Andy Moog

- "I remember the one playoff game we started [Tim] Hunter, [Neil] Sheehy, and [Nick] Fotiu [up front], and they started [Marty] McSorley, [Kevin] McClelland, and [Dave] Semenko. That was pretty wild." —Gary Suter

- "I don't think you could blame one side or the other. Let's just call it a joint partnership." —Lanny McDonald
- "Rivalries grow as teams do. When the games matter, when a lot is at stake for both sides, when feelings are high, when you're fighting each other for something important. The geographical part is obviously already here, in place. So is the history. Hopefully, with the way we're both headed, this is just the start. I'm getting older. When I'm done playing, looking back, it'd be neat to say I was part of the start of it, [to] turn on the TV and see the young guys in here still playing important games against the Oilers." —Flames veteran winger Kris Versteeg, a Lethbridge, Alberta, boy, pushing for a renewal of meaningful hostilities in 2016

44 The Dynasty Dies

The dynasty was over. One year in. The night before, in the broiler better known as the Fabulous Forum in Inglewood, California, in front of John Candy, Tatum O'Neal, John McEnroe, Goldie Hawn, and 16,002 other screaming fanatics, L.A.'s Kings had knocked the NHL's kings off the throne.

The image of the series-winning goal haunted them: Calgary's Mike Vernon on his back, having kicked out a Steve Duchesne shot, then the puck, sent airborne by L.A.'s Mike Krushelnyski from 15 feet out as he was being driven to the ice, floating, in slow motion, like some soap bubble, up over a frantic claw by the little goaltender, and dropping down at 3:14 of double OT. L.A. euphoria. Calgary desolation.

Hockey's best team, carefully constructed to put a run of championships together, was heading home 4–3 losers, taken out in six games, their predicted run of Cups cut off at the bare minimum. "It's a dead feeling," said defenseman Al MacInnis softly. "Empty. But I don't think it'll really hit home until May, when we're watching two other teams fighting it out for old Lord Stanley on TV. I don't think until that moment will we realize exactly what we gave up last night."

Only a year before, in the hallowed place that was the Montreal Forum, MacInnis had lifted the Conn Smythe Trophy (and uttered the immortal "I'm going to Disneyland!" for promotional purposes), as well as the Stanley Cup itself. And now…it all lay in ashes.

"If we play as well as we can and are beaten by a better team, fine," continued MacInnis. "I can live with that. But this…we're a way better team than the L.A. Kings. It's our fault. I don't think they played all that great. We just didn't play very well."

The year before, the Flames dismissively swept the Kings aside in the minimum four games, but Gretzky and his black-and-silver band had taken notes. They made their intentions clear off the hop, winning Game 1 at the Saddledome 5–3 and assuming a 3–1 series lead on the strength of 8–5 and 12–4 batterings after that (both Wayne Gretzky and Tomas Sandstrom gorging on five points apiece).

"What I can't get out of my mind," said Flames quicksilver winger Paul Ranheim in the aftermath of Game 6, "is Gretzky, turning to our bench, laughing, pumping his arm and giving it to us. I just can't forget that."

Nor could they forget—or forgive—referee Denis Morel. The Flames believed they'd sent the series back to Calgary for a deciding clash, but a Doug Gilmour goal was chalked off with 2:23 left in the first OT.

Gilmour was trying to make a pass in front to Brian MacLellan at the time, the puck coming to rest under L.A. goaltender Kelly Hrudey's right leg, which he appeared to drag across the goal line.

Goal judge Ted Metcalfe turned on the red light. The Flames celebrated. After a wildly confusing five-minute delay, during which Morel conferred with Metcalfe—the man who'd called the goal good—it was waved off.

"It was in," seethed Gilmour afterward. "The goal judge said it was in. I was standing behind the net, and I saw it cross the line. I went right to the goal judge. He said it was in, but Morel didn't call it."

Morel initially indicated the puck had never crossed the line. Later, he changed his tune, claiming he'd blown the whistle before the puck had entered the net. Why, then, the Flames wondered, did Morel consult with the goal judge if he'd already blown the whistle?

"He is compounding a lie!" raged Coach Terry Crisp. "One lie leads to another. You know the pattern. He told our guys, 'It didn't go over the line.' There was no whistle. Now he's backpedaling.

"Mistakes I can accept. This isn't sour grapes. It's fact. You know what [Kings coach] Tommy Webster told me when we were shaking hands? He said, 'SOB, Crispie, that goal was yours.' Looked me right in the eye and said it."

Not that the admission did them a lick of good. "That puck," repeated Crisp, 25 years later, "was so obviously in the net. We had it on our TV behind [the bench], but there was no replay at that time. [Morel] wouldn't come over and take a look. And when I looked up and saw him going across the ice with Gretzky, No. 99's arm around his shoulder, I said, 'Whoa, boy.'"

So they were out. They didn't know it at the time, but the best of them as a group was already over and done with. "You've got to remember," said Theoren Fleury, "we lost a big part of our leadership before that season even began, with Lanny and Pep retiring. Hakan Loob went back to Sweden. Rammer [Rob Ramage] left. We were sort of trying to reestablish the leadership of the team.

"And what can I say? It was just one of those weird series. Didn't we give up 11 goals in one game? That just shows you. Everything that could go wrong did. And I don't think the organization ever really recovered after that."

The recriminations were swift. In short order, Crisp—who'd won two Presidents' Trophies and a Stanley Cup in three seasons— was fired and replaced by Doug Risebrough. A year later, following a gutting, epic seven-game first-round loss to the hated Oilers, GM Cliff Fletcher, the man responsible for blueprinting the team, departed for Toronto. The Canadian dollar began to drop. One by one the star names, usually over money, were shipped out of town.

So that disallowed goal, the blunting of the "dynasty" at one, the gnawing feeling of opportunity lost, has carried over though the passing of the years. A quarter century later, Theoren Fleury was still ticked off about the controversial events of that game, still ready to play the conspiracy card. "Gretzky goes to L.A., the league is looking to expand into other warmer climates, warmer markets, and they get a five-on-three in *overtime* in [bleeping] Game 6?" he laughed bitterly. "Then we score and it's not allowed? Are you kidding me?

"Denis Morel was the ref. I remember when their winning goal went in, over Vernie's glove, half the guys sort of sat on the bench, stunned. The other half went right to Morel, surrounded him. And Cooner [Jamie Macoun] speared him right in the nuts. I saw it. And I'm like, 'I can't believe he just did that!'"

So those involved have been left to play the what-might-have-been game. Given the Flames' depth and their championship pedigree from the year before, had the Gilmour goal been given, they certainly could've gone home and won Game 7, carrying all the momentum, and from there, maybe even…

"Not a doubt in my mind," said Fleury evenly.

45 The Risebrough Era

Dog-tired from the long hours and a punishing double workload, Doug Risebrough decided one day to lie down on the floor of the coach's office and snatch a few winks of shut-eye. "It was like 3:00 in the afternoon," he recalled. "I said to myself, 'I gotta lay down. I just…gotta. A quick nap.' So I lay down on the floor because there was no couch or anything. We had a game that night.

"Well, I'm dozing, and in walks Jamie Hislop. He sees me laying on the floor, and he starts screaming, 'Doug! Doug! Doug!' I sit up, and he's like, 'Oh my God. I thought you'd had a heart attack!'"

Calgary's Risebrough era, in its entirely, stretched from September 11, 1982—when he arrived in a trade with the Montreal Canadiens—until November 2, 1995, and his termination as general manager.

During that spell, he had stints as on-ice team captain, assistant coach, assistant GM, head coach and GM (for a grueling 64 games in the 1991–92 season), and finally GM alone when he was replaced as coach by Guy Charron. "When I was in the GM's office," he laughed, "I couldn't wait to get down to the coach's office. And when I actually got to the coach's office, I could hardly wait to get back up to the GM's office."

In assuming the managerial reins from the departing master, Cliff Fletcher, in the spring of 1991, and widely billed as one of the game's rising young management stars, he took on a massive responsibility. "I always say this: you learn more from your mistakes than you do from your successes," said Risebrough now.

"Not to be boastful, but I'd had a lot of successes up to that point. Thirteen years in the league, four Stanley Cups, been to the

141

Finals, I'm an assistant coach [with Calgary] and the team's good, we win a Cup. Everything's great.

"Cliff told me he wanted me in management not in coaching, and I said, 'That's fine.' I'm pitching in, right? The next thing you know, he says, 'We're hiring Crispie [Terry Crisp]. Can you go into coaching?' Sure. Pitching in. No biggie.

"We win the Cup, then I become assistant GM, and all of a sudden Cliff says, 'Crispie's on his way out. Can you coach the team?' Well, I was just pitching in again.

"Then Cliff says, 'Hey, I'm leaving. Want to be GM too?' I'm pitching in again, and he is gone."

The learning curve was a steep one, particularly in an organization—and a city—that had become accustomed to achievement. "Part of the problem," said Risebrough, "is that I'd been playing with half the team only five years before, then I'm coaching the team, and then I'm managing *and* coaching the team. And I had no idea how hard the job actually was.

"It was a learning experience, and it was a lot. During that time, I came to realize two things: One, I was not a good coach. I really tried to figure out coaching, so when I became a manager later on, I knew what I needed in terms of the type of person who would be a good coach. And two, leverage means nothing. When you've got the GM's job and the coach's job, you think you've got total leverage, got it all. It scares the hell out of the players. You don't convince someone to do something just because you've got leverage. It kills them. You've got to find different ways.

"The guy behind he bench was also the guy who could trade them. It's one thing to have their ice time taken away. It's another thing to know that the guy behind the bench can call you tomorrow and say, 'You're no longer here.' Compounding it was the fact that I'd played with half the players, making it almost a personal thing."

During Risebrough's short tenure as head coach, the Flames lost an epic seven-game opening-round series to the Oilers. After handing the coaching responsibilities to Guy Charron for the closing 16 games of the 1992–93 campaign, he hired Dave King as coach for two seasons, followed by Pierre Page.

On November 2, 1995, though, with the Flames listing at 1–8–3, having played 10 of their 12 games on the road owing to Saddledome renovations, Risebrough was axed. The team's executive VP, Al Coates, took command.

Risebrough went on to join the archrival Edmonton Oilers as executive VP from 1996 through 1999 before landing the GM job with the Minnesota Wild, staying 10 years and aiding in the development of that franchise.

The formative, on-the-job training he received in Calgary laid the foundation. "It was wonderful," he said in hindsight. "Maybe it didn't end so wonderfully—these things never do—but when I took the next job, I knew exactly what had to be done.

"I'd seen the development aspect of an organization. So there was no negative. Ideally, you'd like to win a Stanley Cup as a player, as coach, and [as] manager, and stay in the same place. That just doesn't happen.

"I'm the luckiest guy to be able to watch the Montreal organization, with such a high bar, putting the pieces together to win multiple Stanley Cups. But I was also lucky to go to Calgary and watch an organization grow into a champion.

"I knew what was expected in Montreal and saw the benefits, but I needed to go to Calgary to understand how complicated that was."

46 Trading Gilmour

Only the night before, they had celebrated a morale-boosting 3–2 overtime silencing of the archrival Montreal Canadiens in front of a delirious sellout crowd at the Pengrowth Saddledome. A New Year's Eve soiree worthy of the occasion. And the Dead End Kid with that indomitable sneer curling around his lips, Doug Gilmour, was the catalyst, as he had been so often since arriving in town.

Then came that day: January 1, 1992. A day that—for Calgary partisans—will forever live in infamy. The day Gilmour walked out on the Flames.

"Gilmour," said a tight-lipped coach/GM Doug Risebrough, "did not practice today. He came to me this morning and told me he was leaving.

"He said he wanted his contractual status to be looked into. I said I'd do that. I also said I'd prefer he was at practice. He said, 'I've gotta think of myself.' That's not what I want to hear."

At the crux of the long-standing contractual problem: Gilmour wanted two years and an option; the Flames countered with a one-and-one proposal. They could not find common ground. So the two sides went to arbitration. Gilmour reportedly sought $1.2 million; the club upped its offer to $550,000. Gilmour felt the arbitrator would slide in at around $800,000.

Gilmour was bitter over the ruling that awarded him $750,000 and the option year, and incensed that Flames management had been spotted in the stands alongside the arbitrator at the game before the hearing. In fact, he'd called Risebrough and asked for a trade the day the ruling was announced, while the team was in Buffalo, only to relent. At least temporarily.

"Hey, life goes on," said teammate Theoren Fleury the day Doug Gilmour walked out. "We realize we might not have Dougie around for a while. Or maybe ever again."

Risebrough wouldn't back down. Gilmour wouldn't back down. The impasse triggered a 10-player deal the very next day, brokered with his old boss, Cliff Fletcher, now in charge of the sadsack Toronto Maple Leafs: Gilmour, defensemen Jamie Macoun and Ric Nattress, prospect Kent Manderville, and backup goaltender Rick Wamsley in exchange for the erratic but gifted Gary Leeman, defense prospect Alexander Godynyuk, tough guy Craig Berube, much-traveled defenseman Michel Petit, and puck stopper Jeff Reese. No one could realize at the time the impact this one swap would have on two organizations. It has gone down as one of the most lopsided swaps in recent memory.

Fletcher knew each of the players he was acquiring inside out. Outside of Manderville, all were part of the Flames' 1989 championship team. Risebrough, cutting his teeth in the managerial game by comparison, had no such firsthand, battle-tested intel on his new recruits. "It was a mistake by a young general manager," Risebrough admitted later.

More than two decades removed from the events, Risebrough recalled the day: "I remember getting a call from Baxie [Paul Baxter] downstairs, and he says, 'I just ran into Doug Gilmour. He's packing his bags.' I told him to tell Doug to talk to me. Doug came up, we talked; he was disappointed with the contract negotiations. I told him I understood that but it [was] a difference of opinion, and that it wasn't being done maliciously. I told him, 'The business is really complicated. You're under contract. You had your shot at arbitration, and this is what they awarded you.'"

Risebrough told Gilmour that if he left that day, he would be traded, but if he stayed and continued to play, he would reconsider the contract impasse or trade him within 10 days. Gilmour walked.

"My problem," said Risebrough today, "is that I was too impatient in making a deal. I should've let him sit."

There's an old saying: the team getting the best player wins the deal. The best player, by some distance, was Doug Gilmour. Fletcher has often called his acquisition of Gilmour "the trade that pulled everything together" for that 1989 title-winning season. Indeed, he had scored the game winner and the insurance marker into an empty net in the clinching Game 6 at the Montreal Forum. Bringing his special skill and tenacity to Toronto revitalized that franchise. Those sorts of players don't come along very often.

"I'm not going to apologize for anything I said or did," Gilmour said three weeks after the deal was consummated. "I think people did misunderstand my feelings, yes…they just thought I was greedy, that the only thing I was unhappy about was my contract.

"It's time to move on. I think if my situation was going to be resolved [in Calgary], it would've been in camp. But I'm better off now. And the Flames needed a trade." Maybe, but not the trade they made.

The two main components from a Calgary perspective fizzled badly in their brief Alberta tenures. Leeman scored only 11 goals through 59 games as a Flame before exiting for Montreal, while Godynyuk dressed for only 33 games in a year and a half wearing the colors.

Gilmour, as everyone knows, went on to become a Maple Leafs legend in five and a half years in the Big Smoke, twice eclipsing the 100-point barrier (127 in his first full season, a franchise record; 111 the next season) and propelling the Leafs all the way to the Stanley Cup semifinals in the spring of 1993, when they were shaded four games to three by Wayne Gretzky and the L.A. Kings.

On the flip side of the one-sided coin, the trade was a major contributing factor in sending Calgary into a dizzying downward spiral and into the throes of a seven-year playoff drought.

47 Gary Roberts

Legend has the chin-up tally beginning and ending at one. Gary Roberts, however, will argue that total, somewhat sheepishly. "I think I actually did one and a half," he confessed, many, many years after his first, eye-opening pro training camp experience.

He continued, "There are times in your career when you go through ups and downs, and I think we all know my first NHL training camp was a bust. Coach Badger Bob [Johnson] said that I was the worst-conditioned player at camp. Matter of fact, he didn't say my name, but he did say 'Our first-round draft pick is the worst-conditioned player at camp.' So it wasn't too hard for anyone to figure out.

"I gotta say when I think back on it, it kinda made me the player I became and the person I am today. It was embarrassing. I walked into the dressing room, and Paul Baxter was doing chin-ups with a 45-pound plate between his legs. Carey Wilson was doing dips with a 45-pound plate. I didn't even know what those exercises were, let alone doing them with weight."

Roberts arrived in Calgary carrying a lot of fanfare, and a bit of excess body fat, as 1984's first-round (12th overall) pick from the Ottawa 67s, but he turned into a quick study and in no time at all became much, much more than merely Joe Nieuwendyk's Whitby, Ontario, hockey and lacrosse buddy.

Scroll through the annals of the Flames franchise, and you'll find no shortage of star right wingers. Hakan Loob. Lanny McDonald. Theo Fleury. Joe Mullen. Jarome Iginla. The port side? Not nearly so amply stocked. One name towers above the rest: Gary Roberts.

Roberts would get in shape, begin to understand the require-ments of life in the NHL, and find his niche. During the Stanley Cup season of 1988–89, his second full season as a Flame, he did his bit, contributing 38 points and 250 penalty minutes, then a dozen additional points through a 22-game playoff run.

"Guys like Robs," praised Coach Terry Crisp, "bring so much to the table. They play tough, can score, are good in the room. They're fearless, courageous winners. Guys like Robs have the intangibles to help turn mediocre teams into competitive ones, good teams into better ones."

He'd hit anything and fight anyone (a center-ice scrap against Edmonton Oilers superstar Mark Messier perhaps his most famous), all the while continuing to evolve as an all-around player. By 1991 it had all come together. That season ranks as one for the ages, at least organizationally. Not only did the truculent Roberts reach the touchstone 50-goal plateau, his 53 snipes remain the second-highest single-season total of any Flame. Ever. He also topped the club in PIM, at 207. Quite the cocktail of touch and tough.

By then established as a dominant player, he continued to play the type of abrasive game that suited him. That reckless, bumper-car style would soon catch up with him, though. Busted noses. Broken fingers. Stitches. Concussions. They all took a heavy toll. But the worst were the whacks, the cross-checks.

In late 1994 Roberts began experiencing searing pain in his neck and right shoulder. The issue came to a head as he sat alone in the dressing room after a game, confused and frightened. "I broke down," he revealed later. "I cried. The tears just kept coming. I was so scared. I thought about my career. I thought about my life."

The rehab ritual began. He underwent two surgeries to alleviate nerve and disc problems in his neck, in May and October 1994. After missing half the 1994 season, he returned, even scored a goal that first night back. But by June 1996 the pain and stiffness had returned, and he announced his retirement, having undergone two operations on his neck, one on either side.

"The risks are just too high for me to continue," Roberts said that day, fighting back tears during a somber news conference. "I have no bitter feelings at all. I wanted to play the game hard. It shortened my career a little bit, but I'll always feel good about the way I played."

Gary Roberts was only three weeks past his 30th birthday when he retired, but his dream of continuing to play didn't fade away. Roberts continued to strengthen his neck until—having rehabbed for an entire year—he felt reasonably comfortable launching a comeback. "The biggest thing, from our perspective," said Calgary's GM at the time, Al Coates, "was that he'd already signed his disability papers to retire. So our doctors—all great doctors—came to us and said, 'If he's going to come back and play here, that's okay, but we have to resign. We can't sign off and then have him come back and play.' That was a big part of the decision [not to bring him back to Calgary]."

So began a round of stops—in San Jose, on the Island, with the Rangers, etc.—to be examined by team doctors. Among those checkup points was Raleigh, North Carolina. "[GM] Jim Rutherford wanted leadership in their team," explained Coates, "and they were willing to take on a responsibility—let's call it a risk, I suppose—that no other team would. And that's why he ended up in Carolina."

So on August 25, 1997, the Flames dealt Roberts, along with goaltender Trevor Kidd, to the Hurricanes in exchange for center Andrew Cassels and goaltender Jean-Sebastien Giguere. A stubborn cuss, Roberts went on to put 11 more NHL seasons on his odometer, in the service of the Hurricanes, Toronto Maple Leafs, Florida Panthers, Pittsburgh Penguins, and Tampa Bay Lightning.

And he now runs the Gary Roberts High Performance Centre in North York, Ontario, famous across the hockey spectrum, where he acts as a guru to NHLers looking to get that edge in performance via conditioning. Remember, this is the guy whose first-ever chin-up tally began and ended at one. Okay, okay…one and a half.

48 Harley Hotchkiss

Integrity. Honesty. Trust. All the old-fashioned virtues that from time to time may seem out of date today but always, always matter when it counts most. "It may sound corny," Harley Hotchkiss said unapologetically on his induction into the Hockey Hall of Fame in 2006, "but I have a certain set of beliefs, of principles I believe in, and that's how I live, how I conduct myself. And sometimes, you know, corny isn't such a bad thing.

"I love hockey. I believe in how it brings us together as a country. If some people believe that to be motherhood or church or whatever, there's nothing I can do about it."

If any one single person can claim to have shaped the tone and set the standard for the Calgary Flames organization, that man is indisputably Harley Hotchkiss. "Class," replied Jim Peplinski unhesitatingly when asked for one word to describe the man.

Part of the original ownership group that brought the Flames from Atlanta—Nelson Skalbania, Hotchkiss, Ralph Scurfield, Norman Green, Doc and Byron Seaman along with former Canadian Football League star Normie Kwong—Hotchkiss quickly became the team's spokesman. He was frequently around the rink, taking an active interest in the club but in his trademark quiet style. His influence, the respect he generated, cannot be overestimated.

When the Flames were teetering on the brink of relocation in the late 1990s—the team struggling, attendance flagging, and the Canadian dollar dropping—he took the role of the point man to lead a season-ticket campaign that saved the franchise.

When the league was going through arguably its darkest hour, during the lockout of 2004–05, and there seemed no way back, Harley Hotchkiss was called in to help make peace. He had that sort of effect on people, on both sides of the negotiation floor.

NHL commissioner Gary Bettman said any time he thought of Hotchkiss, the famous Teddy Roosevelt quote always popped into his mind: "Walk softly and carry a big stick." Hotchkiss was a self-made success from Tillsonburg, Ontario, who grew up on a tobacco and dairy farm, graduated from Michigan State University, and served in the Canadian Merchant Navy during WWII. Hotchkiss shared the millions he earned in the oil and gas sector with his community.

Within the NHL framework, he convinced the league to adopt a currency-equalization program when the Canadian dollar bottomed out. He championed the league's "small-market" franchises, and for a dozen years he served as chairman of the league's board of governors, the voice or reason in an often-unreasonable setting.

His crowning moment in the game, of course, arrived on May 25, 1989, at the old Montreal Forum—Game 6 of the Stanley Cup Finals. The 4–2 victory that night secured the Flames their first Cup in franchise history. "In Game 6 we had a particularly interesting thing happen," recalled Hotchkiss afterward. "We were already in Montreal, and it happened we had a grandson born that morning. We took that as a very good sign. We talked and joked about naming him Stanley, but he was named Matthew."

Whatever your name—Stanley, Matthew, Joe, Mike, Hakan, or Theoren—Harley Hotchkiss took an interest in you. "He treated you as if you were part of his family," said Theo Fleury admiringly.

He fought the Flames' fight. He fought the league's fight. Gradually, he stepped further back from those roles to enjoy his family and gardening more. No one could begrudge him that; he'd gone above and beyond the call of duty.

In December 2010, after 30 years in the ownership game, Hotchkiss agreed to sell off 22 percent of his stake in the Flames. Health issues, it was learned, were at the heart of the decision. Six months later he died of prostate cancer at age 84.

"I remember being invited over to Harley's house after the team had moved here from Atlanta," recalled former Flames GM Al Coates on the day of Hotchkiss' passing. "Probably the first time I met him. We had a staff of seven, I think, at that point. And this is an owner, right, so you're a little on your guard, worried about making a good impression. But I remember thinking to myself as we were leaving, *You know, that might just be the nicest person I've ever met.* Thirty years later, I had no reason to change that opinion."

So many people associated with the Flames throughout the decades—and within the National Hockey League at large—felt the same. "Harley," summed up Peplinski, "brought an uncommon level of everyday class to the Calgary Flames. That's not easy to do.

"I think of when our [automobile] leasing business got up to over 100 people. The dealership side was 400 or 500. It doesn't seem possible to know everyone. Harley knew all of us and all of our kids. He just had an unbelievable ability to be interested in people, and bring an incredible level of class in an often rough-and-tumble business—to the franchise, to the locker room, to hockey.

"It's too bad there aren't more Harleys. Every organization needs a Harley. But there aren't many fortunate enough to have one."

Top 10 Individual Seasons

1. **Kent Nilsson, C, 1980–81:** Sure the game was loosey-goosey back then, but the Magic Man's 131 points and 82 assists are franchise records that today seem as distant, as unreachable, as DiMaggio's 56-game hitting streak or Wilt Chamberlain's 100 points. How dominant was the enigmatic Swede? Guy Chouinard, runner-up in team scoring that year, was 48 points in arrears. Nilsson finished third in league scoring, behind Wayne Gretzky and Marcel Dionne.

2. **Al MacInnis, D, 1990–91:** Only five defensemen in NHL annals have piled up 100 points or more in a single season—Bobby Orr (six times), Paul Coffey (five), Brian Leetch, Denis Potvin, and Al MacInnis. MacInnis' explosion for 103 in 1990–91 was only one shy of Theo Fleury's team lead for the season and ranked ninth overall, behind the likes of Wayne Gretzky, Joe Sakic, Adam Oates, Brett Hull, and Steve Yzerman.

3. **Jarome Iginla, RW, 2001–02:** The season the inspirational captain should've won the Hart Trophy. He lost to Montreal goaltender Jose Theodore on first-place ballots (26–23) after a deadlock. The game's most complete player at the time, Iginla became the only Flame ever to win the Art Ross Trophy as scoring champion, accumulating 96 points, including 52 goals.

4. **Lanny McDonald, RW, 1982–83:** McDonald's first full season back home in Alberta cemented his legend, deploying the trademark release to pot an astonishing 66 goals. Only Wayne Gretzky, at 71, scored more often that year. Since that season, many Flames have reached the 50 mark, but the closest

anyone's gotten to McDonald's incredible output is 53, when Gary Roberts did it nine years later.

5. **Miikka Kiprusoff, G, 2005–06:** The silent Finn had given everyone a teasing taste of his brilliance in 38 starts his first half-season in Calgary (a modern-day best 1.69 GAA, 24 wins), but the follow-up with an increased workload upped the ante: 74 games played, 42 wins—the Flames as a team won 46—a 2.07 goals-against average and, as a capper, a richly deserved Vezina Trophy.

6. **Joe Mullen, RW, 1988–89:** In terms of complete offensive seasons, Mullen's en route to a Stanley Cup championship certainly ranks right up there: 51 goals, 59 assists, 110 points (second all-time for the franchise), while winning the plus-minus award (plus-51), the Lady Byng Memorial Trophy, and a first-team selection on right wing. Oh, and he led the playoffs that spring with 16 snipes.

7. **Joe Nieuwendyk, C, 1987–88:** The year Nieuwendyk exploded into public consciousness. Pre–Teemu Selanne, the record for most goals by a rookie was held by New York Islanders talisman Mike Bossy, at 53. With 10 games left, Nieuwendyk seemed destined three back, but he stalled in the backstretch and finished at 51. Oh well, he could console himself with a Calder Trophy.

8. **Gary Roberts, LW, G, 1991–92:** Among tough-and-touch seasons, the 1991–92 campaign put in by former first-round draft pick Gary Roberts has no equal. That year, Roberts scored 53 times in 76 games, the second-highest single-season total in club history, while also topping Calgary charts with 207 PIM.

9. **Hakan Loob, RW, 1987–88:** The elfin Swede did something in this remarkable campaign none of his illustrious countrymen had before, or has since: reach the magical 50-goal plateau in the NHL. That year he topped the Calgary scoring charts at

106 points and helped mentor a freshman linemate named Joe Nieuwendyk, also a 50-goal man.

10. (Tie) **Mike Vernon, G, 1988–89; Theoren Fleury, RW, 1990–91:** Yes, the Flames had a powerhouse in their only Stanley Cup campaign, but Vernon went an astounding 37–6–5 with a (for the time) highly respectable 2.65. In 1990–91 Fleury broke the 50-goal plateau (51, tied for second in the league) for the only time in his career and finished with 104 points and at a plus-48.

Miikka Kiprusoff enjoyed a Vezina-winning season in 2005–06.

50 A Dozen Defining Deals

Eight men through the years—Cliff Fletcher, Doug Risebrough, Al Coates, Craig Button, Darryl Sutter, Jay Feaster, Brian Burke, and now Brad Treliving—have controlled the wheeling and dealing of the Flames franchise.

Here, then, are 12 trades that most affected the franchise. The mostly good, the occasionally bad, and (in the case of the Gilmour-to-Toronto transaction) the really, really ugly.

- **November 25, 1981:** Acquired Lanny McDonald and a fourth-round 1983 draft pick from Colorado in exchange for left winger Don Lever and center Bob MacMillan.

  MacMillan and Lever were pretty able contributors, but adding someone who'd quickly become the symbol of your franchise and score a franchise-record 66 goals in one year for you? That's what's known as awfully good business.

- **September 11, 1982:** Acquired center Doug Risebrough and second-round choice in 1983 draft from Montreal in exchange for Washington's second pick in the 1983 draft and Calgary's third in the 1984 draft.

  Risebrough had helped the Canadiens to four Stanley Cups and brought a winning pedigree, an ambitious attitude that Fletcher felt necessary to help move his team along. The feisty centerman later coached and then managed the Flames.

- **June 15, 1985:** Acquired a second-round (27th overall) draft pick in the 1985 draft from Minnesota in exchange for center Kent Nilsson.

  It isn't often that trading away arguably the most gifted player in franchise history turns out to be a good thing. But when you use that selection to land rangy Cornell center Joe Nieuwendyk, who has soft-as-eiderdown hands…

- **February 1, 1986:** Acquired right winger Joe Mullen and defensemen Rik Wilson and Terry Johnson from St. Louis in exchange for defensemen Charlie Bourgeois, Gino Cavallini, and Eddy Beers.

  Mullen went on to score 190 goals and 388 points for the Flames, pocketed two Lady Byng Memorial Trophies and an Emery Edge Award (for top plus-minus in the league), and scored 16 goals during Calgary's 1989 Cup run.

- **August 26, 1987:** Acquired defenseman Brad McCrimmon from Philadelphia in exchange for a third-round pick in the 1988 draft and a first-rounder in 1989.

  The no-frills, stay-at-home blueliner lent an air of veteran solidity and professionalism, and a warrior mentality, to an emerging defense corps that included both Al MacInnis and Gary Suter. His contribution were invaluable through the 1989 run.

- **March 7, 1988:** Acquired defenseman Rob Ramage and goaltender Rick Wamsley from St. Louis in exchange for right winger Brett Hull and left winger Steve Bozek.

  The Flames did lift the Stanley Cup with Ramage playing a significant role in the wake of Gary Suter's broken jaw suffered late in round one, while Wamsley proved to be the ultimate team man. Still, Hull blossomed into a superstar, the greatest pure goal scorer of an era, ringing up 527 snipes over a decade plus, leaving Flames fans to wonder what might have been.

- **September 6, 1988:** Acquired center Doug Gilmour, right winger Mark Hunter, left winger Steve Bozek, and defenseman Michael Dark from St. Louis in exchange for center Mike Bullard, center Craig Coxe, and defenseman Tim Corkery.

  Gilmour's talent and tenacity were just the ingredients the Flames needed as they took aim at glory in 1989. Calgary GM

Cliff Fletcher, the man who brokered the swap, has always listed this as the one that pushed his club over the top.

- **January 2, 1992:** Acquired right winger Gary Leeman, defenseman Alexander Godynyuk, goaltender Jeff Reese, left winger Craig Berube, and defenseman Michel Petit in exchange for center Doug Gilmour, defenseman Ric Nattress, goaltender Rick Wamsley, center Kent Manderville, and defenseman Jamie Macoun.

  This, the largest trade in NHL history, spurred by Gilmour's walkout over contractual differences the day before, sent the franchise into a death spiral. A one-sided dud of historic proportions. Gilmour became a Leafs legend, a Hart Trophy finalist, and propelled the perennial sad sack Torontonians to the 1993 Campbell Conference final. Leeman, the key component in the swap from a Calgary perspective, scored only 11 goals in 59 games as a Flame before being offloaded to Montreal.

- **December 19, 1995:** Acquired right winger Jarome Iginla and center Corey Millen from Dallas in exchange for center Joe Nieuwendyk.

  Dissatisfaction over his contract and in need of a change, the Calgary captain held out until the day of the Christmas trade freeze, when GM Al Coates struck a deal with Stars counterpart Bob Gainey. Millen was a handy pivot who went on to play 92 games for Calgary over a season and a half, but the key for Coates was always Iginla, a first-round pick (11th overall) in the 1995 draft. Considering his hand had been forced, it's hard to imagine a deal working out better.

- **February 28, 1999:** Acquired center Rene Corbet, defenseman Wade Belak, a 2000 second-round draft pick, and defenseman prospect Robyn Regehr in exchange for right winger Theo Fleury and left winger Chris Dingman.

Another money-fueled deal, with Fleury set to become an unrestricted free agent on July 1. Regehr was the player selected from a list of prospects, and again, given the forced hand involved, Coates did exceptionally well. Regehr went on to play more games than any man in franchise history save Jarome Iginla.

- **November 16, 2003:** Acquired goaltender Miikka Kiprusoff from San Jose in exchange for a 2005 second-round pick.

  This was a game-changing addition by GM Darryl Sutter. Sutter knew Kiprusoff from his days in teal but had no inkling of the impact the silent Finn would make. In fact, Kiprusoff was brought in as a backup to Roman Turek. Kiprusoff retired in 2012 holding every major goaltending record for the Flames franchise.

- **March 27, 2013:** Acquired right winger Ben Hanowski, left winger Kenny Agostino, and first pick in the 2013 draft from Pittsburgh in exchange for right winger Jarome Iginla.

  After at least a year of uncertainty, Iginla, the face of the franchise, finally agreed to waive his no-trade clause and was dealt to Pittsburgh to join his 2010 Olympic collaborator Sidney Crosby. Iginla lasted only a few months in Pittsburgh before signing on with Boston. Agostino is now with the St. Louis Blues, while Hanowski is plying his trade in Germany.

51 Top 10 Drafts

1. **Al MacInnis, D, 1ˢᵗ round, 15ᵗʰ overall, 1981:** The third-leading scorer in franchise history, and its hands-down top defenseman. His 103-point season of 1990–91 at the position is certain to stand forever. Sure, Dale Hawerchuk, Ron Francis, and Grant Fuhr were selected ahead of him that year, but so were Ron Meighan, Normand Leveille, and Joe Cirella.

2. **Theoren Fleury, RW/C, 8ᵗʰ round, 166ᵗʰ overall, 1987:** No one seemed willing to take a flyer on a 5'6", 150-pound battler, no matter how gaudy his stats at WHL Moose Jaw, but the Flames, famous for superb late-round picks, did, to handsome dividends. Fleury became the face of the franchise for a decade.

3. **Joe Nieuwendyk, C, 2ⁿᵈ round, 85ᵗʰ overall, 1985:** Wily Cliff Fletcher looked to Cornell University to parlay the selection obtained in the contentious Kent Nilsson trade with Minnesota. It took a while for people to pronounce (and spell) the name properly, but Joe Who? went on to cop the 1988 Calder and pile up 314 goals and 616 points in the colors.

4. **Mike Vernon, G, 3ʳᵈ round, 56ᵗʰ overall, 1981:** Following up their MacInnis pick, the Flames stuck close to home in adding the feisty Calgary product. His elevation from the AHL coincided with the organization's first Cup Finals appearance in 1986 and then backstopped 1989's title win. He held every franchise record at the position until Miikka Kiprusoff made his mark.

5. **Gary Roberts, LW, 1ˢᵗ round, 1984:** Joe Nieuwendyk's Whitby, Ontario, buddy left his own imprint on the franchise. He was skilled, edgy, and willing to fight anyone. He ranks fourth in Flames career goals, with 257, and second in penalty minutes,

with 1,736. His 53 snipes in 1991–92 rank second-highest in franchise history for a single season.

6. **Gary Suter, D, 9ᵗʰ round, 180ᵗʰ overall, 1984:** Not only were the Flames renowned for spotting late-round jewels, they owned the US college market for years. The University of Wisconsin, Coach Bob Johnson's old stomping grounds, provided the second-highest scoring defenseman in club history. He shaded Wendel Clark for the 1986 Calder.

7. **Hakan Loob, RW, 9ᵗʰ round, 181ˢᵗ overall, 1983:** The European option was another one the Flames mined first, and best. Loob dispelled the "chicken Swede" stereotype, and although his stay was relatively brief, his presence was nothing short of immense during the Cup-winning season of 1989. He is still the only Swede ever to register a 50-goal season.

8. **Johnny Gaudreau, C, 4ᵗʰ round, 104ᵗʰ overall, 2011:** Another pint-sized gem. He was a Calder Trophy finalist in 2014–15, and at 64 points, Johnny Hockey spearheaded Calgary's 2014–15 renaissance and first playoff berth after a six-season drought. He followed it up with 30 goals and 78 points in his second year. The horizon for the former Boston College Hobey Baker winner seems limitless.

9. **Sean Monahan, C, 1ˢᵗ round, 6ᵗʰ overall, 2013:** After only two full NHL seasons, Monahan is quickly developing into one of the game's most underrated two-way centermen. A 31-goal, 62-point sophomore campaign foreshadowed stardom. He inspired a fake Twitter account, @boringmonahan, that has attracted 62,000 devoted followers.

10. **Sergei Makarov, 12ᵗʰ round, 231ˢᵗ overall, 1980:** Makarov was already legendary when he arrived at age 31, after negotiations with Soviet Red Army secured his release to the NHL. People giggled when GM Cliff Fletcher selected the *M* of the great KLM line late, late, late into the 1980 draft. He went on to win the Calder Trophy as Rookie of the Year.

52 The Epic Series

The slide—a moment still replayed endlessly on hockey broadcasts everywhere. Theo Fleury stepped in to intercept Mark Messier's ill-advised cross-ice pass through the middle nearing the five-minute mark of overtime, leaving the Edmonton Oilers defense pair of Jeff Beukeboom and Steve Smith skating on a treadmill to nowhere. Then, after coolly sliding the puck through the wickets of goalie Grant Fuhr, Fleury set off on a 180-foot odyssey of joy, arms pumping wildly, mouth agape, as he sprinted down by the Calgary bench, dropped to his knees, and slid, spinning 360 degrees once and finally stopping upside down along the far boards, engulfed by teammates. The first-round series to end all first-round series was suddenly, dramatically tied 3–3 after a nervy 2–1 Flames victory at Northlands Coliseum.

"You know me," said Fleury, years later, harkening back to his slippery flight of fancy. "I always wore my heart on my sleeve.

"Any of those guys, those point-a-game guys, down through the years, they tend to have one goal, one moment, that sort of sums up their career. That was mine.

"Remember, until then I hadn't done a whole lot [in the post-season]. But I was also playing with a second-degree MCL sprain and a separated shoulder. Still, I didn't have a point. Coming off my best season ever, [51] goals, 100 points, and after six games I've got bagels across the board? So yeah, I was feeling the pressure. I remember [Coach Doug Risebrough] sitting me down and telling me to relax, have fun. That helped.

"Then thanks to Mess putting it right on my tape and then having probably two of the slowest defensemen in the game chasing me down the ice…

"I think I got the puck at the red line, Beukeboom was actually in front of me at the [Oilers] blueline, and I just took off. What's that Linda Ronstadt song? 'Blew by You?'"

In the lore of the Battle of Alberta, that entire 1991 series stands alone. For those who witnessed it, those seven games—April 4 to April 16—were the most compelling, unsparing, and bordering-on-vicious they'd ever be lucky enough to savor. "Just plain nasty," summed up Fleury.

The little guy with the indomitable will had his moment, but the Oilers had the last laugh. Arguably the best summation of a series for the ages was caught by photographers post–Game 7, when cousins Joe Nieuwendyk and Jeff Beukeboom congratulated each other and shook hands, totally spent, after having battled hammer and tongs for more than two weeks.

"I remember," said Nieuwendyk, "one of the headlines during that series: No Kissing Cousins. We got into a bit of a slash fest with each other at one point, I remember. But that's just the way that hockey was: brutal.

"It was an incredible series of physicality and hatred [toward] one another. I know I had some personal battles with Kevin Lowe. A lot of individual stuff [was] going on. Tough meat-and-potatoes hockey [that] was kind of unusual for those two teams, because of the skill each team had."

It was a back-and-forth duel, like the shifting of the tides. Edmonton gained a quick advantage, winning Game 1 at the Saddledome 3–1 and racing out to a 3–1 series advantage. Down to their last life, the Flames fought back fiercely, taking Game 5 at home 5–3 and staying alive. Fleury brought it full circle.

The decider, if anything, amped up the superlatives. Calgary roared out to a 3–0 lead on home ice and seemed to be in cruise control, but somehow the Flames trailed 4–3 with 2:10 left in the third, until Ron Stern tapped in a ricochet behind Fuhr from close in after Al MacInnis had hammered a shot off the end boards. Which set the stage for Tiki Time.

As the Saddledome score clock inched toward the seven-minute mark of OT, Esa Tikkanen wired the puck from off the right boards, a shot that clipped Flames defenseman Frank Musil en route and exploded up and in on goalie Mike Vernon, sailing over his left shoulder.

"It was pride," said Tikkanen later. "Everybody in this room knows how to win a Stanley Cup. "They know what it takes."

Which left the Flames to fully comprehend how bad it hurts. "It went off [Musil's] pad and into the top shelf," said a disconsolate Vernon. "It's just one of those things, and it's very frustrating. We carried the play in overtime and they get the bounce—the break.

"We had such a good feeling when we tied it 4–4. I had such a good feeling. We were rolling, and I made that save off Mess early in overtime and then they get a fluke. It's so disheartening.

"The boys worked so hard the last part of the series. We made a lot of progress, and I really thought we were going to go and get it done tonight."

The 1991 series remains one people in Alberta still speak of in reverential tones. "Having had the opportunity to visit the William Wallace monument in Scotland, when I was playing in Ireland, and sort of looking out on the battlefield there at Falkirk, well, that's what that series was like," said Fleury. "Every time you put your equipment—or your suit of armor—on, it was…war.

"If that series was played today, all 40 guys would have all been suspended. You know how they tap each other now and call it slashing? We were full baseball swinging. Trying to hit bone. Not flesh. Bone."

The Oilers reached the semifinals that spring, falling 4–1 to the Minnesota North Stars. For the Flames, the Tikkanen goal triggered a string of deflating first-round losses in Game 7 overtimes.

"You won't see hockey like this again until we meet them again," predicted Fleury back then. The two teams haven't collided in a playoff series since, though we're still waiting, still hoping.

53 Toon Time

In Calgary, the art of the draw wasn't confined to face-off circles. "My favorite Flames cartoon?" repeated cartoonist Dave Elston, delving back into his memory banks. "Top three, I guess, would be the Theo hockey card, where you only see the top of his helmet; changing on the fly, where you see a ladder come over the boards so he can hop on the ice; and the Fleury Christmas tree, where Cliff Fletcher's going, 'Who's the idiot that let Fleury trim the tree?' and it's just the bottom third with decorations on it; the top is all bare."

For 12 years, from September 1989 through 2001, Dave Elston was Canada's only full-time sports cartoonist. His cartoons for the *Calgary Sun* sports pages were, and are, classics. His laugh-out-loud take on sports, the NHL in general, and the Calgary Flames in particular was must-see for anyone remotely interested in the game or the games people play. Including the participants.

"Once, I did a cartoon of Marty McSorley, just before play-offs," Elston recalled. "He had a funnel in his ear, a cement truck is driving off in the distance, and he's saying, 'Thanks for the fill-up!' I remember one of our photographers, Al Charest, coming back to the office from the Saddledome and telling me, 'Marty's not real happy with you.'"

Moving over from political cartooning at the behest of *Sun* sports editor Bill Davidson after chronicling Calgary's Cup-winning 1989 playoff run made all the difference for Elston, sports being his passion. "A bunch of factors came together at once. The Battle of Alberta was in overdrive. All that. The Flames had some great characters on their team at that time—Lanny [McDonald] and Tim Hunter were mainstays. The uniqueness of a daily cartoonist was new, something no one had seen since back in the old days, so people took a look.

"If I really nailed a cartoon, it'd get really good play. If it was a mediocre cartoon, it'd be back in the mediocre part of the section. Our editor, Les Pyette, would throw something I'd done on the front page of the entire paper every once in a while too. So I was lucky; they often got a lot of attention."

And then there was Theo. "When I started, it was just sort of all guns a-blazing," laughed Elston. "I think the naive part of being young and brash is that you assume everyone has the same sort of sense of humor as you do. That's not the case.

"I remember having done a couple of Fleury cartoons, and word came back through the grapevine that his reaction was like, 'Who is this guy picking on me?'

"Someone introduced us finally. When we met face-to-face he kind of softened on me, thought it was a lot funnier, when he saw how tall—meaning how short—I am."

Elston drew one of his best after grumpy Kings coach Robbie Ftorek famously downplayed Wayne Gretzky as "just another player." Elston drew Ftorek as one of the wise men standing around the manger in Bethlehem. "Ah," he's saying in the caption, "it's just another baby."

An Elston cartoon is instantly recognizable: big butts, cracked helmets, name plates across the backs of sweaters. What makes them so memorable, though, are the ideas behind the artwork. It is smart, current, and satiric.

"I've always thought if you have a really good idea, you can always cobble together the artwork, and it'll get the point across. But if you have really, really nice artwork and a mediocre idea, it's just not gonna fly. I've seen interviews with Gary Larson from *The Far Side* saying he wasn't really great at drawing, but he got [these good ideas]. So yeah, it's definitely the idea."

Seven books of Elston's cartoons have been published, and his work graced the pages of the *Hockey News* for years. For Flames fans of a generation, seated behind his easel, pondering the hot hockey topic of the day, Dave Elston captured the tone and times of their team better than anyone, in any type of media, before or since.

54 Those Fickle Hockey Gods

The Russian Rocket had launched and was picking up speed as it exited the Earth's orbit. At least that part of the orbit inhabited by any Calgary Flame close enough to hit an ABORT button.

And from experience, Dave King immediately understood the ramifications. "I'd been watching Pavel Bure a long time, from his days with the Russians," said King. "He always had this tremendous acceleration. So as he began to break away…I can remember, very clearly, when he got the separation and got going, thinking, *Uh-oohhhhh. This is dangerous.*" Fatal, actually.

Imagine this in slow motion: A Jeff Brown outlet pass as true as can be. Bure carving open the Calgary resistance, shrugging off a desperate hook attempt by defenseman Zarley Zalapski before pulling the puck wide on Calgary goaltender Mike Vernon to slip in the series-clinching goal at 2:20 of double OT during Game 7 of the first-round 1994 playoff series. A never-to-be-forgotten moment, either across British Columbia or southern Alberta.

One of a litany of squandered opportunities that encapsulated the Flames' post-Cup failures in the postseason. "The ironic thing," recalled King, "is we'd assigned Mike Sullivan to shadow Bure, and he'd done a great job the whole series. But guys like that, you give them half a chance, the slightest opening…"

Dave King's three seasons coaching the Calgary Flames—1992–93 to 1994–95—were marked by disappointing playoff exits: In his first year, a six-game ouster by Wayne Gretzky and the Kings. In his second year, a seven-game elimination by the Vancouver Canucks, on the Bure goal. Ahead 3–1 in the series, the Flames were beaten in overtime three consecutive games to suffer the ultimate heartbreak. And in his third year, another gut-wrenching, opening-round seven-game loss, this time to the unfavored and widely outplayed San Jose Sharks. The Flames lost four games by five goals in the series. They won three by a total of 14. All close series. A coin-flip winner in each case. Still…

"I know enough about hockey," said King, one of the most respected coaches in the history of the international game. "I've been in enough games over the years to know you have to be well prepared, but there's a certain percentage of the game that is out of our hands. The players on both teams, the coaches…anybody involved. The puck is a funny object; it's going to bounce one way or the other.

"Somewhere in every game there's going to be an aspect of luck, a break, good luck, bad luck—whatever term you want—that exists in the game that you simply have no control over. I just thought the hockey gods weren't kind to us." The Vancouver loss was, and is, particularly hard to bear.

There certainly was plenty to regret about not finishing the Canucks before a Game 7 became necessary. A botched line change cost the Flames Game 6. Paul Kruse, normally a left winger, was being platooned on the right flank that evening. When left winger Ron Stern came to the bench for a line change nearing the 16-minute mark of the first extra frame, Kruse, up next, instinctively hopped on, leaving two right wingers, him and Theo Fleury, on the ice. A too-many-men minor allowed a 23-year-old Trevor Linden to lift the puck over Vernon at 16:43.

Two nights earlier, a miscue by defenseman Kevin Dahl, a Gerald Diduck clearance skipping through his feet, shook Geoff Courtnall free to blaze a shot behind Vernon 7:15 into overtime.

The Sharks series in 1995, compared to Vancouver, was a much different animal. "We carried quite a bit of the play in that series [against the Sharks]," sighed King. "Unlike the Vancouver series, where I enjoyed their hockey and our hockey, this one was really frustrating. Some nights we dominated and could score. Other nights we dominated and couldn't score. Then they brought in their backup goalie [Wade Flaherty], filling in for Arturs Irbe, and he was unconscious. So, very different series." Identically painful outcomes.

With Flaherty playing the game of his life, stopping 56 shots, the Sharks pulled the shocker at 1:54 of double OT in Game 7 at the Saddledome, former Edmonton Oilers stick boy Ray Whitney deflecting a pass/shot from Sergei Makarov behind Trevor Kidd to condemn the Flames to yet another first-round exit.

"One of our shots hits the stick and stays out," said King ruefully, all these years later, "and one of their shots hits the knob of [Whitney's] stick and goes in. How do you explain that?' How many shots did we have? Sixty-something? And we don't win? How do you explain that?"

"We've seen this script before," sighed captain Joe Nieuwendyk, following the loss to the Sharks, his eyes red, his voice shaky. "I think *numbing* is a good word. We're unbelievably disappointed. It's so frustrating to lose when you feel you are the better team."

In short order, King was fired and replaced by former Calgary assistant Pierre Page. Nothing much changed. After capturing the Cup in 1989, the Flames suffered four first-round exits and did not make the playoffs at all in 1992. Page guided Calgary to a postseason spot in 1996, only to be swept aside in four straight by the Chicago Blackhawks.

There followed seven excruciating years of wandering in the playoff wilderness, like kids with their noses pressed up against the toy shop window on Christmas Eve, the outsiders always looking in. "You wonder now," mused Dave King. "If we'd have won that San Jose series, some of the players that left might've finished their careers as Calgary Flames. I might've gotten another contract for three or four years. It's only human nature to wonder [about] the change in direction your career might've taken.

"That's one of the things about hockey. Your career, your life, your family's life, it can all change in an instant. A bad break, a great save, or a weird goal at the wrong time.

"I've often looked back on my seasons in Calgary. It just seemed if something could go wrong at crunch time, it would. We had real good teams, real good regular seasons, had high expectations heading into the playoffs every year. But like I said, a certain percentage of the game we have no control over. Call it 'puck luck,' whatever you want. But sometimes if the stars don't align…"

55 Trading Joe

Al Coates was sitting alone in his office at the Saddledome on the night of December 19, 1995, Yuletide fast approaching. The holiday trade embargo was approaching ever faster.

"Ten minutes before the freeze," recalled Coates, "I've got the New York Rangers on one phone, the NHL on another phone, and Dallas on a third phone. New York opted out—pulled the young component from the package they were offering. But I

170

was determined to get something done. No waiting until after Christmas. Dallas had been persistent. And [Stars GM] Bob Gainey had been pure, pure class throughout the whole thing. And so I made the deal."

Joe Nieuwendyk, Calgary Flame captain and icon, was officially off to the Lone Star State. Coming back the other way: some teenage kid named Jarome Iginla, along with pint-sized center Corey Millen.

The Flames were struggling in the standings—7–19–7 on December 19—their captain was intractable in his holdout, and the team had been waxed 7–1 that very night at the old Igloo in Pittsburgh, while their GM juggled those phone lines back home. So Al Coates, backed into a corner, swung a trade for the future.

At one point, initially, there had been 13 organizations pitching for Nieuwendyk's services. Fully understanding the value of what he was being forced to barter, the Flames' general manager had arrived at a set of criteria for any team interested in doing business. "My message was, 'If you're acquiring Joe Nieuwendyk from us, the guy we're getting back is someone we're going to watch play for the Calgary Flames at a very high level for the next 15 years.' Simple as that. So if somebody came to us and said, 'We're going to give you five of these for Joe Nieuwendyk' and we didn't like what we heard, we'd just say, 'Sorry, not happening.'

"That was part one of the criteria. When we put that criteria in place, the 13 teams were reduced to three in a hurry." Those three were the Rangers, St. Louis, and Dallas.

The Nieuwendyk saga proved to be difficult on all concerned. "He was just...bitter," said Coates. "I don't know how else to describe it. Not about the money he was making. I think he was making $1.2 million Canadian at the time. And the arbitration process had taken him to $2 million. And even put it into US dollars. So it wasn't $1.2 million Canadian to $2 million Canadian.

It was $1.2 million Canadian into $2 million US, with whatever the exchange rate was. So, good money.

"He was just…bitter. Over the arbitration process. Over the fact he knew he was a very good player and there was a battle to keep his salary down, which made for, in his mind, a lack of appreciation for what he'd done, how good he was. Certainly not in my mind. I knew. We all did."

Coates had flown to Toronto that summer to visit with his star pivot in an attempt to soothe trouble waters. "He said, 'Coatesy, I'll come to training camp, but if my heart's not in a different place at the end of training camp, I'm not coming back.' And that's what he did.

"I mean, you could just let him sit out and say, 'To hell with you, Joe Nieuwendyk, you can come back when you're good and ready.' But in doing that, I thought we were really hurting the team. And I knew this wasn't going anywhere. I knew in my own mind that Joe Nieuwendyk was not coming back to play for the Calgary Flames. He would've sat out until his contract ran out. Guaranteed."

The trade—initially panned, now praised—was one of those rare ones that was good for both organizations. Joe Nieuwendyk would help Dallas snare a Stanley Cup. Jarome Iginla would go on to become Calgary's all-time leading scorer. At the time he left, though, Nieuwendyk had contributed 314 goals, 616 points, and a Calder Trophy–winning freshman campaign. He was a star. Iginla was a Kamloops Blazer.

"Obviously, money was a part of the whole thing," conceded Nieuwendyk today. "But a big part of it was that Suter had gone, MacInnis had gone, Vernon had gone, Gilmour had gone. The band was breaking up. So I think at that time it was probably the best thing for myself and probably the best thing for the Flames, too. You don't want it to end that way. Coatesy didn't want it to end that way, either.

"Once I went to Ithaca, I guess it was inevitable. So sure, money played a part, but we'd had such good teams there and such good times, and it was all changing."

"We knew what we were giving up," admitted Coates. "And looking back, I think I should've gotten more. Everybody now says, 'Jarome Iginla. Calgary Flames. Wow! What a deal.' Well, in retrospect I think I should've got more for Joe Nieuwendyk. He was an unbelievable player."

Those sorts of transactions, moving proven commodities, star players, in exchange for future assets, are always extremely tricky business that thrust the deal maker directly in the crosshairs. "You can never be sure," acknowledged Coates. "You just trust in what you're doing, what your people are telling you. I can tell you, though, that soon afterward, I went to the World Juniors in Boston. And suddenly I felt way, way better about that deal…"

56 Iginla: The Greatest Flame

Oddly, what most concerned the Calgary Flames at first wasn't an ability to adapt to the NHL grind or pace. No, it was a reluctance to roll out of bed in the morning. "This kid sleeps like a bear. Other guys nap. He hibernates," laughed Coach Pierre Page, speaking about Jarome Iginla way back in 1997, during the soon-to-be icon's first full NHL season.

"You worry about where other guys are at night, about what they're doing. Not Iginla. The question is: 'Will you be able to get him out of bed?'" That concern passed quickly enough. During his 16 seasons in southern Alberta, Jarome Iginla donned many hats:

captain, leader, beacon during some awfully dark seasons, Olympic hero, spokesman.

He is also indisputably the greatest Calgary Flame ever. no one has played more games (1,219), scored more goals (525), or accrued more points (1,095) in the colors than Jarome Arthur-Leigh Adekunle Tij Junior Elvis Iginla. His 11 consecutive seasons of 30 goals or better is astounding. He's the only Flame ever to snare the Maurice Richard Trophy (2002, 2004) as top goal scorer and/or the Art Ross Trophy (2002) as the league's leading scorer. He is famously the final piece in an amazing domino effect: the equation whereby Kent Nilsson translates into Joe Nieuwendyk translates into Jarome Iginla, each one better than the last.

As so often happened during those lean years, with no salary cap and a lousy Canadian dollar, the trade that shipped Iginla's rights, along with pint-sized centerman Corey Millen, to the Flames in exchange for star pivot Joe Nieuwendyk was triggered by—you guessed it—money.

Captain Nieuwendyk had been embroiled in a contract holdout since the season opened when Calgary general manager Al Coates pulled the trigger with Stars GM Bob Gainey on December 19, 1995.

The highly regarded Iginla had been the 11th overall pick in the 1995 draft by Dallas and was playing for Team Canada at the World Junior Championships in Boston—where he would lead the tournament in scoring and propel his country to a fourth consecutive gold medal—when the trade came down.

For someone backed into a corner, Coates, as it turned out, did wonderfully well. "The most important thing was where are we going with the future of our team," explained Coates, "and our organization for this city, for the franchise, and we're going where Jarome Iginla goes."

The initial return on investment wasn't exactly off-the-dial stellar. In 1996–97 Iginla scored 21 times and contributed 50 points to finish fourth on the Calgary scoring charts. The next season, he dipped to 13 goals and 32 points, and the grumbling began anew. The turn of the century, though, coincided with the blossoming of an elite power forward. The 2000–01 campaign produced the first of 11 straight 30-plus goal campaigns for No. 12. He'd found his stride.

As the years rolled on, Jarome Iginla developed into, quite simply, the most complete forward, the most effective player, in hockey. His 2002 Hart Trophy loss to Montreal goaltender Jose Theodore remains one of the most mystifying major award votes

Jarome Iginla gave fire to the Flames.

in memory. That year, he copped both the Ross and the Richard, a first All-Star team slot at right wing, and the Lester B. Pearson Award as seasonal MVP, as voted by his peers.

Too often, his surrounding cast didn't begin to measure up to the quality of the star, the exception, of course, being 2003–04. That year, all the planets and stars came into alignment. Iginla propped a team on his shoulders and, with the able assistance of goaltender Miikka Kiprusoff, piggybacked it to within a game of a Stanley Cup. He scored (22 points), he fought, he set the example, he took responsibility. The Game 7 loss cut deep at the time. No one could know then that it would be as close as Jarome Iginla would come in his days with a franchise he will forever be tied to.

On April 1, 2011, he netted his 1,000th point, scoring the winning goal in a 3–2 win over the St. Louis Blues. And on January 7, 2012, he scored goal No. 500 against Minnesota's Niklas Backstrom, one of only 15 players to snare their first 500 with one club, joining the likes of Maurice Richard, Jean Beliveau, Mario Lemieux, Wayne Gretzky, Brett Hull, and Mike Bossy.

Atypically, his 500th didn't arrive on the wings of a trademark scorcher from off the right boards. No, a searching pass to the front of the net actually glanced off the skates of two Wild players to befuddle Backstrom. "It's definitely a lot more special to do it here at home, and as part of a win," Iginla said afterward. "The crowd was great tonight; they were into the game. I've been very blessed in hockey to have some great moments and memories that will stick with me—been part of different games and scoring some different goals, but that's one that I'll definitely remember."

It would be his final season as a Flame. In truth, the organization needed a refresh. Ultimately Iginla realized he did, too. So on March 27, 2013, an era ended when Iginla waived his no-trade clause and GM Jay Feaster dispatched the franchise leader in virtually every major offensive category to the Pittsburgh Penguins.

There have been many great players to don the flaming *C* over the years: Kent Nilsson, Lanny McDonald, Al MacInnis, Joe Nieuwendyk, Joe Mullen, Hakan Loob, Doug Gilmour, Mike Vernon, Miikka Kiprusoff. All made indelible contributions to the cause in their own ways. But factoring in longevity, productivity, and influence, one man alone reigns. Iginla's position atop the pile was, and remains, unassailable.

57 The Age of Austerity

In 1995 the Canadian dollar fluctuated around 71.6 cents per American dollar. By 1998 it had slid to 70.2 cents, and by 1999 it had bottomed out to 66.3 cents. Salaries went public, giving players comparables and driving asking prices through the roof. In such challenging economic times, the "small-market" Canadian franchises struggled to keep pace.

"I'm not sure that I knew then how difficult it would be to take over" said Al Coates, Flames GM from December 1995 to 2000. "And it was challenging. In my mind, if I had it to do over again, I wouldn't even attempt to try and continue to win and entertain the people while rebuilding at the same time. I'm not sure that's actually doable, then or now."

Size matters. Particularly when it comes to quantities of available cash. "Nobody changed the size of the ice surface," laughed Coates. "The size of the ice surface was still 200 by 85. But nobody told Philadelphia and New York, Toronto, and Detroit, that they couldn't spend $70 million." In Coates' final year at the helm, the Calgary payroll topped out at $24.8 million, including bonuses.

"[It was] nobody's fault. That was just the way things were. I accepted—we accepted, Brian Sutter and that whole coaching crew—the reality of the situation. That's what we had to work with. And within that framework, we'd do our best to make it happen."

With Pierre Page behind the bench, the Flames qualified for the 1996 playoffs and were swept aside by the Chicago Blackhawks in four straight games. When Sutter took control in 1997, it began an agonizing string of seven consecutive postseason-deprived springtimes.

The landscape had shifted—seismically, economically, and competitively. "I mean we were talking about moving out of Calgary," said Theoren Fleury. "Actually moving. I mean that's... crazy.

"The night I broke the record for most points as a Flame, Jeff Shantz is my centerman and Bobby Bassen is my left winger. Nothing against those guys. But I went from playing with Nieuwendyk and Roberts to Jeff Shantz and Bobby Bassen. This is sort of where we were and where we sort of went. It was tough. Because the first six or seven years in Calgary, expectations [to win] were huge. And we did win, consistently, just not in the playoffs. So it was really difficult going through it."

During that stretch of freefalling, they accumulated only 67 points in 1997–98, a franchise low that still stands. Meanwhile, stalwarts such as Joe Nieuwendyk (netting the organization Jarome Iginla) and Fleury (bringing back Robyn Regehr) were being offloaded over —what else?—finances.

"People talk about the salary cap coming in, when, in 2005?" said Coates. "Well, back then we had our own salary cap. It was our budget. I paid a lot of attention to the budget. We worked around it. We had to be creative, look ahead. We made deals like the [Jonas] Hoglund–[Zarley] Zalapski deal for Valeri Bure with Montreal that turned out to be a really good hockey deal. But there was a money component to that deal. There was a money component to every deal. Zalapski was making $1.3 million, if memory serves me correctly, [which was] a lot at the time. Hogie, I believe, was around $400,000. But there was a big switch in money in that transaction. Them taking on, us giving up."

When Coates traded down in the draft to acquire center Marc Savard from the Rangers in a multipronged deal that involved the rights to Jan Hlavac, there were familiar conditions involved. "The Rangers had the wherewithal to finish paying the signing bonus due Marc Savard. They took that on. Then they also had to go sign Hlavac, who we didn't have the money to sign. Like I said, it was nobody fault. You're managing the situation as best you can," Coates said.

The Flames were receiving a bit of a break on a Canadian equalization program then in place, championed by Calgary co-owner Harley Hotchkiss. "Only three teams qualified: Ottawa, Edmonton, and Calgary. So there was some money there. I want to say $3 million, maybe, in Canadian funds. There [were] criteria you had to meet, but we got a part of that. It helped," said Coates.

Still, the playing field could scarcely have been less level. "I give our ownership credit," Coates said. "They ran the business as a business. It wasn't okay to go way over the budget for some reason that may have seemed to make sense at the time. It was difficult, but we had a great group of people. We accepted the position we were in."

Coates smiled when asked how frustrating those years were. "Hey, if it's frustrating, quit. I never dreamt I'd be a general manager in the National Hockey League. There's only 30 of you in the entire world. And it's a pretty good job. They're not easy to get, and they're not easy to keep, quite frankly. So you won't hear me complaining. It just seemed that annually we came up one player short of where we wanted to be."

58 Two That Got Away

Brett Hull and Martin St. Louis. Illustrious names. Illustrious careers. And both began their NHL careers as Calgary Flames. Hindsight is always 20/20, of course, and every organization can look back with regret at certain decisions, but relinquishing two generational talents continues to gnaw at the innards of many long-time Flames boosters.

Both Hull and St. Louis were at the start of their careers when they were dealt away (Hull) or released (St. Louis). Between them they went on to four first All-Star team selections, four Lady Byng Memorial Trophies, two Hart Trophies, a pair of Art Ross Trophies, 14 All-Star Game appearances, and two Stanley Cups titles. The Golden Brett went on to score 714 goals and add 625 assists with three other organizations (plus a five-game, one-helper cameo to cap a career in Phoenix); Martin St. Louis had 387 goals and 626 assists with two other clubs.

Brett Hull arrived in Calgary as the 117th overall pick in the 1984 draft out of WCHA Minnesota-Duluth. After playing two playoff games during the Flames' 1986 run to the Cup Finals, he spent the entire 1986–87 season with the team's AHL affiliate in Moncton, New Brunswick, scoring 50 goals in 67 appearances. Super shot, great release…clearly a star in the making. The next season, Hull gave everyone a hint of his latent ability to score goals at the top level, notching 26 in 52 starts with the big club.

Then on March 7, 1988, he was shipped to St. Louis. The deal—via which the Flames added backup goaltender Rick Wamsley and sturdy defenseman Rob Ramage—looks woefully lopsided now, in the hard, pitiless mirror of reflection.

At the time, though, the man who completed the swap with the Blues, the author of the NHL version of *The Art of the Deal*, Calgary GM Cliff Fletcher, understood the possible ramifications of the move. But he'd decided the time was ripe to take a run at Calgary's northern rivals, the Stanley Cup champion Edmonton Oilers, and felt one or two veteran pieces were required to put the deal across. He was proven correct, but the price turned out to be staggeringly high.

"Trading Hull, we knew what we were doing when we did it. I think," Trader Cliff mused years later. "By that, we understood what kind of potential he had. I said then, when we made the deal, that he'd score 150 goals the next three years. Turns out, he got 160.

"But we got Wamsley, who was very important to the group, and we got Ramage, and if you remember back, Gary Suter got hurt in the first round"—of the 1989 run, versus Vancouver—"and Ramage had a helluva playoff. At the time we had three right wingers who had scored 50 goals—Lanny [McDonald], Hakan Loob, and Joey Mullen. So I felt I could do it."

And the Flames did lift the Stanley Cup in the spring of 1989. So there was, at least, brief consolation. But McDonald retired, Loob returned home to Sweden, and suddenly Calgary's right side wasn't quite so formidable.

The Martin St. Louis situation was completely different. He didn't arrive with a high-powered last name but as a pint-sized undrafted free agent in an age of size, penciled in as a checking winger and a penalty killer (just goes to show). The Flames, at least, were willing to take a chance on him when no one else would. St. Louis spent parts of the next three seasons toiling for the American Hockey League's Saint John Flames.

After three goals and 18 points during a 56-game call-up in the 1999–2000 campaign, the Flames released him that summer. Tampa took a flyer. And the rest is…well, awfully good or awfully bad, depending on your rooting interest.

"No excuses on my part for not knowing Marty St. Louis better," candidly admitted TSN hockey analyst Craig Button, in the early days of his Calgary managerial career, on the day St. Louis announced his retirement in 2015.

Button was in the early days of his first big-league managerial opportunity when St. Louis left the Flames. "I'd watched him since he played midget in Quebec. I'd seen him a little bit in the minors. That was part of my job: player personnel, scouting, evaluation. That's on me.

"But when we as a group sat down and talked players, there was only one person in the entire organization that really had a strong voice for Marty St. Louis, and that was Tom Watt. At the end of the day, only one person was going to bat for Marty St. Louis, and that was Tom. Nobody outside of Tom Watt.

"You know what the real frightening thing is? There was far greater support for Andrei Nazarov—who I ended up trading for Jordan Leopold—than there was for Martin St. Louis. Looking back, you think, *Well, of course*. But then…

"So I'll take my share of the responsibility. I was the one with the final say, but no one, believe me, was clamoring to get Martin St. Louis."

The lack of belief, of foresight, came full circle to haunt the Flames in Game 6 of the 2004 Stanley Cup Finals, St. Louis scoring in OT to send the series back to Tampa, the Bolts returning to win the championship on home ice.

"The people that liked me [in Calgary]—cared about me, so to speak—they were all gone," St. Louis reflected in 2014. "So it's not like I felt betrayed. I felt good about what they were doing with me, and vice versa. Al Coates. Brian Sutter. Nick Polano, the assistant GM. I felt they could see that I had something, that it was kind of a matter of time, so to speak. I felt my role that second year I was here—I ended up playing 56 games—I was getting better. They had confidence in what I was trying to do. But when everybody gets fired, it's hard. So I don't hold any grudges."

59 "It's Not the Size of the Bull..."

To make the hour and a half drive south from the family farm outside Red Deer, Alberta, and attend his own introductory media conference, Brian Sutter literally dragged himself out from underneath a broken-down tractor. When this guy said, "I can be just as happy out in the rain, riding a horse, rounding up cows," you believed him.

Brian Sutter was raw, basic, totally devoid of any manner of pretense or shiny veneer. Which was exactly the way he played for a dozen seasons as the beating heart of the Blues, nine of those as team captain. And then after he turned to coaching, he enjoyed four years in charge of St. Louis and then three as bench boss in Boston, where he pieced together a .608 winning percentage, before heading to Calgary to coach the Flames. When once asked about fielding an undersized Flames lineup, he shot back defiantly: "It's not the size of the bull, it's how well he's hung!"

As a coach, he didn't talk in technicalities, in *X*s and *O*s, in breakout systems or defensive zone coverage, but in general, simplistic terms of commitment, self-effacement, values, and earning the faith of the guy sitting next to you. He deplored slackers, whiners, and anyone who otherwise shortchanged himself, his employers, or his teammates.

"I think it's a privilege to coach in this league," Sutter declared often. "I really do. And I believe the players should look on what they do in the same way. They get a certain amount of notoriety.

They get paid piss pots full of money. They get everything first class. So I don't think it's too much to expect that they give you more than the average. You need 'extra.'"

"Extra," in his eyes, was standard—and nonnegotiable. "Brian was a hard-nosed coach," recalled defenseman Denis Gauthier, a first-round pick in 1995 who was 21 when Sutter took control of the Flames. "Well intentioned. Very, very, very old-school. At the time, I thought he was the hardest coach I'd ever played for. I was a little intimidated by him, a young kid, trying to make my room there.

"Typical Sutter, he liked to press buttons looking to get the best out of a guy. He got me going a few times, being harder on me than I thought he should've. Looking back, though, it was a good learning experience for me. I grew out of it. I matured very quickly.

"He wasn't a very tactical coach, but you had to respect how much he cared about his players."

Care. If there was one word that defined Brian Sutter—as a player, as a coach, as a person—that might be it. "I care," he said once, with flat finality. "If caring is a crime, then lock me up. I'm guilty as charged. When I let off a little steam, it's not 'cause I'm mad at them. I just want them to be the best they can. Now is that so terrible?"

The care, the fierce desire to pull, pry, or prod as much out of those in his charge as possible, manifested itself in many ways. "I remember him one time in the locker room," Gauthier reminisced, "calling Chris Dingman 'Chrissie.' Chris wasn't playing physical enough, wasn't playing the body enough, for Brian's liking. So he was trying to get him going. 'Hey, Chrissie, don't hit anybody.' 'Hey, Chrissie, you wouldn't want to hurt yourself.' He repeated *Chrissie* maybe 20 times. Now, Chris Dingman's 6'4" and maybe 240 pounds. I can't remember whether it lit a fire under Chris or not, but it sure did get him mad."

If Brian Sutter felt an individual had more in him to give, by heavens he considered it his job to unearth whatever was being withheld. One night in Greensboro, North Carolina, Gauthier was knocked silly by a mid-ice hit from towering Keith Primeau of the Hurricanes. "I think I tried to get on their bench first—they were side by side back then—but finally got close to ours. I stayed down because I was basically knocked out," Gauthier said.

The trainer hauled a wobbly Gauthier back to the dressing room. The period ended. Sutter demanded to see the woozy defenseman in his office. "I didn't want to come out, I didn't want to say I was hurt. But he opened a can of whup-ass on me—'This is not the [bleeping] Quebec league! You don't show an opponent you're hurt! You stay on the ice, you...' This was actually the first time I ever told a coach to go [bleep] himself. I was hot. But you know what? The weirdest thing—I had the sense, after that, that he finally respected me. He probably saw a guy that stood up for himself, got mad, and wasn't going to take it. That he could appreciate."

Brian Sutter's tenure in charge of the Flames lasted three seasons. Both he and the man who hired him, GM/VP Al Coates, took the long walk the same day—April 11, 2000—following a third consecutive playoff miss. In attempting to achieve the improbable, the Sutter-skippered Flames had finished 9, 6, and 10 points shy of postseason hockey, respectively. He assumed the reins during an age of development, a sorry Canadian dollar, and during Calgary's Young Guns phase—Cory Stillman, Derek Morris, Val Bure, a youthful Jarome Iginla, Todd Simpson, Gauthier, et al.

The ask—competing on a vastly uneven financial playing field with a young group—always shaped up as a daunting one. "In two years you don't build a team," Sutter shot back the day of his ouster. "Last year the players could see the playoffs, but they never felt them. This year they got a taste of it, and they felt it. It's devastating. The part that really hurts is that Coatesy did a hell of a job with what was available to him."

But that care that he considered his mantra, the unwillingness to compromise on standards or efforts—so often interpreted by young players as overbearing or unfair in the immediacy of the moment—stuck with many of them later on. "I saw Brian, I want to say 10 years after he left," said Denis Gauthier now, older and wiser. "I was in town at one point, at Japanese Village, with my wife, for old time's sake, remembering our days in Calgary. And Brian was there. I didn't see him right away, but the waiter came up with a bottle of wine and said, 'The gentleman down there would like you to have this.' I look over, and it's Brian.

"He came up to the table, asked how the family was. He remembered Stephanie, my wife's, name. He remembered my son's name. That, to me, is a tell. He paid attention to people. Maybe you didn't like his methods all the time, and he wound me up pretty good a few times, but you had to respect how much he cared about his players, the team, and trying to win games."

60 "Hello, Hockey Fans"

He was already known—and this is by no means a stretch—world-wide, as the voice of Stampede Wrestling, famous for his signature, "It's gonna be a ring-a-ding-dong dandy!" and the exit line, "In the meantime, in-between time..."

But when Ed Whalen—or Wailin' Ed, as he was affectionately dubbed for his unique on-air delivery—wasn't extolling the exploits of Abdullah the Butcher or the Great Gama grappling in the squared circle, he had the call on Lanny McDonald rifling home a goal off the right wing in the Corral or Joe Nieuwendyk deftly deflecting an Al MacInnis shot into the bottom corner or Tim Hunter and Dave Semenko shucking the mitts and squaring off. For 19 years, from the time the Flames arrived in 1980 until his retirement in 1999,

Whalen provided television fans, on 2&7 and then Calgary 7, what Peter Maher did on radio: a voice to people's dreams.

His "Hello, hockey fans" pregame intro, whether originating from the Saddledome or the Fabulous Forum in Inglewood or the ol' Chicago Stadium, became a staple for Flames aficionados. The hockey was what he truly loved. "All the setup stuff with the Sheik, Ed hitting people over the head with the microphone, and the Stampede Wrestling is what made him a household name," said Whalen's 2&7 longtime broadcast booth sidekick John Garrett. "Hockey brought him into the real world."

"I'd rather do it than eat," Whalen once confessed of Flames play-by-play. "I'm not the best ever, by any means, but I think I'm one of the most exciting."

Ed Whalen was one of those outsized personalities that television could scarcely contain. Even today, whenever anyone tells a Whalen story, the voice automatically rises an octave higher, bends to that familiar inflection, imitating Wailin' Ed.

"Back in the old days of the Saddledome, when the broadcast booth was halfway up the stands," recalled Garrett, "people would walk by and Ed would be too busy saying hello to everybody to do the game. 'Hey, Ed! Hey, Ed!' [He'd say], 'How ya doin', big guy?' 'How are ya?' [He] didn't know anybody's name. But he sounded as if he was their best friend. He had that way about him.

"He was good at it. He was excited. As soon as you heard his voice, you immediately identified with the team. He was such a big fan. He lived and breathed the Flames. I thought he should be in the broadcasters wing of the Hockey Hall of Fame. I still do."

Grant Pollock, host of the broadcasts at the time, said Whalen wasn't even first choice for the job. "Either the Flames or Molstar owned the rights, and they didn't want him. And Ed knew that. But our general manager, Noel Wagner—remember, local stations back then had more power than they do today—insisted on Ed.

"So he wanted to be good. He was nervous before games. For Ed, calling Lanny McDonald's 500th goal and 1,000th point were the high points. He was proud of those calls. He did them well. Every broadcaster, I think, wants to have a couple of those signatures during their career. For Ed, those were the calls."

The focus of those milestones, the mustachioed one himself, is an unabashed Whalen fan. "You look at what Ed meant to the organization, sure," said McDonald. "But also look at what he meant to the city. He was larger than life, as recognizable as any player. Think about what he did for the children's hospital and the [Children's] Miracle Network telethon. He was someone who cared. About what he did. About his family. About community."

Everyone in Calgary, it seems, has an Ed Whalen yarn. For some, there's the one of him holding his hairpiece on the ferry ride across the bay from San Francisco out to Alcatraz for a tour, while the San Jose Sharks were playing in the Cow Palace in Frisco. "Better safe than sorry, kid!" he said.

He could be wonderfully self-deprecating, once remembering a producer muttering into his headphones while he was in the midst of calling a game: "Ed Whalen. The only guy in the world who's older than dirt."

In 1998, a year before putting down his microphone, Ed Whalen celebrated 50 years in the business. "God, what a time I've had," he admitted to *Calgary Herald* columnist Tom Keyser. "It's kinda staggered me, really. Forty-three years in this market, and I'm still greeted warmly. There's always danger of wearing out your welcome. But it hasn't happened." Never would. Never will.

So the sad, shocking news in early December 2001 hit the Calgary sports community, hard: while on vacation with his wife, Nomi, in Venice, Florida, Ed Whalen had suffered a cardiac arrest. On December 4 a local icon passed away. To signify his contribution to the city and the organization, both the press box and media lounge at the Saddledome were named in his honor.

"Everyone loved the guy," said Lanny McDonald. "And really, how could you not? To see the smile, the enthusiasm, every day he arrived to call a game, it was infectious. Such passion, for whatever was going on. He just loved life. That was Eddie. Everyone could learn a lesson from the guy: Enjoy what you do. And enjoy every day. He certainly did."

61 Coatesy

Sometimes, reflecting, Al Coates wonders how his path would've been altered if Jiggs McDonald had made a different call.

"When the announcement was made about the team moving here," Coates explained, "Jiggs had been working as the broadcaster and public relations director in Atlanta. But Jiggs didn't want to move.

"Much the same as Bearcat Murray. The trainer there at the time, Norm Mackie, made the decision not to come, either. That gave Bear his chance.

"So, looking back, if Jiggs feels differently about the move, there's a very different landscape for me. He would've been the broadcaster and likely stayed the public relations director. But his decision opened up a spot for someone. That someone turned out to be me. Really interesting how you can sometimes catch a break and hopefully make the most of it."

Jiggs McDonald, of course, went on to become the voice of the New York Islanders, calling play-by-play during their dynastic four-season Stanley Cup streak. Al Coates spent two decades in the Flames organization, doing what was required, advancing up the pecking order, beginning in that role as PR czar and working all the way up to the general manager's office by November 1995. He was the ultimate multitasker, a good soldier among good soldiers. No detail was too small, and no task was too great.

"One of the things I'm proud of is that I've done just about everything there is to do in hockey," said the Listowel, Ontario, product, now serving as senior director of special projects for Hockey Canada. "So I understood Bear's role, [equipment manager] Bobby [Stewart's] role, Cliff's role, and anybody's in between. There hasn't been much in the game I haven't taken a stab at."

His name is there on the Stanley Cup with the Flames' 1989 team, as assistant to then-president Cliff Fletcher. Graduating to that job, then the top job a half dozen years later, he found himself overseeing the organization's most problematic days, endeavoring to rebuild a roster on a tight budget with a free-falling Canadian dollar.

He'd subsequently go on to work in other organizations, including as part of the title-topping Anaheim team of 2007 in the role of senior advisor to the president, but it's in Calgary, with the Flames, that he left his mark. "I think the most enjoyable part of my career was working with the ownership group back in the early days. People today don't believe you started an NHL franchise with a staff of seven or eight people in three trailers adjacent to the Corral and two offices inside the Corral.

"So the neat thing about it was that you were involved in everything. We were really proud—and I think we were right to say it—that we were somewhat of a model franchise, in terms of class. Class...that's a characteristic we were constantly striving to attain.

"Myself, I went and called Jean Beliveau when we were in Montreal one time, and he graciously gave me 20 minutes of his time. The Canadiens and the Philadelphia Flyers organizations were two models we could pattern ourselves after, the way they did things and treated people. There's a right way to do things, and I think we always tried to follow that route."

Dominoes, of course, have a hand in the course of any career. Jiggs McDonald turning down the move north got the ball rolling for Al Coates. Then assistant GM David Poile accepted the managerial job with Washington two years into the Calgary Flames' existence, increasing Coates' responsibility.

"A lot of things David had done before he left, I inherited. Looking after the farm team, minor league contracts, being on the road with the team, that kind of thing. Also being on the pricing strategy for next year's season tickets and the community-relations part of it. I really enjoyed that we were involved in the whole gamut of responsibilities within the organization. It was a great, broadbased education for me."

Cliff Fletcher's departure for Toronto following the 1991 playoffs proved to be another pivotal turning point. "In a lot of cases," Coates admitted, "I happened to be there, to be handy. But I also think that I earned my way along the journey, to gain trust of the ownership group, or certainly tried to. And it just…evolved."

When Doug Risebrough was fired on November 3, 1995, Coates, then executive VP of the Flames, took over the GM position. "There are no magical solutions," he warned that day, as the man handed the keys to a kingdom he knew intimately. In the final analysis, the perfect storm of challenges that led to Risebrough's ouster contributed to his replacement's too, four and a half years later.

The Al Coates story is proof positive that advancement to top levels in the pro sports fraternity is, in fact, possible, wherever you may start. He told a story of his tenure in SoCal. Disney, at that time, owned the Ducks and Major League Baseball's Anaheim Angels. "The fellow running the business side of the baseball team"—Kevin Uhlich—"was also doubling up with the Ducks until someone was hired, which turned out to be me.

"So we're sitting around BSing one day, and he says, 'How'd you ever get into this business in the first place?' And I told him,

'Well, to tell the truth, you've got to start wherever the opportunity is, and for me, I'd taken a bunch of physiotherapy work, so I started in the American Hockey League as a trainer. How about you?' And he says, 'I was the bat boy for the Angels.' And he went on to become [vice] president! So we had a lot to talk about."

62 Trivia Time

In honor of goaltender Mike Vernon's retired No. 30, here's a quick 30-question quiz on the Calgary Flames through the years.

Some questions are a snap. Some are stumpers. Just remember: real Flames fans don't peek!

1. What signature Flame's first number was 24 before switching to the double-digit he will be forever known for?
2. Who was the team's first captain after the move from Atlanta?
3. In the 34 regular seasons as the Calgary Flames, how many of those have been .500 or better?
4. The Flames established an NHL record at Quebec's le Colisée on October 17, 1989, that still stands, via Doug Gilmour and Paul Ranheim in an impossible-to-wrap-your-head-around 8–8 OT tie against the Nordiques. What's the record? (Bonus points for naming Quebec's goaltender that night.)
5. The first year in Calgary, the team's top farm club affiliate was based where?
6. Which four-year Flames defenseman holds the distinction of being the all-time penalty-minutes leader in the rival World Hockey Association?

7. Lanny McDonald's 500th career goal arrived at the Saddledome, fittingly, on March 21, 1989. Team and goaltender?
8. Jarome Iginla's 500th career goal arrived at the Saddledome on January 7, 2012. Team and goaltender?
9. Name the two players who share the club record for most regular-season hat tricks as Flames.
10. When goaltender Miikka Kiprusoff was acquired from the San Jose Sharks, a second-round pick (35th overall) went back to Silicon Valley in the exchange. That draft pick is still wearing teal. He is?
11. Lanny McDonald, of course, made the No. 9 his own. Which two players wore it in Calgary before the mustachioed one arrived from Colorado?
12. Where did current captain Mark Giordano play junior hockey?
13. At fourth overall, Sam Bennett is the highest-ever draft selection to don the flaming *C* for at least one game. Who is the lowest? Name and position, please.
14. During the 1998–99 campaign, an injury plague forced a staggering *six* goaltenders to play at least three games for the big club. Name three. (Bonus points for the entire half dozen.)
15. The franchise's leader in playoff game appearances is?
16. The Sutter clan has been well represented in the organization over the years, in various coaching, scouting, and management positions. Name the only two from the family, an uncle-nephew tandem, to play for the team?
17. During regular-season jousts, the Flames have won more games against which team than any other?
18. The only Flame to score five goals in a game is this former captain. Name him.
19. Jarome Iginla began his amazing run of leading the team in scoring for 11 straight years in the 2000–01 campaign. Who topped the point list the season before Iginla took over?

20. Before joining the Flames as head coach, Bob Johnson piloted the University of Wisconsin to seven national US tournaments. How many of those did the Badgers win?

21. In the mid-1980s, what three players made up the Dice Line, and why the name?

22. The 1988–89 Stanley Cup–winning entry lost only 17 games in piling up 117 regular-season points. How many of those games were dropped at home?

23. Who is the only man with two separate stints as Flames head coach?

24. When future Hall of Famer Al MacInnis was dealt to the St. Louis Blues, name the future Hall of Fame defenseman who came to Calgary in the deal.

25. Can you name the four goaltenders taken by the Flames with their first draft selection in a year?

26. Who is the only Flames player to graduate to become the team's head coach?

27. Miikka Kiprusoff holds virtually every franchise goaltending record. But this immensely popular puck stopper pieced together an unequaled 19-game personal undefeated streak (12 wins, 7 ties) during the 1983–84 season. Name him.

28. Seven men have scored 50 or more goals during a season while wearing the flaming C. They are?

29. Johnny Gaudreau, of course, received the 2014 Hobey Baker Award as the top US college player of the year before turning pro and joining Calgary. Who are the other three Hobey winners to suit up for the Flames?

30. In 1983 Calgary boy and future Flames standout goaltender Mike Vernon backstopped the first US-based junior team to capture a Memorial Cup. Name it.

Answers

1. Jarome Iginla
2. Brad Marsh
3. 20
4. Fastest two shorthanded goals, four seconds apart, at 19:45 and 19:49 of the third period to send the game into OT with their own goalie, Mike Vernon, pulled for an extra attacker. Bonus answer: the unfortunate Stephane Fiset
5. Birmingham, Alabama (the CHL Bulls)
6. Paul Baxter (962 PIM)
7. New York Islanders, Mark Fitzpatrick
8. Minnesota Wild, Niklas Backstrom
9. Theo Fleury and Kent Nilsson, with 13 apiece
10. Marc-Edouard Vlasic
11. Don Lever and Denis Cyr
12. Owen Sound of the OHL
13. Pavel Torgaev, LW, 279th overall, 1994 NHL entry draft
14. Fred Brathwaite (28), Ken Wregget (27), Jean-Sebastien Giguere (15), Tyler Moss (11), Andrei Trefilov (4), and Tyrone Garner (3)
15. Jim Peplinski (99)
16. Ron Sutter, 21 games in 2000–01, and Brett, Darryl's son, 18 games split between 2008–09 and 2009–10
17. Winnipeg Jets
18. Joe Nieuwendyk
19. Valeri Bure, 75 points (Iginla collected 63)
20. Three
21. Colin Patterson, Carey Wilson, and Richard Kromm, whose numbers were 11, 22, and 33, respectively
22. Four. Their Saddledome record was 32–4–4, for 68 points
23. Al MacNeil: the first two full seasons in Calgary and an 11-game interim stint from December 3, 2002, to December 27, 2002
24. Phil Housley
25. Jason Muzzatti (21st overall in 1988), Trevor Kidd (11th overall in 1990), Brent Krahn (9th in 2000), and Leland Irving (26th in 2006)
26. Doug Risebrough
27. Reggie Lemelin
28. Lanny McDonald, Hakan Loob, Joe Mullen, Joe Nieuwendyk, Theoren Fleury, Gary Roberts, and Jarome Iginla
29. Brendan Morrison, Chris Drury, and Jordan Leopold
30. Portland Winter Hawks

63 Draft Disappointments

The study of 18-year-old hockey players has been proven, over and over, to be that most inexact of sciences. Every NHL franchise has suffered its share of blushes and disappointments on draft floors across North America over the years. That's why it's called the lottery. The list of misses inevitably far outnumbers the number of hits for each franchise.

So many negative variables go into the development of a player—bad luck, injury, a bad situation, you name it—let alone one capable of revitalizing a franchise. Still, even taking the relatively low overall batting averages into account, from 1985 to 2004 the Flames organization drafted only two authentic impact players with its first selection in a given draft year. Two. Those are truculent left winger Gary Roberts, chosen 12th in 1984, and bruising defenseman Dion Phaneuf, picked 9th 19 summers later. Other than that…

Oh, there were some serviceable-to-good choices. Center Dan Quinn—chosen 13th in 1983—contributed 52, 58, and 72 points before being dealt to Pittsburgh in the mid-1980s. Another pivot, Cory Stillman, a sixth-overall selection in 1992, scored 109 goals and played nearly 400 games for the franchise, but his greatest successes came elsewhere.

Defensemen Denis Gauthier (20th, 1995) and Derek Morris (13th, 1996) provided solid service, playing for the Flames in 384 and 343 games, respectively. Morris was also an All-Rookie Team selection.

Billed as the heir apparent to Cup winner Mike Vernon, the Flames famously traded up the 1990 draft to snare goaltender Trevor Kidd at the 11th spot (bypassing a certain Martin Brodeur;

of course, so did Montreal, the NYR, Buffalo, Hartford, Chicago, Edmonton, Vancouver, and Winnipeg, but none of them had identified goaltending as a top priority). The rangy puck stopper from Dugald, Manitoba, never cemented No. 1 status in Calgary. He played 178 games for the Flames.

Eric Nystrom, Chuck Kobasew, and Oleg Saprykin? They were okay...but merely that. And Mikael Backlund, their 2007 selection, has just begun to bloom.

Here, then, in the safe haven of hindsight, is a selection of the disappointments:

- **In 1985, D Chris Biotti, Michigan, 17ᵗʰ overall**

  "He is arguably the best defenseman in the draft," lauded general manager Cliff Fletcher following the selection of the mobile, puck-moving blueliner. "He has the talent to be a legitimate star. He could be the best draft the Flames ever had."

  Well, Biotti never really recovered from major knee surgery performed during his first year at Harvard, and was released after three seasons of minor league service to play in Italy, never having suited up for an NHL regular-season game.

  Flames games: 0

- **In 1987, LW Bryan Deasley, U of Michigan and the Canadian National Team, 19ᵗʰ overall**

  After turning pro, Deasley toiled for three seasons with the AHL Salt Lake Golden Flames before being offloaded to Quebec prior to the 1992–93 season. He retired a year later and became a player agent, never having played an NHL game.

  Flames games: 0

- **In 1988, G Jason Muzzatti, Michigan State, 21ˢᵗ overall**

  One of those goaltender-of-the-future gambles, Muzzatti played all of two games in two seasons with the big club before being plucked off waivers by the Hartford Whalers.

  Flames games: 2

- **In 1991, RW Niklas Sundblad, AIK IF, 19th overall.**

  He played one season in North America before returning home to Sweden.

  Flames games: 2

- **In 1993, RW Jesper Mattsson, Malmo IF, 18th overall**

  He played two and a half seasons in North America before returning home to Sweden.

  Flames games: 0

- **In 1997, C Daniel Tkaczuk, Barrie Colts, 6th overall**

  At the time, this was the highest-ever draft pick by the franchise. Though Tkaczuk was compared to departed star Doug Gilmour, concussion issues cut short the Barrie Colts sniper's path to the NHL, and he counted a meager 11 points in Calgary.

  Flames games: 19

- **In 1998, RW/C Rico Fata, London Knights, 6th overall**

  The lickety-split winger from the Knights scored 27 NHL goals in brief stints at five succeeding NHL whistle stops, but none as a Flame. One assist for such a high selection is hardly a great return on investment.

  Flames games: 27

- **In 2000, G Brent Krahn, 9th overall**

  Krahn was meticulously studied by the team, as he was so close to home, playing for the Calgary Hitmen. A recurring knee problem hindered Krahn's progress and he eventually drifted off into the minor league mists. He played 20 minutes of one NHL game before retiring.

  Flames games: 0

- **In 2004, RW Kris Chucko, University of Minnesota, 24th overall**

  Chucko spent all four of his pro seasons in the Calgary organization, eventually retiring due to concussion issues.

  Flames games: 2

- **In 2008, RW Greg Nemisz, Windsor, 25th overall**

  Projected to be a dependable power forward at the top level given his 6'4", 207-pound frame, he never reached the level of being an everyday NHLer, spending two short stints in Calgary before being dealt to Carolina and then retiring from active play at age 25.

  Flames games: 15

64 Pssst! Santa's a Flames Fan. Pass It On.

He's known by everybody around the Saddledome as simply Santa. But he will answer to Kim Thomas too, in a pinch. That is, after all, what's printed on his birth certificate and driver's license. "I've been playing Santa since 1972," explained Thomas. "I did it as a lark to start with. I had dark hair and a beard, so to start I had to wear a fake one. Well, I've still got the beard. But as the years went by, it whitened up on its own."

At 67 years old, he's cut back the Yuletide gig to a few corporate parties, and makes a run on Christmas Eve with family and then on Christmas Day. "The suit's a little snug this year, but no, it hasn't been retired," he said.

There's something immensely comforting in the fact that Santa is arguably the Calgary Flames' No. 1 superfan. Born and raised in the city and retired for years from the telecommunications business, Santa/Thomas isn't technically a day one season-ticket holder but began attending games at the Corral by purchasing someone else's seats in 1980, the year the franchise shifted north from Atlanta. He said, "I used those tickets for three years and then got my own when they moved over to the Saddledome. So I myself think I'm a day oner.

"Those games in the Corral, you were *so* close, right on top of it. I had seats on the blueline just as you come up the chute. So electric.

"Growing up, I was a Leafs fan. That's all we had, Toronto or Montreal. My dad was a Montreal fan, so I had to cheer for somebody else. The day we were able to get our own NHL team and I was able to go to NHL games, I couldn't believe it. Like a kid in a candy store." Or Mr. Claus in his toy workshop.

Thomas reckons he's seen close to 1,500 Flames games live. Wherever. Whenever. He tailed them to Japan for their two-game season-opening set against the San Jose Sharks and to the Czech Republic and Soviet Union for the Friendship Tour in the fall of 1989.

During the improbable 2004 run to the Stanley Cup Finals, inspired by Jarome Iginla and Miikka Kiprusoff, he went to 21 of the 26 games the team played, missing only Game 5 and Game 7 of the Vancouver series and the Game 5s of the other three rounds.

Unfortunately, he wasn't in the stands at the venerated Forum on the night of May 25, 1989, to soak in the franchise's touchstone moment. "I couldn't justify the cost at the time, flying out for one game," he confessed. "But I ended up out on Electric Avenue with everybody else in town. [In hindsight] it's certainly one of my regrets."

Santa's favorite all-time Flame? A toss-up between Lanny McDonald, Tim Hunter, and Craig Conroy. Among his most prized memorabilia are a seat from the old Montreal Forum ("I attended five games in the Forum, all involving the Flames and four in Stanley Cup Finals") and a framed ticket from the December 7, 2003, game against the Pittsburgh Penguins that features his picture on the ticket. That year the team honored season-ticket holders by using photos of them on game tickets.

"Sports has always been a big part of our family," said Thomas. "My father took me to my first Stampeders game when I was three years old, down at the old Mewata Stadium. I used to go to a lot of hockey games, too. But once the Flames came to Calgary, it was a no-brainer.

"Do I follow them religiously?" A small laugh. "I guess you could say that."

These days, Thomas owns nine season tickets at the Saddledome for home games. He normally sits in Section 208, Row 12, Seat 8. He's a regular, a fixture. "I love it," he said. "Truly love it. I'll always be a Flames fan."

There can be the occasional drawback, however. "The year they swept L.A. [in 1989]," recalled Santa, "I was in the can, with my Flames jersey on, naturally. As the old Fabulous Forum tended to be, it was just a trough. And all of a sudden I hear some guy behind me say, 'Let's put out the Flames.' So I take a step up, figuring, *Okay, whatever, pal.* Then all of a sudden, he peed on the back of my pant leg." Talk about a way to get yourself on the naughty list until the end of eternity...

Giving Back

Thirty-seven years ago, the concept began with a single initiative, 18 holes of golf, and it raised $25,000. Fast-forward to 2014–15: it saw 80 beneficiaries and close to $3 million poured back into the community. The Flames Foundation for Life, the charitable arm of the hockey club, has funneled more than $30 million into southern Alberta over the past three decades.

The foundation was the brainchild of the Flames' original ownership group that helped bring the club north from Atlanta—Harley Hotchkiss, Doc and B.J. Seaman, Ralph Scurfield, Normie Kwong, and Norm Green.

Among the worthy organizations supported annually are Camp Kindle, a camp for children affected by cancer, the Alberta Children's Hospital Rotary Flames House, and the Comrie's Sports Equipment Bank. The Flames' EvenStrength and HEROS programs help make hockey more accessible to all, while Alberta Junior Hockey League and Canadian Women's Hockey League programs do as well.

Fund-raising initiatives include 50/50 draws at home games, contests, and special events such as the annual golf event and Flames Ambassadors Celebrity Poker Tournament.

What's amazing about the foundation is that its level of community commitment has never wavered through the years, even during difficult financial times for the franchise. "It's a wonderful exercise," explained executive director Candice Goudie, "sitting down now with charities and working on their needs and how we fit into those based on why we're here and what the initial framework was."

She continued, "Harley and Doc had invested in Project 75, for Hockey Canada and [the Canadian Hockey] Centre of Excellence, which was obviously very important to hockey, and the foundation was created after that.

"We started quite small, but now it's obviously very, very large and focused on developing the game. The mandate is still the same as it was in 1983, and that's to improve the lives of southern Albertans. They really put an emphasis on why hockey's here, and we still think about that when we're making funding decisions, not based on what we've done in the past but why the foundation was created in the first place. Obviously we have health and wellness and grassroots sports, but hockey has always been at the root of it."

The scope of the endeavor has spread steadily over the last 22 years, and now has at its helm an 11-person board of directors made up of Flames executives and Calgary business leaders. "In the '80s and '90s there were usually one or two fund-raisers, and a relatively small amount of money went to one or two charities. Now we have a different fund-raiser every day. Around 1998 to 2000 we started the 50/50 draws, and the growth there has been phenomenal."

What began with 18 holes of golf 37 years ago has become an endeavor that has benefited thousands upon thousands of southern Albertans. Its imprint is there for all to see. "The idea," said Flames icon Lanny McDonald—among the most tireless of charity advocates—"has always been to make sure you put something back. To leave a community better than when you got there. And that's a pretty wonderful thing, don't you think?"

66 Land of the Rising Sun

The Flames weren't originally even supposed to be part of Game 1, in 1998, which would see two NHL teams play two season-opening games in Tokyo; originally the Oilers were supposed to go. But owing to an ongoing ownership imbroglio, Edmonton was forced to pull out of its commitment to travel overseas.

So it was left for the Calgary Flames to pinch-hit in early October 1998 and make the trek to Tokyo to face the San Jose Sharks in a two-game, regular-season set; to deal with the 15-hour time difference; and hopefully to kick-start their year as positively as possible. And they certainly needed a big kick off the hop.

They were coming off their lowest full-schedule point total in franchise history—67—and consecutive seasons of missing the postseason. And their star player, Theo Fleury, was coming up on the end of his contract and was at an impasse with the organization over dollars (he would later be dealt to the Colorado Avalanche). All that made 1998–99 an important season for the franchise.

The grumbling over the unique opening in Japan started early. Sharks boss Darryl Sutter had spent some nomadic playing time in the Land of the Rising Sun. And eyeing the horrific starts suffered by both the 1997 participants in the event, Vancouver and Anaheim, he viewed the adventure with pragmatic suspicion. "My problem with this deal has always been the travel," was Sutter's frank admission. "We logged the second-most miles of any team in the league last season, behind Dallas." Grunting sarcastically, he added, "So I suppose what's another 5,000 miles, one way?"

Flames boss—and Darryl's big bro—Brian Sutter tried to make the best of the situation. He may not have learned fluent Japanese for the trip but did acclimate himself with a couple keynote words: *dozo* and *arigato*. "*Please* and *thank you*," he explained, "are the two most important things you can say in any language."

As with the previous year's visit by the Ducks and Canucks, the two games would be housed in the 10,500-seat Yoyogi Arena, situated in the Harajuku section of the city. Built for the 1964 Summer Olympic Games as a swimming and diving facility, a three-meter board loomed at one end of the ice surface. (Tom Renney, coach of the Canucks the year before, had offered up some pre-trip info on the site: "The benches are huge. The atmosphere is good. If you don't break through the ice and hit a pipe, you'll be just fine.")

And indeed, the playing conditions were an instant concern. The boat carrying a huge refrigeration unit required to maintain the ice actually ran into a typhoon en route from Los Angeles to Tokyo and suffered significant damage to one side. The unit—designed in Edmonton and used on some movie shoots—such as the Anthony Hopkins–Alec Baldwin survival drama *The Edge*, shot in Canmore, Alberta—was repaired, and at least the NHL had learned from its first Asian experience, this go-round bringing its own ice-flow panels, boards, and glass.

Instantly, Theoren Fleury, Calgary's tiny terror, morphed into a local celebrity. When the Flames' Japan Airlines flight touched down at Narita International Airport in Tokyo on October 8, local media was there to greet him 30 strong.

There was sightseeing to do, yes, but more vitally there was hockey to play. Back-to-backs, in fact. The first game ended 3–3 with the Sharks' Mike Ricci squaring accounts with 2:18 remaining in the third period. The second? All Fleury. Five points, including his 12th career hat trick, to smote his old Stanley Cup–winning pal Mike Vernon in the San Jose net and give the Flames the 5–3 win.

So despite all the uncertainty, the Flames returned home with three points from a possible four. And memories to last a lifetime: The search for the best sushi. Wonderful gardens. Crowded trains. Lanny McDonald visiting the Cavern Club in the Roppongi party district—named for the Liverpool club made famous by the Beatles—which featured three sets of Fab Four impersonators doing songs that sounded as good as listening to the original records. Flames mascot Harvey the Hound endeavoring to climb the three-meter diving board for a bit of hijinks, only to be officially censured by the NHL ("Get that [bleeping] dog off that board!" hollered Arthur Pincus from the league office).

"It was a pleasure," summed up Fleury. "When people approached you, always 'thank you' and 'please.' Never 'Sign this!'

Nobody shoving stuff in your face. They were just so happy to get your signature. Honestly happy. Nobody doing it only to turn around and resell what you'd signed. They respect you, respect your space, and expect you to show them the same sort of respect back. Now is that a good basis for living, or what?"

67 Young Guns

The marketing campaign certainly had a catchy western motif: "The Young Guns Are Coming!" Youth. Energy. Enthusiasm. That was the sales pitch. The winds of change were wafting throughout the Saddledome. Attendance had begun to lag, the average down to 17,000 through the previous season, 21st in a 26-team league, as the Flames missed out on the postseason party for the first time in five years in 1996–97. A new order, with an emphasis on revitalization, was due as the 1997–98 NHL campaign drew near.

Oh, sure, there were old hands still on deck—Theo Fleury, Michael Nylander, Tommy Albelin, and James Patrick among them—but a shift to the future, a goal of reaching a point out there on the horizon, had begun in earnest. Forwards Jarome Iginla, Hnat Domenichelli, and Aaron Gavey, along with defensemen Todd Simpson, Derek Morris, Cale Hulse, Jamie Allison, Chris O'Sullivan, and Denis Gauthier, hinted at brighter times ahead.

Former sixth-overall pick Cory Stillman was still only 23 and entering his fourth NHL season, ready to move into his prime years. Shifty winger Valeri Bure, 23, would arrived in a swap with Montreal during the season, along with rugged 21-year-old pivot Jason Wiemer from Tampa, adding to the demographic profile being implemented by GM Al Coates.

With steel-spined Brian Sutter installed as coach, replacing Pierre Page, optimism swelled. "We're definitely going to make the playoffs," predicted the rugged Simpson. "It's just something you know, something you can feel."

A 20-year-old Iginla, entering his second full NHL season, couldn't shake those warm vibes, either. "Fans seem supportive of it," he gushed of the new direction, "and we're excited too. It's good for competition, when everybody's pushing for spots. That way, nobody gets comfortable or complacent. If you're not working hard, there's someone there ready to take your spot.

"The atmosphere around the city feels good. I definitely think the organization is going up. The past few years, the team has been rebuilding, but each year now, we're better than we were the year before."

Reality soon reared its ugly head, though. To open the 1997–98 season, the kids stumbled out of the gate—badly—leading off with a 3–13–4 record, plagued by defensive miscues and the unavoidable pitfalls of youth. Then bad went to worse when 23-year-old center Gavey, projected as possible captain material down the road, suffered an abdominal strain and dressed for only 26 games that season. After conditioning in AHL Saint John most of the season, he was traded to Dallas for 33-year-old Bob Bassen the following summer.

The rock 'em / sock 'em Simpson—one of those prominently featured in the Young Guns ad campaign, with taglines such as, "Todd: All Heart, No Ache"—also struggled with injury, hurting a knee in training camp that cost him 10 games, followed by a shoulder injury that sidelined him for another four games and then a concussion that ended his season prematurely.

And the Flames finished with a franchise-low 67 points. The succeeding two seasons would show improvement, but only incrementally at 72 and 77 points, respectively. And no playoffs.

The mercurial Bure thrived under Sutter's tough-love approach, scoring 35 times in 1999–2000, but grew increasingly dissatisfied when the oldest brother in the legendary Viking, Alberta, hockey clan was ousted in favor of first Don Hay and then Greg Gilbert. Coates, the man who drew up the youthful blueprint, took the fall with Sutter in April 2000.

Even before the change in regime, though, old hands such as Ken Wregget, Phil Housley (in a second tour of duty), and Steve Smith started to arrive to plug holes. Gauthier gave the organization 384 games of service, Morris a solid five seasons, and Iginla, of course, went on to become the greatest player in franchise history. Yet most of the kids ticketed for stardom, counted on to push the organization forward and return it to relevant status, fizzled and either left or were shipped out. In truth, the much-ballyhooed Young Guns era was over almost before the kids had time to clear the holster.

68 Ultimatum

In this city, fans once bequeathed season tickets in wills, passed them on generation to generation. They were as valuable in their way as the crude oil that pumped dollars into the economy. By the early summer of 1999, though, sales of Calgary Flames season seats had plummeted to a reported 8,700, a shocking drop of nearly 5,000 over three years. Three years in succession of being on the outside peering in come playoff time had translated into a growing apathy within the community. The team was in danger of losing out on the $3.4 million currency-equalization payment established by the league—a vital windfall in those days—that was tied to ticket sales.

Doug Gilmour, Mike Vernon, Gary Suter, Joe Nieuwendyk, Gary Roberts, and Al MacInnis were long gone. That spring, the team's one remaining superstar, Theo Fleury, had been offloaded because of—you guessed it—a money squabble. Rather than lose the pending unrestricted free agent and prime bargaining chip on July 1 for nothing, Flames general manager Al Coates made the hard choice and dealt Fleury to Colorado. It was yet another sign to increasingly disgruntled patrons that their team simply could not compete anymore.

Escalating salaries, a small market base, a non–salary cap world to buffer them, along with a painfully weak Canadian dollar were all conspiring to bring down the onetime giants. As this was unfolding, the specter of the Winnipeg Jets and Quebec Nordiques—since sold off to US destinations—hovered uneasily in the imagination.

Once the undisputed Rolls-Royce of the NHL, the Flames were in danger of veering off the Yellow Brick Road and into the ditch. And the tone soon became very clear, all the way out of Calgary. "Our intention is to stay here," admitted the point man among the ownership group, Harley Hotchkiss, in an interview, "but if the financial situation doesn't improve and people don't come out to support the team in this tough time—and I understand people have the right to stay away—we could be put in a situation where we might not be able to fulfill that commitment." It was an ultimatum: fans weren't required to buy tickets, but owners losing money weren't required to stay and continue to suffer either. A public backlash over the implied ultimatum ensued.

"We don't just need fans, we need supporters," pleaded team president and CEO Ron Bremner. "We need people who are there for us when we are building and growing and improving and getting better. Not just fans who are going to say, 'We will be there when you get into the second round of the playoffs. Then we will come and see you.'

"If I were giving the team a physical, checking its blood pressure and cholesterol, I'd say there are definitely some things we have to pay attention to, to monitor. We're going back to basics. Clearly, we have to get more people out to see the product and enjoy it. We need to enlist the support of the NHL fans, the hockey fans, in this city. We've got a hard-core base right now of 9,000. That has to be expanded."

Looking back, former general manager Al Coates pointed to renovations inside the Saddledome as a major contributing factor in dipping attendance. "For sure—the renovation of the building hurt. Really hurt," he conceded. "That was a mistake. There were 8,700 seats in the lower bowl of the Saddledome prior to the renovation. Even today, the lower bowl is less than 4,000 seats. I remember at the time, the amount of people displaced from the lower bowl was roughly 6,000. They tried their new seats and they didn't like 'em. A lot of those people had been sitting next to other fans who had become friends over the years, had become a real part of their experience at games. Suddenly, that was gone. That part of it was underestimated.

"You look at that and the fact that we were starting to rebuild the team then. I'd say our fan base had been spoiled with the success over a number of years, and it all sort of came together."

The team stumbled through another playoff-deprived campaign in 1999–2000, and if anything, the ultimatum was being driven home even louder, with more urgency.

Faced with a possible loss of its one overriding passion, the city and corporate community stepped up. The vital 14,000 season-ticket minimum criteria was reached (14,014), triggering the currency-equalization payout. And there was a restructuring with the Saddledome Foundation regarding the team's operating lease on the building.

Additional infusions of cash were forthcoming from a multi-year, multimillion-dollar arena-naming agreement with Pengrowth Management Limited, increased advertising prices, and the formation of a provincial lottery to assist both the Flames and their northern rivals, the Edmonton Oilers.

So on July 1, 2000, the announcement Calgarians had been waiting for arrived: their hockey team was saying put. "There's no move to sell the team now, and I don't believe there will be, but we still have some hurdles to get over," a relieved Hotchkiss told a jam-packed media conference.

"While it would have been great to have concluded all our goals by June 30, it was unrealistic to expect the Saddledome Foundation, the city, and the province to deal with these issues until it was clear we had solid fan support."

Crisis averted. The Flames had survived, but it would be four more years before they would capture the city's imagination again.

69 Ten Memorable Goals

1. **May 25, 1989:** Not just *any* old empty-net goal. *The* empty net goal to end 'em all for Flames fans everywhere. Doug Gilmour slotted into a vacated Montreal net at the majestic old Forum to seal the deal, and the Stanley Cup, 4–2 in Game 6 over the Canadiens. Cue the party.
2. **April 15, 1989:** The carom shot glancing off Joel Otto's right skate 19:21 into the first OT period in Game 7, ending a surprisingly grueling opening-round squabble against Vancouver, lifting the pressure and setting the soon-to-be-champs off on their destiny.

3. **April 19, 2004:** After the favored Canucks had tied Game 7 late, the Eliminator, Martin Gelinas, counted his second OT winner of the first-round series to push the underdogs past Vancouver at Rogers Arena.

4. **April 14, 1991:** For sheer heart-pounding drama, Theo Fleury's pickpocketing a Mark Messier pass to score a break-away on Grant Fuhr and send the compelling 1991 first-round series to Game 7 back home (where Calgary lost) is difficult to top, and impossible to erase from memory.

5. **May 3, 2004:** That man of the moment again, Martin Gelinas, eliminated the Detroit Red Wings and sent the Flames to their first Stanley Cup Finals appearance in 15 seasons at 19:13 of overtime in Game 6 at the Saddledome.

6. **May 25, 1989:** Many people remain convinced Lanny McDonald's Game 6 strike, on a lovely hookup with Hakan Loob and Joe Nieuwendyk, stood as the Cup clincher. In fact, it wasn't, but the image of McDonald's face in joy, peeling away after beating Patrick Roy, is forever young.

7. **March 21, 1989:** Icon Lanny McDonald counted career snipe No. 500 on a wraparound against Mark Fitzpatrick of the New York Islanders. It turned out to be the final regular-season goal of his illustrious career. The top almost popped off the Saddledome in celebration.

8. **January 7, 2012:** Icon Jarome Iginla counted No. 500 of his career. Not exactly in spectacular fashion, as his pass ricocheted off the skates of two Minnesota players to befuddle goaltender Nicklas Backstom. No matter, he had scored his share of beauties before in becoming the 42nd player in league history to hit 500, and only the 15th to do so in one organization.

9. **May 8, 1988:** A signature Al MacInnis beebee 15:05 into OT gave the Flames a 2–1 victory over Chicago at the magnificent old Stadium and a 3–1 stranglehold on their semifinals series.

10. **March 12, 1988:** Twenty-one-year-old center Joe Nieuwendyk's second goal of the game versus Buffalo at the Saddledome put him at 50 for the season.

70 Hall Monitoring

General admission, ages 14 to 64, is $18.00 Canadian. So if you happen to be out east in Toronto, for whatever reason, and you're modeling a replica Johnny Gaudreau No. 13, a Mark Giordano No. 5 or, say, a classic throwback Lanny McDonald No. 9, wander down to the Hockey Hall of Fame, at 30 Yonge Street, on the corner of Front Street, the site of the old Bank of Montreal building.

There's plenty for Flames fans to see inside the Hall of Fame's 60,000 square feet of lore. Of the 271 players, 104 builders, and 16 on-ice officials honored there, 15 men with ties to the organization and two media stalwarts are enshrined in the temple of the game.

Any list of worthy Hall of Famers begins with right winger McDonald, the most enduringly popular Flame ever and, fittingly, the first honoree from the franchise inducted, class of 1992. The mustachioed one only happens to be the current chairman of the Hall.

On the players' side, you move from there to another pair of franchise icons, center Joe Nieuwendyk and defenseman Al MacInnis, the 1988 Calder Trophy recipient and 1989 Conn Smythe Trophy winner, respectively.

Right winger Joe Mullen left for Pittsburgh and collected two additional Stanley Cup rings but earned his first in Calgary, and scored 16 playoff goals in 22 games during that quest. Center Doug Gilmour was the catalyst behind Mullen being acquired from St. Louis.

Defenseman Phil Housley, who had two turns and 328 regular-season starts as a Flame, made the Hall grade in 2015. Longstanding nemesis Grant Fuhr, meanwhile, who inflicted more than his share of pain while in the employ of the dynastic Edmonton Oilers in the 1980s, ended his playing career in Calgary, notching his 400th regular-season game. Fuhr spent three additional seasons as the team's goaltending consultant.

In 2016 Sergei Makarov, the 1990 Calder Trophy–winning Soviet superstar, entered the Hall. In four seasons as a Flame, the *M* of the Red Army's and Soviet national team's fabled KLM Line scored 94 goals and contributed 292 points over 297 regular-season games.

Guy Lapointe, one of Montreal's Big Three on defense during the 1970s, earned a Hall nod in 1993. Lapointe spent a decade in Calgary's employ, as an assistant coach and scout. Sniper Michel Goulet of Quebec Nordiques renown, inducted in 1998, has been a scout for the team from 2010 until today.

Glenn Hall, Mr. Goalie, the man whose 502 straight appearances in goal for the Chicago Blackhawks will never be equaled, helped Mike Vernon, among others, learn his trade as goaltending consultant in Calgary from 1988 to 2000.

In the builders category, Harley Hotchkiss, the engine room of the original ownership group that brought the team to Calgary from Atlanta in 1980, and Doc Seaman, another original owner and key player in bringing the 1988 Winter Olympics to the city and the launching of the Olympic Saddledome, are enshrined. And, of course, there's Badger Bob Johnson, he of the immortal "It's a great day for hockey" line and the trendsetting professor behind the Flames' first run to the Stanley Cup Finals, in 1986.

On the media side, longtime radio voice of the team, Peter Maher, the man who made "Yeah, baby!" a listening hallmark, has a richly deserved spot as winner of the 2006 Foster Hewitt Memorial Award, while Eric Duhatschek, whose prose graced the *Calgary Herald* through two decades, from the Flames' Calgary inception, received the Elmer Ferguson Memorial Award for service to hockey writing in 2001.

Each and every one worth the price of admission during their playing, coaching, managing, troubleshooting, play-calling, writing days. And now, gone from the immediacy of the doing into the realm of legend, no less so.

71 Hart Breaker

The curio cabinet had already been amply stocked: A miniature Art Ross Trophy as the NHL's leading scorer. The Rocket Richard Trophy as its top goal scorer. Tack on the Lester B. Pearson Award as the loop's top performer, as voted on by his peers. So it's not as if Jarome Iginla had been left empty-handed, or could've felt snubbed, the night of the NHL's annual awards soiree in Toronto in late June 2002. That said…

By that moment in time, Calgary's inspirational captain had reached the summit, inarguably the game's most complete player. Hit? Fight? Score 50? Lead by example? All good.

"My first four games, I remember opening the paper and reading, 'What's the matter with Iginla?'" he reminisced the night of the big awards show at the Metro Toronto Convention Centre.

"I could never have dreamed it would go like this. I had 18 goals in the first 20 games and I thought that was pretty wild. But it wasn't until after the All-Star Game, after the Olympics"—in Salt Lake City, where he helped Canada end a half-century gold-medal drought—"that I really thought about the scoring championship or scoring 50 goals. Before that? It just felt like some good streaks."

The man earned some Lady Byng love, despite his rock 'em–sock 'em style, and a few Frank Selke Trophy votes. An astonishing variety of respect, all in all. A season for the ages just wasn't enough to also walk away toting the Hart Trophy, presented annually to the NHL's "player judged most valuable to his team." It was the biggest, brassiest bauble of the evening. That, controversially, was carted off by Montreal Canadiens goaltender Jose Theodore, also the Vezina Trophy recipient as top goaltender.

A historic ballot-point deadlock between the two—434 points apiece—was decided by first-place votes: Theodore 26, Iginla 23.

No one could diminish Theodore's accomplishments. His goals-against average was miserly, 2.11. But Patrick Roy went lower, 1.94. Theodore posted 30 wins, but Martin Brodeur notched a chart-topping 38, and Roy hit for 32. Theodore rang up seven shutouts, but Roy edged him yet again, with nine.

Iginla, meanwhile, set the standard in virtually every offensive category, finishing six points ahead of Vancouver's Markus Naslund atop the scoring chart (at 96), and ending a 21-year run of Ross dominance by three superstars—Wayne Gretzky, Mario Lemieux, and Jaromir Jagr. He performed like a driven man.

Iginla's buddy Craig Conroy, a Selke finalist himself that year, told reporters in Toronto, "All these guys were trying to catch him, trying to catch him. There were charges from all over the place. And those were the greatest players in the world.

"They'd get close, then he'd have a four-point game. And I think they're looking, too, saying to themselves, 'Oh, man, he's not slowing down.'"

What must have been a tipping factor for a deciding few of those voting: the Habs reached the playoffs, and the Flames—in spite of all Iginla's brilliance—did not, for the sixth of seven consecutive seasons.

Typical of the man, if there was any rancor inside, Iginla hid it well. "I was very honored to be a nominee," he maintained, "but once I was nominated, I really wanted to win it. It's a very prestigious award, and a lot of great players have won it, like Wayne Gretzky and Mario Lemieux.

"But Jose Theodore had an unbelievable season, and he was a very deserving winner, as Patrick Roy [the other finalist] would have been."

The guy posing with the hardware seemed a trifle taken aback. "After I got the Vezina," admitted Theodore, "I said to myself, 'That's good; at least I got one of them.' I couldn't believe it when Wayne Gretzky announced my name [for the Hart]. I'm on rubber legs right now." So were more than a few Flames partisans, utterly convinced of their candidate's worthiness.

The Pearson, arguably a truer judge of value given those casting ballots, tickled Iginla to no end. "In a game like hockey that is fierce and with the physical battles that go on all season," he said, "it's a special feeling to think that some of those same opponents voted for me.

"I couldn't ask for more of a dream season, except for making the playoffs and winning the Stanley Cup. So there are more dreams, but a lot of them have been delivered this year."

72 By the Numbers

A few fun Flames figures:

1: Number of Stanley Cup wins

2: Number of Flames jerseys retired—Lanny McDonald (No. 9), Mike Vernon (No. 30); number of Presidents' Trophies captured (1987–88, 1988–89)

3: Number of seasons with 40-plus wins by a goaltender (all courtesy of Miikka Kiprusoff)

4: Highest-ever draft position (Sam Bennett, 2014); number of regular-season home losses during the Stanley Cup season of 1988–89 (32–4–4)

6: Most All-Star Game appearances representing the Flames (Theoren Fleury)

7: Most playoff goals scored in one series—Hakan Loob vs. L.A., five games, 1988 *and* Theoren Fleury vs. San Jose, seven games, 1995

8: Number of seasons of 100-plus points registered by Calgary Flames—Kent Nilsson and Theoren Fleury have two apiece; Hakan Loob, Mike Bullard, Joe Mullen, and Al MacInnis have one each; number of general managers in Calgary Flames history (Cliff Fletcher, Doug Risebrough, Al Coates, Craig Button, Darryl Sutter, Jay Feaster, Brian Burke, and Brad Treliving)

Theo Fleury is all over the Flames' record books.

11: Consecutive seasons Jarome Iginla led the team in scoring—2000–2001 to 2011–2012; number of Flames goals scored by Gary Leeman, the Calgary-bound centerpiece of the infamous Doug Gilmour deal with Toronto; first jersey number worn by Al MacInnis (in 1981–82) before switching to his signature No. 2

13: Most goals scored by the team in a game, 13–1 over San Jose, on February 10, 1993; record for most career hat tricks (Theoren Fleury, Kent Nilsson)

19: Number of captains in franchise history

21: Number of seasons the Flames qualified for the postseason while based in Calgary

23: Number of playoff games vs. Edmonton (8 wins, 15 losses)

28: Penalty shots scored in those games, in 59 chances

30: Combined PIM total (14, 16) of RW Joe Mullen's two Lady Byng Memorial Trophy–winning seasons as a Flame

31: Playoff point total of 1989 Conn Smythe Trophy winner Al MacInnis over 22 games; Willi Plett's franchise-high penalty-minute total for a playoff game, vs. Philadelphia on April 2, 1981 (three minors, one major, two game misconducts)

35: Most playoff goals in a career (Joe Mullen)

41: Playoff OT games since the team moved to Calgary (18 wins, 23 losses)

45: Goalkeeper Miikka Kiprusoff's regular-season win total in 2008–09, a franchise record

51: Number of goals scored by Joe Nieuwendyk during his Calder Trophy–winning season of 1987–88

53: Second-highest one-year goal total, by Gary Roberts, in 1991–92; first number worn by Johnny Gaudreau, for one game to close out the 2013–14 season (he switched to No. 13 for his first full NHL season)

54: Lowest point total to top the team's scoring chart in a full / non–work stoppage campaign (Jiri Hudler—17 goals, 37 assists—in 2013–14)

59: Most shots in a game (February 23, 1991, vs. Quebec)

66: The first jersey number worn by T.J. Brodie (who, wisely, in short order ditched Mario Lemieux's legendary number and switched to his current No. 7); Lanny McDonald's franchise single-season-best goal windfall (1981–82)

82: Kent Nilsson's assist total, a Calgary record, during his never-to-be-approached 131-point 1980–81 season

93: Jersey number for Sam Bennett and, previously, Michael Cammalleri, the highest double-digit ever worn by a Flame, edging out Michael Nylander's No. 92

96: Jarome Iginla's point total in 2001–02, in becoming the only Flame to collect the Art Ross Trophy as NHL scoring champ

193: "Badger" Bob Johnson's coaching win total in Calgary, a franchise best

279: Lowest draft position at which the Flames selected a player (C Pavel Torgaev)

283: Defenseman Kris Russell's 2014–15 shot-block total, a league record

397: Most goals scored as a team during a single season (1987–88)

1,095: Jarome Iginla's career Calgary points total

2,405: Tim Hunter's Calgary career penalty-minute aggregate

6,475: Hockey seating maximum at Stampede Corral, the Flames' first Calgary home

73 All-Time All-Stars

Of all the players and coaches who have passed through the Stampede City over the course of their careers, these men stand out as Calgary Flames all-time All-Stars.

Goal

First Team—Miikka Kiprusoff: The redoubtable Finn owns club records for shutouts in a campaign (10), wins in a season (45), games played (576), career victories (305), lowest seasonal GAA (1.69), and highest seasonal save percentage (.933). He is the only Flames puck repeller ever to accept the Vezina Trophy.

Second Team—Mike Vernon: The Calgary kid played a major part in felling the Oilers juggernaut in 1986 and celebrated Stanley Cup euphoria three years later. He had a 262–187–57 record, and another 77 wins come playoff time, a franchise high.

Honorable Mention: Reggie Lemelin

Defense

First Team—Al MacInnis: Topped 100 points in 1990–91 (103), third all-time in club scoring (822 points), and first in helpers (609). Two-time first-time All-Star, three-time second while in the colors. And, in case it's slipped your mind, he won a trinket called the Conn Smythe Trophy in 1989.

First Team—Gary Suter: Powerful-skating offensive D-man. Fifth franchise-wise in points (564). Ideal complement to MacInnis on the power play. Calder Trophy recipient and NHL All-Rookie team in 1986. Second-team All-Star in 1987–88.

Second Team—Brad McCrimmon: No-nonsense, uncompromising, Suter's mentor and longtime pairing sidekick. A towering presence through the 1989 Cup run. A second-team All-Star and NHL plus-minus leader in 1987–88.

Second Team—Robyn Regehr: Carnival ride owner and operator of the Tunnel of Death. Superb closing hitter down the boards. Second in games played as a Flame (826), trailing only Jarome Iginla.

Honorable Mentions: Mark Giordano, Paul Reinhart

Center

First Team—Joe Nieuwendyk: Fourth among all-time franchise scorers (616 points) and third in goals (314) in only 577 games. Calder Trophy winner, two-time 50-goal man. Softest, deftest, most cunningly lethal set of hands in Flames history.

Second Team—Doug Gilmour: Doesn't rank high in any franchise career categories, spending but 266 games as a Flame, but his impact on the touchstone moment in franchise history is inarguable.

Honorable Mention: Joel Otto

Left Wing

First Team—Gary Roberts: A truly marvelous 1991–92 campaign, scoring 53 times (second among all individual seasons) while compiling 207 penalty minutes. Eighth on the franchise points list (505).

Second Team—Kent Nilsson: A bit of a cheat here, as he was a natural center, but the Magic Man is too sublime to be left off this team, and was so innately talented he could've played anywhere anyway. His 131-point season the year the Flames moved in from Atlanta is unassailable, his skill set unparalleled, his ability to astound and anger (often at the same time) without peer.

Right Wing

First Team—Jarome Iginla: Tremendous competition at this position, but the numbers are overwhelming: 525 goals, 1,095 points, 831 PIM. The franchise's all-time leading scorer and long-serving, iconic captain. Three-time first-team NHL All-Star nods, twice the Rocket Richard recipient, one Art Ross Trophy. Then—inhale—we move on to the King Clancy Award, Mark Messier Leadership Award, etc. For a spell, the game's most complete, dominating player.

Second Team—Theoren Fleury: Propped up a team. Second all-time in points (791) and goals (364), to go along with 1,339 penalty minutes. So richly, vastly entertaining. A second-team All-Star in 1994–95, tied for tops in the Plus-Minus Award in 1990–91.

Honorable Mentions: Joe Mullen, Lanny McDonald, Hakan Loob

Coaching Staff

Bob Johnson, Terry Crisp, Darryl Sutter, Bob Hartley: Between 'em, 578 regular-season wins, and at least triple that in great one-liners (Sutter's a tad more pointed); three trips to the Cup Finals; a Stanley Cup; and a Jack Adams Award

General Manager

Cliff Fletcher: The architect who carefully constructed the franchise's one golden moment. Hockey Hall of Famer for a reason.

74 Mr. Popularity

For one of the most popular players ever to don the silks, the relationship got off to a rather rocky beginning. "I remember my wife calling, in tears," Craig Conroy recalled of the March 13, 2001, trade that made him a Calgary Flame for the first time. "She's really upset, and says: 'Have you read the paper in Calgary? I've gone online and was reading all the articles. They *hate* you.' I'm like, 'What?' I'd met the team on the road, flown to Philly, then Columbus, and then I [flew] home. I [hadn't] even reached Calgary yet. And already they *hate* me?"

Today, such ill will seems impossible; Craig Conroy ranks among the franchise's most popular players ever. Two spins as a Flame, the most productive center ever to distribute the puck to Jarome Iginla, Conroy retired to Calgary and joined the organization's hockey management staff.

Outgoing, underrated, and a consummate team guy, he played 507 games in the colors, contributing 308 points and distributing more gratis goodwill than any franchise has a right to expect of any employee. But back then Cory Stillman was the top point producer (45 in 66 games) on an offensively challenged team, and Conroy, largely unknown in the city, was viewed as nothing more than an industrious, defensive-minded center.

"Even Jarome made the comment, 'Why would we trade our leading scorer for another checker?' I'm talking to Tyson Nash, my linemate in St. Louis, and he says, 'This Jarome Iginla is the nicest guy you'll ever meet. You're going to love him.' After what he'd said, I'm like, 'Really?'"

"I understood people's take on it—they got rid of their leading scorer for a guy whose role was as a third-line checker in St. Louis. But it was tough. A young team here, not a playoff team, I don't know the city and I don't feel welcome...at all."

Compounding the problem, Conroy met Flames coach Don Hay for the first time at a morning skate, received a pep talk about how much he was wanted, etc., and felt better about things. Then Hay was fired...later that day.

"I'm thinking, *What is going on around here?*" Conroy said. "It was a lot to take in. I knew Val Bure, and Val was great to me when I got here, but he wasn't happy. Clearly. The minute after practice was over, he'd be gone. So it all seemed a bit dysfunctional to me. Honestly, I couldn't wait for those 14 games to end."

The one saving grace for Conroy was that Hay's replacement turned out to be Greg Gilbert, who'd coached him in the minors and understood his hockey gifts were more than simply, strictly as a checker.

The next season, the pivotal point in Craig Conroy's pro career arrived. Center Marc Savard was hurt at Joe Louis Arena in Detroit, and Conroy hastily shuffled up to the big line with Iginla manning the right flank. On the ice and off, they connected. "Jarome had 20 goals in 20 games," Conroy recalled. "We developed a bit of chemistry. So even when Marc came back, I stayed on the line. That's how it evolved."

In 2004, against all logic, with Iginla scoring goals, Miikka Kiprusoff saving shots, and the flinty Sutter prodding personalities, the Flames reached the Cup Finals, but a lockout the next year signaled change. Despite the long springtime run, coach/GM Darryl Sutter decided on an extensive retool. So Conroy was looking at a one-year deal. There were four-year offers in other cities, and so, despite wanting to stay in the city that had once seemed so unwelcoming, he signed on with the L.A. Kings.

But fate stepped in, only a year and a half into his SoCal tenure. On January 29, 2007, he received a call from L.A. GM Dean Lombardi. "We were in Alberta for the game. He says, 'You've been traded,'" Conroy recalled.

"I say, 'Where?'

"He says, 'Calgary.'

"That was pretty emotional. Nice of Dean to get a deal done with Darryl to bring me back. It couldn't have worked out better."

Given a second chance at a welcome, it seemed as if the entire city of Calgary put its arms around the product of Potsdam, New York, for a group hug.

The very next night, in his first game back—against the Kings, no less—Conroy scored twice to only sweeten the moment. Earlier, as he sat on the bench during the national anthem, the Jumbotron crew flashed his image in high definition, and the 19,000-plus gathered at the Saddledome stood as one and cheered the returning hero.

"That was just fantastic," he said now, softly. "You know people still come up to me and tell me, 'I was there that night you came back and scored the two against the Kings.' It felt 'right' this time. I still remember sitting on the bench thinking, *This is great. This is where I belong*. I was home."

75 All Ducks on Deck!

Mayhem. Anarchy. Multiple line brawls. Records established for delinquent behavior. And the Edmonton Oilers were nowhere in the vicinity? Nope. Nary a Dave Semenko or a Tim Hunter, a Don Jackson or a Jim Peplinski, a Ken "the Rat" Linseman or Neil "the Butcher of Harvard" Sheehy anywhere in sight.

It hardly seems plausible, given that raw, almost visceral enmity, the legendary bad blood and bile built up between the Flames and Oilers that kept the Battle of Alberta hopping through the years. Yet the wildest, most unruly of nights in Flames history involved a team named after a feel-good family flick starring Emilio Estevez: the Mighty Ducks of Anaheim—yes, the G-rated Disney darlings—in town at the Saddledome on December 8, 2001.

The visitors were cruising, up 4–0 with 4:30 left to play when all hell broke loose on a routine enough play: Calgary defenseman Denis Gauthier dumping the puck in behind the Anaheim net.

Flames robust winger Craig Berube took dead aim, clattering into goaltender Jean-Sebastien Giguere, out behind his net to play the puck. Giguere, clearly incensed, maintained his balance but not his composure. With no small amount of trepidation, in tiptoed Ducks D-man Niclas Havelid, taking a couple cuffs from the bruising Berube. A charging penalty to Calgary's enforcer. Everything was sorted out to everyone's satisfaction, right? Hardly.

The antics *really* started when Kevin Sawyer—the league's fight leader at the time—made a beeline for Calgary's Mike Vernon in retaliation for the Berube hit, and as 1989's Cup-wining hero covered the puck in anticipation of a whistle, Sawyer drilled the unsuspecting goaltender with a cross-check to the face, knocking off his helmet and drawing blood.

In short order, Calgary defenseman Robyn Regehr tracked down Sawyer, Jarome Iginla got into a prolonged tiff with Denny Lambert, and the Flames' Dean McAmmond threw Lambert's jersey at Oleg Tverdovsky. Then things settled down...for a moment or two.

On the very next faceoff, the four Flames on the ice—Bob Boughner, Denis Gauthier, Steve Begin, and Clarke Wilm—shed their mitts simultaneously and the gong show was well and truly on.

On the next faceoff, Rob Niedermayer and Mike Leclerc decided to tango, as did Toni Lydman with Pavel Trnka. Not to be left out, Ronald Petrovicky and Dan Bylsma—yes, *that* Dan Bylsma, later to coach the Pittsburgh Penguins to a Stanley Cup—began exchanging shots. Seconds later, Scott Nichol and Tverdovsky mixed it up inside the Anaheim zone, Giguere leaving his goal crease to stick up for his teammate, earning an immediate ejection.

But wait, hostilities still hadn't concluded. With 8.4 seconds left, Berube exited the penalty box and began chasing Anaheim winger Jeff Friesen around the ice in slapstick fashion.

When the ice chips had finally cleared, the Flames had eclipsed an NHL record for most penalty minutes by a team in a period (190), bettering the number set by the Broad Street Bully Philadelphia Flyers on March 11, 1979, in a donnybrook-filled game against the L.A. Kings.

In the final 85 seconds, a whopping 279 PIM to both teams were distributed—182 minutes to the Flames, including seven misconducts, four game misconducts, and one gross misconduct to Nichol; and 97 minutes to the Ducks, including one misconduct, two game misconducts, and a pair of match penalties.

"Let's put it this way," challenged Calgary coach Greg Gilbert to reporters postgame, after the shenanigans had finally come to a conclusion. "Craig Berube probably could have put Giguere in the hospital if he'd wanted to. He bumped him. If the goalie's going to play the puck, the rulebook still says he's fair game.

"The way Kevin Sawyer came from the far blueline and made a straight beeline for Mike Vernon? That's unacceptable."

"That," declared Calgary captain Dave Lowry, marking his 1,000th NHL game in unforgettable fashion, "was old-time hockey."

The fans ate it up, of course.

The NHL wasn't quite so enthralled. For starters, Gilbert was suspended two games expressly for the lineup he put on the ice prior to the first line brawl. "The deterioration of this game in the final minutes is clearly unacceptable and, in particular, coach Gilbert and the Calgary club must be held accountable," said NHL lawgiver Colin Campbell in a release. "The message should be clear to all teams that this type of conduct will not be tolerated."

Nichol received a two-game sit-down and Berube three. Sawyer, meanwhile, received a five-game ban, and the Flames as an organization were fined $25,000.

76 Rockin' Red Socks

Denis Gauthier calls it, rather perfectly, "the mercy towel." A 21-year-old student lay on his back on the Saddledome ice, unconscious, totally naked except for a pair of cranberry red socks and a wristwatch. Luckily, Flames athletic therapist Morris Boyer came to the rescue.

"You see streakers in other sports, like soccer, where it's a little warmer," recalled Gauthier, now an analyst for RDS TV. "But hockey…well, it's obviously a little cooler. And the cold got to the guy. Because we saw…uh…physical evidence of how cold it was."

Time was winding down on what would end up being a 3–3 tie between the Flames and Boston Bruins on October 17, 2002, when a streaker—apparently on a $200 dare/bet, ostensibly to be used to buy new textbooks—decided he'd go all *Playgirl*.

"The socks...now that was a nice touch," said Scott Nichol, then a pesky checking centerman and today director of player development for the Nashville Predators.

The socks might've been a nice touch, but it turns out they were a bad idea. After scaling the nine-foot-high glass, the au naturel interloper dropped to the ice, lost his footing because of the socks he was wearing, and...*crack!*...suffered a severe concussion and temporary amnesia. The entire unbelievable stretch lasted only six minutes, but it seemed to go on for an hour.

"What sticks out in my mind most vividly," said Gus Thorson, Calgary's equipment manager at the time, "is Mo dropping the Gatorade towel over the guy's crotch. The whole thing just happened so fast. Nobody had ever seen anything like it. We were all kind of [like], 'Whaaaaat?' But then it's, 'Okay, somebody's gotta handle this.' And, hey, Mo got out there and handled it the best way he could—professionally, quickly, and relatively quietly."

The incident has stood the test of time. "I remember it being on a TSN Top 10 a little while ago, and that really brought back some memories," recalled Gauthier. "Before I actually saw him, there was kind of a ruckus in the crowd. We knew something was going on; I just couldn't see where it was coming from.

"The first time I glanced at him, he was riding the glass. I started giving the guys the elbows, like, 'What the hell? Look at this cuckoo.' Then he fell. He's lying there. And we're sitting there thinking, *Do we help him? Do we laugh at him? Is he hurt?* We weren't sure what the protocol was in that situation."

"I thought he was dead," confessed Nichol. "The best part [was], after they finally got him on the stretcher, as they're wheeling him off, he makes this little peace sign. There was this picture

I remember seeing the next day—this lady in the stands, as he's climbing over the glass buck naked, she's right behind him and she is...snortin'.

"I think the funniest part of the whole story, though, was actually the next day at practice. That game might've been the first time Rob Niedermayer had ever been a healthy scratch. He was struggling a little bit. So the next morning, we hung a pair of those red cranberry-colored socks in his stall. And we're bugging him like, 'Hey, buddy, it's not *that* bad. It's just one scratch. You don't have to jump over the glass and knock yourself out.' Well, I thought that was pretty funny, anyway. He didn't think so."

Postgame, the Bruins and their one point gained were lost in the antics. "Well, that's a shame," complained bruising blueliner Bob Boughner. "It's never a girl. It's always a guy."

Chimed in plucky Steve Begin, "I mean, everybody was in shock. What is this guy doing? I guess he'd had a few cocktails."

The wandering miscreant nudist was identified as Tim Hurlbut, who was studying professional golf management at Lethbridge College in southern Alberta. Hurlbut's mother, Jackie, was definitely *not* amused. "I'm embarrassed for all mothers all over the world," she told the Canadian Press. "I can't believe this is happening. He has really embarrassed his mother, and that's not right."

Hurlbut later pleaded guilty to public intoxication, paid a $2,500 fine, and spent six months on probation.

77 Darryl

That very first day, remembered Craig Conroy, put everyone on alert. "He had [GM] Craig Button and [president] Ken King leave the room," the veteran centerman recalled. "And he wasn't asking. So it's just him and us. And he says, 'I'm here. To stay.' And while he's looking around at every player individually, he says, 'A lot of guys in here will be gone. This will not be the team I win with.' And you're like sitting there like, 'Whoa!'

"Understand, there'd been a lot of change in coaches before Darryl. Donny Hay. Greg Gilbert. Boom, boom, boom. He was telling us all that there was only one boss. Like, 'This is my show. You're going to play my way or you won't be around long.' That familiar 'The players got the coach fired' scenario? Uh-uh. Sorry, boys. Not happening here."

It's not a stretch to say Darryl Sutter threw the franchise a lifeline. Through his badgering and bullying, his cunning and his coaching acumen, he resurrected the Calgary Flames. Dragging, kicking, and screaming sometimes, he pulled the most out of his players. "What he set was a standard," said Conroy, now the Flames' assistant GM. "A standard that he would not allow to be compromised."

Oh, he could be sarcastic, condescending, and downright acidic. (Sutter's way with a poison-tipped jibe preceded him. After one subpar effort from Tony Granato when the men were in San Jose together, Sutter met one of the game's fiercest warriors at the bench with a caustic "Nice shift...Cammi.") As much fun as being rubbed with a hunk of pink asbestos insulation fiber.

Sutter didn't give a damn. "Doesn't bother me," he said flatly. "Why? Because I know what I'm about, what my motives are, and what's important. I know me. There are always 5 guys in the dressing room who hate your guts, 5 who like you, and 10 who are undecided. The trick is to keep the 10 undecided guys guessing."

Four weeks after being fired in San Jose, Darryl Sutter came home, to Alberta, close to his spread in Viking, and began the task of remodeling the team. He was the eighth man to coach the Flames in 13 years.

His dour, bitter-beer face quickly earned him the nickname the Jolly Rancher. That first half season, the Flames went 19–18–8–1, fifth in the Northwest Division and out of the playoffs for a seventh consecutive season. Sutter scowled and vowed to change all that. He was a man of his word. In short order, with the axing of Button, he was retooling the organization, taking on the managerial duties as well, and consolidating the power base at the Saddledome.

"I said at the outset that my challenge and my responsibility as head coach was to restore credibility and respect to the Calgary Flames," Sutter told a media conference announcing his dual role. "We've made strides at that downstairs. We're going to make strides at that upstairs, too."

The tide was beginning to shift. Through Sutter's first season in complete control, the perennial doormats were bucking for a playoff spot. He brought in Miikka Kiprusoff from San Jose, the pesky Ville Nieminen, and the stalwart Markus Nilsson. They were starting to get noticed.

"We've played them three times in here and once at home, and every game is the same: hard," said Colorado Avalanche defenseman Rob Blake after one battle at the Saddledome.

He continued, "That's the sort of team Darryl Sutter coached in San Jose that took us to seven games a few years back, scared the heck out of us, and had a legitimate shot at the Stanley Cup. Physical. In your face. On the puck all the time. They may not have a bunch of household names over there, but they're a team in the best sense of the word. People waiting for that team to go away might be waiting a long, long time."

And so began a stretch that's still spoken of in reverential terms in Calgary. The Flames qualified for the playoffs for the first time since 1996 at 42–30–7–03, then a wild, improbable, exhilarating springtime run through favored Vancouver, Detroit, and San Jose that ended one goal from sending Game 7 of the Stanley Cup Finals against Tampa Bay into overtime. One sign held aloft at the Saddledome that winter read: IN SUTTER WE TRUST! He could do no wrong.

"Sometimes you think [his methods] are unfair," acknowledged Conroy during the run. "Sometimes you think it's personal. Sometimes you want to scream. Sometimes you want to cry. But the thing about Darryl is that he plays no favorites. Sure, he's got guys in here who he likes, likes the way they play. That's natural. But it doesn't mean they're immune if they screw up. No one is off his radar. No one gets out unscathed. He treats everyone the same. And the next day, you start fresh with him."

Everyone predicted more big things ahead. After a 46–25–11 season in 2005–06, following a lockout washout year, the Flames were surprised in a seven-game opening-series set by the Anaheim Ducks, themselves on the verge of big things.

Darryl Sutter, having reached a Stanley Cup Finals, won a divisional title, and piloted the first 100-point season since 1991, then made the decision to punt himself upstairs and install trusty lieutenant Jim Playfair as coach.

As a general manager, he made a great coach. After Detroit eliminated Calgary in six games, Sutter replaced Playfair with an old mentor, Mike Keenan, and started bringing in assorted retread veterans rather than building through younger players. Keenan eventually made way for Sutter's brother Brent, and their relationship became strained under the close, intense working conditions.

In the wake of four consecutive years of first-round exits, his acidic style not playing quite so well without the results, Darryl Sutter stepped down as GM on December 28, 2010, eight years to the day after he'd signed on.

"It's surprising in one sense when a big change does happen," admitted captain Jarome Iginla. "Everybody takes it personal. Some of us more so. We've been through a lot with him and have been here a long time and benefited from a lot of his moves. A lot of us have got[ten] to know him, become friends, been through a lot of battles together. It's a hard day. I had a good relationship with Darryl. Yeah, if you're not going, he'd definitely let us know. But I learned a lot from him, about players on other teams, different situations… He was hard, but I respected him.

"One day in Montreal, when he first got here, Connie [Conroy] and I had just a terrible game. You're going bad and your name's not being called anymore; you're pretty much benched. He doesn't say it [in so many words], but then he does say, 'Hey, you two! Don't worry, I won't put you back on that big, bad ice. You're all done. I wouldn't want you to go out there and break a nail!' That's a printable one."

Sutter went on to even greater glory coaching the L.A. Kings, of course. And no matter what anyone thought of his methods or his style, Darryl Sutter's vital imprint on the Flames franchise when it most needed a boost is undeniable.

78 The Tunnel of Death

Even the most lightly obsessed of Flames devotees would have no trouble answering when quizzed about the franchise leader in games played. Jarome Iginla. Easy. At 1,219 regular-season starts. Next, the No. 2 man on the list is far more problematic. Al MacInnis, maybe? Or Theo Fleury? Joe Nieuwendyk? Joel Otto, perhaps? Nope. The answer: Robyn Regehr, of course. No shame in getting that one wrong. You certainly wouldn't be alone.

"Didn't know that," Regehr confessed back on February 27, 2014, marking his first game back at the Scotiabank Saddledome as an enemy intruder, in the black-and-silver garb of the L.A. Kings. "I did know that I'd passed Al [MacInnis] for most among defensemen."

Amazing. Particularly so when considering that at 19 years old, all of 15 years earlier and before his pro career had even begun, Robin Regehr lay in a bed at the University Hospital in Saskatoon, one leg broken and the other fortified by screws, following a horrific head-on car crash in Warman, Saskatchewan, 40 kilometers northeast of the city. Two people died and five others were injured in the accident on July 5, 1999. Regehr's dad, Ron, went out to survey the wreckage and found one of his son's sandals crushed between the brake pad and the floor.

Yet four months later the former Kamloops junior star had recovered sufficiently to be back on the ice. After five conditioning-stint games with AHL, he made his NHL debut for the Flames on October 28, 1999. Regehr went on to play 825 more through 11 seasons modeling the flaming C, topped only by Iginla. Together, along with netminder Miikka Kiprusoff, they were the beating heart of the franchise for more than a decade.

Originally drafted 19th overall by the Colorado Avalanche in the 1998 draft, the teenage Regehr was the key Calgary component in the trade that sent franchise icon Theo Fleury to Denver. In the exchange, the Avs submitted a list of prospects for Flames GM Al Coates to choose from. The only name excluded was that of the superslick Alex Tanguay, later to be a Regehr teammate in Calgary. Turns out, Coates chose wisely.

There were, naturally, some initial bumps. Regehr spent some game nights in the press box that first NHL season, making way for Petr Buzek and Igor Kravchuk, believe it or not. In short order, though, his size coupled with a competitive zeal and appetite for the big hit cemented his spot along the blueline.

During his long heyday defending Calgary interests in general and goaltender Miikka Kiprusoff in particular, the 6'3", 225-pound Regehr was among the most feared of NHL defensemen. His moon-shot body checks soon had the pathway leading down the left-side boards at the Saddledome dubbed the Tunnel of Death. It was a privately owned and operated ride that ranked among the scariest anywhere across the NHL spectrum. Once inside, there was no turning back, no escape.

"What does Reg bring?" pondered another hard-rock defense-man, Steve Staios. "Fear, for one thing. Ask any winger in this league who likes to cut across the middle or go into the corners. They know who he is, what he can do, the damage he can inflict. He plays that nasty type of game.

"Guys are looking for him. They'd be crazy not to. You see their heads jerk up trying to see if he's on the ice or not as they're coming through the neutral zone. As a defenseman, getting an offensive guy off balance, or thinking, is a major part of winning the battle."

Quiet, unassuming, Regehr transformed himself from merely an open-ice belter into one of the game's top shutdown defense-men. Like so many of his mates, he pushed his game to its zenith during the never-to-be-forgotten spring of 2004, as the startling Flames dispatched Vancouver, astounded Detroit, and poleaxed the San Jose Sharks en route to an improbable Stanley Cup Finals date against the Tampa Bay Lightning. For Regehr, as for so many on that edition, that Cinderella trip through to the Finals was his watershed moment as a Flame.

"You can tell the difference in him," lauded Detroit's truculent winger Darren McCarty—another future teammate—during the Flames' six-game ouster of the prohibitively favored Red Wings. "It's all confidence. He plays strong. Mean. A ton of minutes. And he's not a spot-picker. With Regehr, you know you're going to get hit. And you know he'll go into the corner and take a shot too. You can't help but respect a guy like that. He's become a great defenseman."

During his Calgary career, he went through five general managers (Coates, Craig Button, Darryl Sutter, Brian Burke, and Jay Feaster) and seven coaches (Brian Sutter, Don Hay, Al MacNeil, Greg Gilbert, Jim Playfair, Mike Keenan, and Brent Sutter). In 2011, having waived his no-trade clause, the Flames flipped Regehr, Ales Kotalik, and a second-round pick to the Buffalo Sabres in exchange for defenseman Chris Butler and jack-of-all-trades forward Paul Byron.

From there, after a season and a half, he was off to L.A., to reunite with Darryl Sutter and join a team that had hoisted the Cup the year before. That playoff ended prematurely for the Kings, and Regehr required off-season elbow surgery.

During the 2014 postseason, Regehr injured a knee in the opening-round series vs. San Jose that ruled him out the rest of the way. When the Kings clinched their second Cup in three years, though, L.A. captain Dustin Brown handed the big, jug-eared silver mug to Regehr after concluding his own victory lap.

A year later, after the defending champs were shockingly eliminated from playoff contention, in Calgary, of all places, Robyn

Regehr called it a career—1,089 regular-season games later, 826 of them in Calgary. So it was only fitting that on January 11, 2015, he signed a one-day contract to retire as a Flame.

79 Kipper

He slipped into town with virtually no fanfare. Viewed as nothing more than a stopgap acquisition by coach/GM Darryl Sutter in exchange for a second-round draft pick. A hunk of Finnish Polyfilla to patch up and paste the team together while starting goaltender Roman Turek recovered from injury. He left a franchise legend.

The importance of Miikka Kiprusoff to the resurrection of the Calgary Flames cannot be overemphasized. Implacable, hiding a fierce competitive drive behind the most nonchalant of veneers, most nights he found himself propping up a mediocre-to-poor team. His durability was nothing short of amazing, averaging 73 appearances a season over a distinguished seven-year block of work.

Kiprusoff never seemed to be hindered by a performance ceiling. He just kept topping himself. "There seems to be something every day," marveled defenseman Mark Giordano "that sorta makes you lean back and say, 'Wow!'"

Sutter had known Kiprusoff from their days together in San Jose, where he languished in the minors, eventually deemed surplus requirements behind Evgeni Nabokov and Vesa Toskala. But the Flames boss could never have envisioned the return on investment he'd enjoy. In short order, Kiprusoff became not merely the de facto No. 1 in net at the Saddledome but the undisputed cornerstone of the franchise—more valuable, arguably, than even Jarome Iginla. That first season, he finished with a modern-day-low 1.69

goals-against average, and the Flames reached the playoffs for the first time in seven years.

And then they went on the memorable springtime run, bolstered by Iginla's follow-me leadership and backstopped by Kiprusoff's brilliance, all the way to Game 7 of the Stanley Cup Finals against the Tampa Bay Lightning.

If that 2004 playoff run cemented his status among the elite, coming back from a wasted lockout year, the 2005–06 season produced his finest run in the colors, a master class that netted the silent Finn his first and only Vezina Trophy: 42 wins, a 2.07 goals-against average, and a .923 save percentage. Predictably, Kiprusoff had no interest in being on hand in Las Vegas to pick up his hardware. He was most likely off on a boat in Finland somewhere, fishing.

Kiprusoff became nearly as famous for his inscrutability as his goaltending. He used to tiptoe out of the dressing room while the media horde interrogated Iginla, actually putting an admonishing "Shhhhh!" finger to his lips to demand silence so he could escape undetected. There hadn't been a goalie this laid back since Grant Fuhr was in his Cirque du Soleil prime with the Edmonton Oilers. "For a lot of us," said teammate Michael Cammalleri, "there's probably a lot to learn about personal happiness, the way he goes about his business and his life. Whatever he's doing, he's enjoying it."

Despite his reluctance to give anything away, Kiprusoff's popularity soared. Nearly as many No. 34 jerseys could be spotted around the Saddledome as No. 12s. Embodying the phenomenon was the Kipper Kid (or Mini-Miikka, whichever you prefer). Brendan Peters began attending games at nine years old, during the 2005–06 season, dressed in Kiprusoff garb—mask, sweater, pads, the lot—in tribute to his idol. He'd delight the hometown crowd by mimicking No. 34's every movement during warmups (Peters, by then an 11th-grade student at Notre Dame High School, returned for one last performance at Kiprusoff's second-to-last home appearance, seven and a half years later).

Kiprusoff continued to shine, but Calgary's deep playoff run had been a one-off. By the 2012–13 season, the end seemed near. The direction of the organization was changing. Bob Hartley had been installed as coach. Kiprusoff was 36. Iginla, his iconic sidekick, had been dealt to Pittsburgh. Kiprusoff had been deeply unhappy over dwindling playing time. So there was an air of finality about April 20, 2013, Calgary's final home game of the season, although nothing had been formally announced. And Miikka Kiprusoff, the silent showman, did not disappoint, stopping 36 Anaheim shots in a 3–1 Calgary win, the end of another dispiriting campaign that resulted in missing the playoffs.

One last time the Scotiabank Saddledome faithful had the chance to stand as one and make the joint reverberate with the familiar chant of "Kip-PER! Kip-PER! Kip-PER!"

"I *love* watching him," murmured goaltending coach Clint Malarchuk that night. "I *love* working with him. For me, he's the best. The very best. My hero. I'm so proud of the guy. So I'm a little misty about it. Yeah, I am. I'm a goalie, he's a goalie, okay? If I had his talent and my personality? I'd be a frickin' movie star."

"I've been doing this for a living for a long time," admitted Kiprusoff, tipping his hat ever so slightly. "Even before I came over here, I played in Europe. That's been my life. Nothing else. It takes lots from you."

The official announcement arrived on September 10, only confirming expectations. And true to form, Kiprusoff exited as he'd arrived: with no fanfare, no formal media conference, no tears, no good-byes, no nostalgic reminisces. He just...vanished into the mists. "It is quintessential Kipper," agreed the Flames GM at the time, Jay Feaster. "It was difficult enough to get him to do these kind of things when we were paying him, and in theory as a player we had some leverage..."

No matter. What he left behind—the memories, the highlight-reel saves, the 2004 run—was more than ample.

In nine seasons as a Flame, his GAA rose above 3.00 just once and his save percent dipped below .900 just once—both in that final, uncharacteristic 24-appearance final season—and by then he had usurped every franchise record at the position from Mike Vernon. As Clint Malarchuk said in tribute: the very best.

80 The 2004 Run

The greatest player in all of hockey at that moment in time looked so totally of character. Oddly lost, confused, disbelieving. "We thought," said Jarome Iginla softly, engulfed by media inside the visitor's dressing room at the St. Pete Times Forum on the night of June 7, 2004, "that was going to be us out there, hearing that music, listening to the crowd, lifting that Cup. We wanted to win it for Calgary, our city, the fans who've been so great to us, best in the league. They showed what a sports city is."

Iginla paused, searching for words. "We wanted to win it for so many reasons," he went on haltingly. "This is going to sit with me for a long time. This is an indescribable sting. This is the worst feeling you can have, the worst I've ever felt, anything I've been a part of. The toughest loss by a thousand times. We worked...so hard. We got...so close."

They had pushed so far, overcome so much, beaten three favored opponents—the Vancouver Canucks, Detroit Red Wings, and San Jose Sharks—en route to an improbable, illogical Stanley Cup Finals against the Tampa Bay Lighting. And then they were left to try and make some sense of a 2–1 Game 7 loss that shattered the fairy tale.

Of the three Stanley Cup Finals involving the Calgary Flames, 2004 remains unique, for the sheer confounded unexpectedness of it all. The 1986 run, too, came out of nowhere, but the vibes being given were nowhere near this powerful. In 1989 nothing less than a championship was expected of a 117-point, Presidents' Trophy–winning group. In 2004, to everyone's utter amazement, a team dismissed by virtually everyone ended a seven-year franchise playoff absence and pushed past the first round for the first time since the Cup-capturing season.

They were driven relentlessly on by the pointed cowboy kickers of coach/GM Darryl Sutter, powered by Iginla's unparalleled mix of mojo and moxie and by Miikka Kiprusoff's brilliance in goal. But there was so, so much more to those 2004 Flames.

They were a cast of characters straight out of a Dickens novel. Ville Nieminen's maniacal Heath Ledger / Joker grin. The dramatics of serial series clincher Martin Gelinas. The defense-playing Doors—Steve Montador and frizzy-haired Mike Commodore—lighting a fire that would've pleased even the Lizard King, Jim Morrison, himself. The articulate Andrew Ference. The human sound bite, Craig Conroy. Senses-sapping defenseman Robyn Regehr's Tunnel of Death at optimum operation.

The road was difficult and dramatic, set in motion by beating the Canucks at Rogers Arena on a Gelinas OT goal. Slaying the Detroit Red Wings—15 points their better over the regular season—in six on another Gelinas goal at the Saddledome, and then dispatching the San Jose Sharks in another half dozen games in the Western Conference Finals.

In snapping a 2–2 series deadlock and dusting Darryl Sutter's former employers, Calgary became the first Canada-based team since the 1994 Montreal Canadiens to reach the Finals. "This," said Iginla, "is the chance of a lifetime."

Flames assistant coach Jim Playfair likened the captain's quest to that of a friend, Dr. Dennis Brown, who twice had made an assault on Mt. Everest's summit, getting as far as the Hillary Step—a shelf a tantalizing 100 feet from the end of the quest—before being forced to turn back. "And that," said Playfair, "is where Jarome's at. He's at [the Hillary] Step. And now he's only a hundred feet from the summit."

The final series was a back-and-forth affair, the teams trading 4–1 wins, then splitting the next two games via shutout. Calgary took Game 5 3–2 in overtime on a goal from Oleg Saprykin to assume control of the series. Game 6 will forever be remembered in southern Alberta for "that" non-goal, a puck deflected off one of the skates of Gelinas that appeared to cross the goal in OT that would've (should've?) clinched a second Stanley Cup win for the franchise.

Waved off on the ice and not reviewed, the debate as to whether Tampa netminder Nikolai Khabibulin had in fact kicked the puck out with his right toe before it inched across the line rages on to this day. Rubbing itching powder into an open wound, old Flames spare part–turned–Tampa superstar Martin St. Louis sniped 33 seconds into double overtime to send the series back south.

As is often the case, Game 7 itself failed to fire to life. Both sides looked spent from nearly two months of slogging through adversity. The homestanding Bolts jumped in front 2–0, but the Flames, as was their custom, continued to fight uphill, swimming desperately against the current. A goal by Craig Conroy shaved the deficit in half, but a late save from Khabibulin off defenseman Jordan Leopold was as close as the visitors would come.

Sutter admitted afterward that his team was running on fumes. "In the end," he acknowledged, "we ran out of gas. The longer the series went, the tougher it was going to be. I think we tried to summon all we could in terms of energy. In the end, they had more legs than we did."

Anyone who says that time heals all wounds has never come up a nickel short in a Stanley Cup Finals Game 7. Years later, defenseman Rhett Warrener harkened back to that. It marked his third time to a Stanley Cup Finals. And his third time coming away empty. "Remember that movie *The Perfect Storm*?" mused Warrener. "They think there's sunlight there for a little bit, and they think they're going to get out of that storm. But the guy says, 'It's not going to let us go.' That's how I felt."

They couldn't have realized it at the time, such was the raw, immediate feeling of emptiness, but that season, that run, revitalized a stagnant franchise and kept it vital for the next four seasons. Only the passage of time can add that perspective.

Asked Conroy bitterly on that night of such crushing disappointment, "Whoever remembers who finished second?" More than a decade later in Calgary, no one has forgotten.

81 OT Hero

Over the course of one unforgettable springtime, the Flames spawned more heroes than Marvel Comics: Jarome Iginla's peerless leadership skills. Miikka Kiprusoff's acrobatics. Ville Nieminen's nefarious Joker sneer. Mike Commodore's finger-in-the-light-socket hair and Grizzly Adams beard. Darryl Sutter's bitter beer face. Craig Conroy's gift of the gab. Robyn Regehr's Tunnel of Death. And as memorable as any of it, Martin Gelinas' incredible run of dramatics.

Over that springtime, the 33-year-old well-traveled winger had a better knockout percentage than Sonny Liston, George Foreman, and Mike Tyson. "Oh, yeah, I still get people talking to me about it all the time," said Gelinas. "Not the kids, of course. But their dads. The people who were here and Flames fans at that time. And that's nice.

"It's such a great market, Calgary. When you win, the city just rallies around you, wraps its arms around you. Such a fun time in my career. I'll always remember it. We came out of nowhere and became a great story, had a great run.

"My game in the 2004 playoffs was a hardworking, blue-collar game, get to the blue paint and get it done. People appreciated that, they were happy for me, and more important, they enjoyed our team winning."

In the spring of 2004, Gelinas was christened the Eliminator. And small wonder. He scored three consecutive series-winning goals (only the second player ever to do so) as the Flames embarked on a journey that took them to one game of an improbable—no, impossible—Stanley Cup victory.

In order:

- **First round:** At 85 seconds of overtime to eliminate the favored Canucks, 3–2 in Game 7 at Rogers Arena
- **Second round:** At 19:13 of the first OT period to stun Stevie Y, Brett Hull, Nicklas Lidstrom, and the rest of the favored Red Wings 1–0 in Game 7 at the Pengrowth Saddledome
- **Third round:** At 3:46 of the second period in Game 6, a goal that provided the Flames with a 2–1 lead and would hold up the rest of the way to stand as the game-winning goal to slay the favored San Jose Sharks

"The biggest one, in my mind," said Gelinas, now an assistant coach for the Flames, "was the goal against Vancouver in the first round. We weren't even supposed to make the playoffs, let alone win a round.

"And it had been so long"—15 years—"since the franchise had won one. Everyone in the city wanted it so badly. That goal made us believe we could go further. Made us believe we could beat anyone.

"It was special for me for two reasons. One, it was my daughter's birthday, April 19, which was fantastic. And two, I remember four days before I scored that goal, Darryl Sutter said, 'If I had another left winger, you wouldn't be playing.' That fired me [up] to just want to prove him wrong and, more importantly, prove myself right. That goal was a turning point for me, and for the team."

Dramatically, the Canucks had tied matters with 5.7 seconds left in regulation. But with Ed Jovanovski perched, fuming, in the

The Eliminator strikes again, this time against the San Jose Sharks in the 2004 Western Conference Finals.

penalty box, Gelinas cashed in from the side of the net after captain Jarome Iginla had made a patented power move to the front of Alex Auld's cage.

"We came into the room after they tied it so late," recalled Gelinas, "and it was *so* quiet. And then, I'll always remember this, Jarome stood up and said, 'Look, if someone had told us at the beginning of the season we'd be in overtime of Game 7 against the Canucks, we'd have said great.' The attitude changed right there."

During that 26-game odyssey, Gelinas poached eight goals, second on the team to Iginla's 13. And when he scored, he made it count. "I mean, you don't want to think about it too much. Or try to explain it. You just go with it. Just enjoy it. Because something like that doesn't happen very often, if ever."

Even more remarkable, a potential Game 6–winning, series-winning, Cup-clinching goal that would've been credited to No. 23 was chalked off. A puck deflecting off one of Gelinas' skates appeared to cross the goal line before Tampa Bay's Nikolai Khabibulin curled the toe of his right pad and booted it out. That goal would've given the Flames a lead in a game they eventually lost in double OT.

"It's upsetting," admitted Gelinas. "Still. Because it was right there for us. The Stanley Cup. And sure you have to overcome those kinds of things and just play through them.

"I remember after I went in and talked to Collie [Campbell] about it, and they were all saying, 'The angle of the camera where the puck is suggests it's not in.' But a picture is a picture. They dropped the puck, and it was done." So were Gelinas and his gallant mates, beaten 2–1 at Tampa in Game 7, their adventure grinding to an unsatisfying end.

Calgary has never forgotten or forgiven. "You always wonder 'What if?'" conceded Gelinas. "Most of the time, I'm a big believer in things happening for a reason. But I still struggle to find a reason for that."

82 The Heritage Classic

Nothing much ever fazed Miikka Kiprusoff. Not, say, Brett Hull, dead center in the slot, wrists cocked, and the puck laying flat on his blade. Not screens or tips or 100 mph howitzers. Not the inevitable jostling in and around his blue-painted domain. Not even, as it turned out, practicing his particular magic outside in temperatures that, factoring in the wind chill, dipped to minus-21 degrees Celsius.

Following in the footsteps of the frigid but highly memorable and hugely successful inaugural Heritage Classic at Edmonton's Commonwealth Stadium eight years earlier, the Calgary Flames hosted the second edition in 2011. On February 20 of that year, a crowd of 41,022—bumped up from the site's customary football capacity of 36,650—huddled (tightly, for warmth) in McMahon Stadium, home of the CFL's Calgary Stampeders. The protagonists certainly had a history: the Flames and the Montreal Canadiens had collided in both the 1986 and 1989 Stanley Cup Finals.

In the lead-up to the game, the original weather forecast had dipped from a livable plus-2 degrees Celsius to a minus-15. "Minus-15?" blurted Flames left winger Alex Tanguay. "Yeah, that's cold. But Carnaval in Quebec City? That's *cold*."

Turns out, even Bonhomme Carnaval, the snowman synonymous with Quebec City's annual winter extravaganza, would've felt right at home. "It's not like it's going to be a total shock to us," said Calgary coach Brent Sutter, "because we already know what's going to happen. It's winter in Alberta. It's February. We know what time it's going to get dark. The lights will come on. It'll just be like a baseball game when you get to play under the lights."

The ice, predictably, was a chippy concern, the tone prior to puck drop light. Habs goaltender Carey Price had a Jacques Plante tribute model mask fashioned, following in the footsteps of the tuque—complete with pom-pom on top—predecessor Jose Theodore had favored to much acclaim in the first Classic. The Flames, meanwhile, had new duds whipped up for the occasion, complete with tiger-striped jerseys, cream-colored pants, and striped socks. Not the easiest on the eyes but a marketing bonanza.

For the ins and outs of such a unique experience, there were a few old hands to seek out. Calgary defenseman Steve Staios, for instance, had played in the Edmonton game eight years earlier, while one combatant per side—Montreal's Mike Cammalleri and the Flames' David Moss—had been part of the historic 2001 Cold War outdoor game at Spartan Stadium between Michigan State and the University of Michigan that drew a then-record hockey crowd of 74,544.

"We definitely want to enjoy this," said Flames captain Jarome Iginla. "It's a rare opportunity. It's exciting for the city, our fans, our families. We'll enjoy it, I'm sure. But it hasn't felt like we've been over-the-top excited. 'Oh my gosh, this is so cool' or anything like that. We've been taking things as they come.

"I've always enjoyed playing under the lights"—Iginla had a rink built in his backyard in Calgary—"so that'll be pretty cool, as the sun sets. That'll be unique. And yeah, you can't block all of that out."

Weekend festivities leading up to the Classic itself included two outdoor games at McMahon, including an alumni game that featured many of the stars from the 1986 and 1989 Cup battles, and the Western Hockey League's Calgary Hitmen versus the Regina Pats. Inside, at the Scotiabank Saddledome, Calgary's AHL franchise from Abbotsford, British Columbia, tangled with the Edmonton Oilers' top farm club from Oklahoma City. They were all just opening acts for the main event.

During the game, NHL ice guru Dan Craig had the ice continually flooded by hoses, fearing the weight of a Zamboni would cause disaster. The action had to be stopped numerous times to try and improve the playing surface. Once they got going, and between stoppages, the game itself (as did so many during his eye-popping tenure in southern Alberta) turned into an advertisement for the silent Finn, Kiprusoff.

He had a fairly uneventful first period, facing only eight shots, as his group dominated play and jumped ahead when Rene Bourque opened scoring via the power play at 8:09. During the middle stanza, however, the 2004 Vezina Trophy winner turned on the style. The Canadiens, warming to the cool conditions, fired 21 pellets at the Calgary net and came away frustrated, Kiprusoff stopping the lot. Ten more saves in the third translated into a 39-shot shutout for the game's first star. And even more crucially for the playoff-chasing Flames, an invaluable two points in a 4–0 whitewash. Defenseman Anton Babchuk, shorthanded got one score, Bourque another, and Tanguay scored the other Calgary goals.

"The first period was really cold," said Kiprusoff afterward, peeling off layers built up for warmth. "You had to stand outside there a little bit, and there were some problems with the ice, so it took quite a bit of time before the game started.

"Second and third periods, I felt good. I had something underneath and I felt better. I tried that diver's wetsuit yesterday, but it was too hot. Nice in the practice, but a little too much, I thought, for the game."

83 Dealing Dion

In only four and a half seasons in Calgary, Dion Phaneuf had certainly made himself a magnet for attention. Whether launching some idling interloper into the 10th row of the pricey seats just above the glass or driving the fan base crazy with a puzzling lapse in defensive concentration, his detractors and champions queued up in equal measure.

No one, though, on either side of the fence can argue Phaneuf failed to pack more than his share of debate and achievement into a Calgary stay that on first blush seemed destined for a longer run than *Les Mis* in London's West End.

As the ninth overall pick in the 2003 NHL Entry Draft, he went on to play his first NHL game two years later, on October 5, 2005, against the Minnesota Wild. Raw-edged, possessed of a rocket of a shot from the point and an apparently inexhaustible appetite for body contact, he did that most difficult of things for a young, unvarnished player—he made people *notice* him.

The Edmonton kid who moved halfway to Calgary to complete his junior commitment for the WHL Red Deer Rebels, coached by Brent Sutter, Alberta hockey royalty, then completed the journey south to fulfill his professional destiny. "To be honest, he's the first player I put my eye on," said Flames GM/coach Darryl Sutter, who was so tickled on draft day that he gave Phaneuf a hug up onstage at the Gaylord Entertainment Center (now Bridgestone Arena) in Nashville.

Sutter said, "Hey, remember what we're doing here. I just came from my daughter's graduation at high school. She's the same age as these guys, and I don't think she's going to be a professional in what she wants to do next year, either. We drafted Dion Phaneuf because we think he's going to be a hell of a player in the NHL. But he'll be a hell of a player at his own pace.

"But he's a kid with a lot of character. An Alberta boy. He's still a project—but a pretty good one. He's a great kid, full of piss and vinegar. And I love it."

Phaneuf's first two seasons as a pro bore out Sutter's boundless enthusiasm. As a rookie, he was only the third man ever to score 20 goals from the defense position, while eclipsing Gary Suter's 19-year-old franchise freshman record of 18. He was an All-Rookie Team selection and received a Calder Trophy finalist nod (the other two to survive the cut-down, Sidney Crosby and winner Alexander Ovechkin, didn't turn out too badly, either). Two years later, he was a finalist for the Norris Trophy as the NHL's top defenseman (no shame in losing to Nicklas Lindstrom on his sixth of eight wins) and received a spot on the NHL's first All-Star team.

The road ahead seemed littered with trophies, achievements, and a long stay at the Saddledome. Yet just 24 and only a couple years removed from that scintillating start, Dion Phaneuf's game tailed off to the point where he'd become such a lightning rod for controversy in Calgary that he found himself rumored to be on the trading block.

And on January 31, 2010, with the floundering Flames clinging to the eighth and final playoff spot in the Western Conference like a shied cat to the living room curtains Darryl Sutter shipped the not-long-before-untouchable/-untradeable/-unassailable defenseman to the Toronto Maple Leafs along with utility winger Freddie Sjostrom and Keith Aulie in exchange for center Matt Stajan, wingers Niklas Hagman and Jamal Mayers, and rear guard Ian White. Whether out of perceived necessity or growing panic is anyone's guess.

The deal itself was big enough—a blockbuster. But the implications went beyond its sheer scope. Phaneuf was the first of the Big Four cornerstones—which also numbered captain Jarome

Iginla, defenseman Robyn Regehr, and goalie Miikka Kiprusoff (a group Sutter had envisioned propelling the Flames to the Stanley Cup glory denied them in 2004)—to be shipped out, signaling an admission that the blueprint that had been put in place was flawed.

Only three weeks before pulling the trigger, the GM had scoffed at speculation Phaneuf was being shopped around. "Everything is false," he growled. "Whoever makes up that stuff is not doing anything. We've worked really hard at building a top young defense in the league, and our intention is to keep them, so that's [rumors] just from somebody who didn't have anything to do on that day. All that stuff is crap." Yes, well, one man's crap is the same man's…

"I still do think very highly of him," Sutter said in the wake of the trade. "But you have to remember how the economics affect that core group. You have a lot of money tied up in four or five guys.

"I'm not convinced that's the best route. Being able to spread [the salary dollars] out…reflects why we brought the forwards in. Because it balances it out. If you do the math, it's just about even."

Sutter reasoned that the off-season signing of Jay Bouwmeester and the emergence of a certain Mark Giordano—just back from self-imposed exile in the KHL—to go along with Robyn Regehr gave him a surplus on the blueline. "What impacted this…there's a gap on our team in terms of productive forwards," he continued. "The last seven or eight weeks, it sort of played out that we weren't getting that [expected offensive punch]. So we had to deal from the strength."

Phaneuf himself was stunned by the news. "If Wayne Gretzky can get traded," he reasoned, "anybody can get traded. But I was… very surprised."

It was rumored that Coach Brent Sutter, Phaneuf's junior mentor in Red Deer, had been kept out of the loop as the details to the mega-swap were being worked out, but he too put on the company face. "We all know what Dion has accomplished and the potential he has to move forward. I've known Dion a long time, from such a young age, 14. But this is part of the business. This is what happens at times, and it's happened here."

Reaction to the deal in Calgary was, predictably, mixed—met with either disbelief or relief. Dion Phaneuf had that effect on people. What's indisputable is this: the Flames went on to miss the postseason that spring…and four more in succession after that.

84 Family Ties

The only thing missing was the sight of a lonely tumbleweed skipping down a dusty main street in front of saloon doors swinging in the breeze. A double slug of Sutter—straight back, no chaser. Let the good times roll.

Yes, the southern Alberta horizon seemed so bright, so blue, so limitless the day of the hire—June 23, 2009—as Brent Sutter took coaching control of the Flames, to be backed by GM brother Darryl upstairs. "Can I just clear all of that up in a hurry?" said the GM that day, waving a hand toward his older sibling and incoming assistants Ryan McGill, Dave Lowry, and Jamie McLennan. "All four of these guys sitting here, I coached them all. They're all very strong guys in the locker room. Great team players. You could flip all their last names around, put the first names where you want. I'm the general manager and Brent's the head coach. This is the coaching staff. They were the very best people available. It didn't really matter what their last names were."

Two weeks earlier, Brent Sutter had resigned as coach following two seasons in New Jersey, citing a desire to be closer to his

Alberta roots. That was a possibility both he and Devils general manager Lou Lamoriello had agreed to when he took the New Jersey job. By chance, "Iron" Mike Keenan had been fired as big boss of the Flames three weeks prior to that.

By the end of Brent Sutter's tenure behind the Calgary bench, his brother—the man who'd turned the franchise around eight years before—had been fired amidst loud whispers of interference with the coach and a simmering unrest between the two. "So much was made of the relationship between Darryl and I," Brent Sutter said later. "Most it was overblown.

"At the end of the day, Darryl was the GM and I was the head coach. I do think there was no question that he thought he should still be coaching the team, though. He loves coaching. And the reality is: Darryl's a great coach. He's shown that in L.A. So that part was tough. Not unmanageable but tough.

"When he got to L.A., he talked about that—it's not easy being a GM/coach and then stepping down to be the GM alone. It was not Darryl's wish to step away from coaching. I know that.

"But people saying there was a disconnect between management and the coaches at that time…not true. There were certainly discussions held on the direction of the team, but that's normal. And the reality is you don't always get your way. Were there issues that had to be dealt with? Absolutely. And they were. The idea that it was dysfunctional, though…people ran with it."

Sutter's three years at the Flames helm produced 118 victories, 90 regulation losses, and 38 OT losses. Certainly not a poor record. But vitally there would be no postseason follow-up. In those years, Calgary was close, finishing 10th (five points out), 10th (three points out), and 9th (five points out), but couldn't quite find the formula to crack the top eight in a competitive Western Conference.

"Disappointing in the sense we never made playoffs in three years, and let's face it, that's what professional hockey is all about," Sutter acknowledged. "And yet there's also no question, looking at the team and the conference we were in, [that] the Calgary Flames were an 8th- to 10th-place team. They were not a 102-, 104-, or 105-point team. That was the reality. I came in with my eyes very wide open."

The most formidable obstacle in Sutter's view, then and now, was the demographics of the group at his disposal: older, entrenched, too secure. "I look back," Sutter said, "and probably the best we played was when we brought in the young kids. There was enthusiasm, there was excitement then. When a certain percentage of your players have played somewhere for a very long time, they become very comfortable. Too comfortable. And that makes getting the most out of them very, very difficult from a coaching perspective.

"Back then, the star players weren't getting younger; they were getting older. They were there for a reason; their contracts dictated it, but it certainly hurts the level of how the team can play. All you're doing is sitting in the mud, spinning your tires, and no progress is being made.

"Funny how after you leave, after you're gone, things you had discussions about, changes that had to be made, get made. That's disappointing, but that's the way it works. It's all about timing."

Bob Hartley ultimately replaced him behind the bench, a seismic shift in organizational philosophy was undertaken, and that dreaded *R* word (*rebuild*) was actually uttered aloud before the Flames' fortunes began improving.

Now back in familiar territory as owner, GM, and coach of the Western Hockey League's Red Deer Rebels, Brent Sutter still pulls for the team located an hour and half north down Highway 2. "Certainly no resentment, no hard feelings, on my part. I learned a lot. The Calgary ownership group is second to none. I have a tremendous amount of respect for every one of those people. I'm an Albertan. I want to see both the Flames and Oilers do well. Hockey's a part of us, right?

"Do I wish some things had been different during my time there? Of course. That's only natural. But there's no bigger fan of the Calgary Flames than me."

85 Iginla Exits

The whole night had a surreal, Rod Serling–ish feel to it. Speculation had been building as the 2013 trade deadline neared. Whispers grew ever louder, ever more persistent that Jarome Iginla, the smiling, stalwart superstar face of the franchise for more than a decade had waived his no-trade clause. And now, game on between the Calgary Flames and Colorado Avalanche that March 27, and no sign of the captain. Not even the lame, customary "upper body" or "lower body" subterfuge rolled out by the club to throw curious bloodhounds off the scent. Not only wasn't Iginla in the lineup, he wasn't anywhere in the building.

An audible buzz fizzed around the Scotiabank Saddledome when his name was announced as among that night's scratches. TSN's Mike Johnson, working between the benches, was grilled by Flames players about the latest info on a possible landing place.

The end had been hanging in the air for a while. In the previous home game a few days earlier Iginla scored the game-winning goal in the third period, the 83rd of his career, to slay the St. Louis Blues, and the building erupted in tribute. The by-now-familiar "Ig-GY! Ig-GY!" chant had washed over him one final time as a Calgary Flame. That reaction, the adulation, would serve as a good-bye.

In the dressing room following the Colorado game, Iginla's gear hung in his stall, as always. An eerie sight. The list of teams he'd approved as potential destinations was reported to comprise Boston, Pittsburgh, L.A., and Chicago. (By the way, the Flames did beat the Avs, 4–3. Not that anyone much noticed.)

"He's been a superstar in this league," said Iginla's left winger and pal Alex Tanguay in tribute (the two would, of course, reunite a year and a half later in Denver). "He's going to be a Hall of Famer. It's been a privilege playing with him.

"He's a role model. The kids that have grown up in this city the last 15 years, for most of them, Jarome Iginla is their idol. It's sad to see it come to this day, but it's the business we're in.

"We've had some great years together. What a player. What a person. I mean, what can I say?"

There wasn't anything left to say. The only thing left to do was wait. The evening ground along. Speculation increased. Finally, a deal seemed a fait accompli and involved the Boston Bruins: Iginla to Beantown for a conditional first-round pick, defense prospect Matt Bartkowski and Providence Bruins center Alexander Khokhlachev. At least Bruins GM Peter Chiarelli thought so.

Turns out Iginla had say, he was hedging, and the chance to play with Sidney Crosby—his Olympic gold medal collaborator—and Evgeni Malkin simply proved too enticing. So when Flames general manager Jay Feaster strolled into the Ed Whalen Media Lounge at 11:30 PM MST and announced Iginla had been shipped to the Penguins for two college prospects and a first-round pick, the news threw everyone for a loop.

"We as an organization owe a tremendous debt of gratitude to Jarome," said Feaster, "not only for what he did for the franchise during his tenure as a player here and as our captain, but also for the fact that now, as we recognize that despite our best efforts, and despite the work we've put in, we've fallen short of the goals we set for ourselves as an organization."

The next day, Iginla reflected on his time in Calgary and the hard-to-wrap-your-head-around idea of playing somewhere, anywhere, else. "You hear it all the time—mixed emotions," he said, pausing at times to compose himself. "My teammates, the city, the organization. To leave, it's tough. But I'm also very excited about the opportunity to go to Pittsburgh to play with [Crosby and Malkin] and do some good things there.

"It's a very difficult day and feeling right now, because this has been my home—I've grown up here. I've obviously only played here, but I do appreciate fans when they say that they hope I go and win. I hope I do too."

86 Iginla Returns

It was his homecoming night—December 10, 2013—and he had returned to a place that nurtured him both professionally and personally. Jarome Iginla tried to leave the ice. He honestly did. But the way was blocked by his Boston Bruins teammates. So what was a guy to do? Take another couple spins. The decibel level continued to rise. The spotlight sought him out. The Bruins weren't about to let him leave. Neither were the 19,000-plus fans who had found in him the ideal leader, the everyman star, the consummate icon.

"It was pretty forced," laughed Iginla, a humble sort, finally allowed to escape into the sanctity of the visiting dressing room. "Z [Zdeno Chara] and the guys were great and wouldn't let me off the ice. I went for a loop, and they said, 'No, no—one more.' And I went for another, and they said, 'No, no—one more.' It was nice for the fans, and by the end, they also probably wanted me off the ice."

There had been other emotional homecomings down through the years. Many, in fact, as one by one the players from that championship team of 1989 were dispersed to other locales, different challenges: Al MacInnis, Joe Nieuwendyk, Doug Gilmour, Theo Fleury, Gary Roberts, Mike Vernon. But this return had something more, something special. This was, truly, the Return of the King.

"No, never anything like this," chuckled Boston lineman Milan Lucic at the circus that awaited Iginla when the Bruins reached the Scotiabank Saddledome, flying in from Toronto to practice the day before their meeting with the Flames. "[I've never] experienced anything like this before. With anyone. But if you look at the last generation, from, say, 2000 on, I don't think anyone's left an imprint on their team and organization as much as Jarome Iginla did here."

Even the new crop of Calgary Flames were caught up in the buzz. Center Joe Colborne, for instance, had grown up in town, loving the team, idolizing its captain. "The sweater?" blurted Colborne, taken slightly aback that one even had to ask. "Oh, yeah. Of course I had one. A No. 12. With the name plate? What do you think? With everything. Can't remember when I got it exactly. Christmas? Birthday? I don't know. I got it just…just because. Because he was my favorite player. Because he was everyone's favorite player. It seemed every person in town had one of those sweaters. You'd see so many 12s walking around on game days you couldn't keep count."

Those No. 12s were back in force on December 10. Slightly more than eight months after Iginla had waived his no-trade clause and been peddled to Pittsburgh, he was back…as a Bruin. It didn't matter. If he'd come back as an Edmonton Oiler, the city would still have (grudgingly) wrapped its arms around him for one final hug.

Before puck drop, a 1:15 montage of Iginla moments flickered triumphantly on the Jumbotron as the players leaned against the boards, heads tilted, to take in the show. And what a show it was.

"I had a great sleep last night, actually," Iginla admitted after the game. "I wasn't sure how it was going to be. But I had a real good sleep. Honestly, just excited about the game. Kinda like a little kid."

And maybe it took a little kid—four-and-a-half-year-old Ryan Howden—to epitomize how an entire populace was feeling. At the morning skate of game day, Ryan was there for an autograph, outfitted with a red Calgary Flames jersey adorned with autographs in black Sharpie. A No. 12 on the back, naturally. On the front, though, a Boston Bruins crest had been attached.

"Going back," Jarome Iginla had mused the week before, "makes me realize how fast the time does go. I remember older players telling me that when I was young, and I was like, 'Yeah, whatever.' Now I'm telling 26-year-olds the same thing! They're telling me. 'Ah, I'll only play until I'm 31 or 32.' And I'm like, 'Okay, we'll see.' Funny, the way your perspective shifts. I mean I did my best. As a team, we did our best. We didn't win a Cup, but I played as hard as I could; we played as hard as we could. I hope the reaction is positive."

He needn't have worried.

87 The Flood of 2013

The first photographs, released a few days after the fact, had an eerie, almost *Titanic* discovery feel to them. Debris floating in murky water that has risen eight rows high in the lower bowl. Mud everywhere. The reality proved even worse than the images.

The southern Alberta floods of 2013 were devastating in so many ways. On June 19, 2013, after days of increasingly heavy rain, the unthinkable became reality. A total of 32 states of emergency were declared and 28 emergency operations centers were established as water levels rose and communities were placed under threat.

Among the hardest-hit areas near downtown was low-lying Stampede Park. More than 30 million gallons of water cascaded from the overflowing banks of the Elbow and Bow Rivers and into the Scotiabank Saddledome, the then-30-year-old home of the Calgary Flames. Water levels submerged the back parking lot, destroying the ice plant, television control room, event-level kitchen, more than a quarter million dollars of food, dressing rooms, and one-of-a-kind franchise memorabilia. Flames president Ken King described the damage on the Saddledome's lower floor as "a total loss."

The $5 billion in damage and $1.7 billion in insurance claims caused by the flooding in southern Alberta made it the costliest natural disaster in Canadian history. In a documentary on the flood, *Back in the Saddle: Face Off With the Flood*, Calgary mayor Naheed Nenshi admitted, "It was like a stab in the heart for every Calgarian to see the Saddledome underwater."

In the aftermath of the carnage, the idea of beginning a National Hockey League season on time seemed utterly impossible. Contingency plans for relocating early season Flames games were bandied about as the city began to recover from a natural disaster unparalleled in its scope.

Ironically, the scope of the loss became an ally. "We quickly came to the realization that a full gut was what was required, and we weren't going to be able to salvage anything," said Libby Raines, VP of building operations. "And in a way that actually helped the process because you're just in full demolition. You're not waiting to make decisions—'Can this be saved? Can that be saved?'"

Less than 69 days after disaster struck, the Cana restoration teams turned what had seemed at the moment of crisis to be a lost cause back to the hockey club. Director of building operations Robert Blanchard estimated that 650,000 man-hours had been put in to make the Saddledome functional and puck-ready.

To a city's relief, California country rockers the Eagles reopened the Saddledome on September 11, 2013. Then, three nights later, the building was in good enough shape to host the Calgary end of the annual split-squad games against the northern rival Oilers. Workers who tirelessly toiled in the cleanup efforts were invited. And on October 6 the Flames kicked off their regular season, on time, at home, against the Vancouver Canucks. *On time.*

Photographs showing how the Saddledome looked after the initial cleanup now hang around the walls of the building, as a reminder of the disaster and the group effort that pulled out the venue from a deep state of decrepitude.

The efforts of the cleanup crew were not lost on the building's most famed tenants. "If we would have been all over the place during training camp, I can't guarantee that we would have been this prepared at this time, with all the traveling and changing rinks," praised Flames coach Bob Hartley. "Thanks to those people, we were in our rink, in our facility. What these people have done is amazing. Just amazing. We're always preaching teamwork to our players. Well, this...this is the greatest example of teamwork I have ever seen."

88 Gio

Mark Giordano can be called the quintessential self-made man. Initially unheralded. Undrafted. Now there isn't a team among the 30 organizations that wouldn't, in a heartbeat, stick Giordano on their blueline in any key situation.

"You look at Mark Giordano's story, and it's a story every player can look at and take something from," lauded former Flames coach Bob Hartley. "Hard work. Determination. Self-belief. He's had nothing handed to him. People see that and they respond to it. He instinctively knows how to do things the right way.

"The one great quality Gio has is he makes people around him better. I know you hear this all the time. It sounds easy. It's not. He's a pillar for us. Our compass. For me, the perfect captain." And Hartley is a man, for anyone in need of reminding, who was lucky enough to be able to call on Joe Sakic during their winters spent together pushing the Colorado Avalanche forward.

Hartley compared No. 5 Giordano to his skipper in Denver, Hall of Famer Sakic. "You talk to Joe, you talk to Gio, and the

With Gio on the ice, the future looks bright for Calgary.

conversations are very, very similar," he said. And Calgary GM Brad Treliving likened Giordano to Arizona Coyotes veteran stalwart Shane Doan after his time in the desert. Lofty praise, indeed.

Now 33, Mark Giordano has become a mentor to the young, emerging Calgary defense corps—to pairing sidekick T.J. Brodie, to Dougie Hamilton. He's an example for all the young Flames—Sean Monahan, Johnny Gaudreau, Mikael Backund, etc.—to emulate.

He succeeded icon Jarome Iginla as captain when he was traded, which, in context of team and influence, is somewhere along the line of following Sinatra at the Sands or the Beatles on *Ed Sullivan*. Yet he is already regarded as being among the game's finest leaders.

Yet the Giordano story, then to now, is far from straightforward. In 2004 Calgary GM Darryl Sutter signed the unheralded defenseman after taking stock of his skills at a summer camp held by the Flames. Giordano had just spent two years playing for the Owen Sound Attack of the Ontario Hockey League and would go on to spend his first two pro seasons toiling for the Flames' minor-league affiliates of the day: the Lowell Lock Monsters and Omaha Ak-Sar-Ben Knights.

But there was always something extra there—something that just needed coaxing out, needed nurturing. Phoenix Coyotes associate coach Jim Playfair, a Calgary assistant coach at the time and one of Giordano's early pro mentors, said, "You could tell early on when I was [in Calgary], he was going to be the next captain of the Calgary Flames. I mean you could just…tell. I said that to a lot of people over the years. And that doesn't make me a genius, by any means. It was just…obvious.

"Did I know at that time he'd one day be this caliber of player? Of course not. But you could see the potential, the qualities in him, almost right away. The way he carried himself, the way he worked on and off the ice. He's got an air, a quiet demand of excellence around him."

Giordano's first sizeable slice of NHL activity arrived in 2006–07, when he played 48 games for the big club.

The next season, unable to reach a contractual agreement with the Flames and feeling nothing more could be mined out of another term in the AHL, he shocked many by opting to head overseas, agreeing to terms on a one-year deal with HC Dynamo Moscow of the Kontinental Hockey League. Many in Calgary wondered if he'd ever be seen again, if he hadn't thrown his career away. "He didn't make a big noise, he didn't sit out, didn't go home, didn't pout," said Playfair. "I don't think he went to Russia because he liked the weather there. I don't think he went to Russia to learn Russian. He didn't go to make a bunch of money. He didn't do it to stick it up anybody's ass. He went over there to play."

In 2014 he was on Canadian GM Steve Yzerman's Olympic radar for Sochi. In 2015 he played in his first NHL All-Star Game, and the rest of the hockey world began to realize what Calgarians had been onto for a while.

In the 2014–15 season he had 48 points, was a plus-13, and was on the ice in virtually every key situation for a team afforded little room for error. He was a clear front runner for the Norris Trophy as the loop's top defenseman before suffering a torn bicep in the dying seconds of a February 25, 2015, 3–1 victory at New Jersey. An awkward-looking play, with Giordano falling to the ice after appearing to be accidentally tripped by Devils forward Steve Bernier. His season was cruelly over. As the only player to be a part of the last Calgary playoff team, in the spring of 2007, he was forced into the role of uneasy spectator for their long-awaited return to the postseason.

So how far has Giordano come? Well, back in 2007, still trying to establish himself as an everyday NHLer, he forsook the Flames and the NHL, fleeing to Russia and HC Dynamo Moscow of the

KHL over a contract impasse and a lack of playing assurances. Fast-forward eight years to late August 2015, and he's upgraded to the franchise's single-most-vital asset, signing a six-year contract extension worth $40.5 million. And now that he's signed, sealed, and delivered—on board for an additional six years—he remains a major part of why the future is full of such possibilities.

89 Sean Monahan

Understand, Darryl Sutter isn't known as a floral-arrangement kinda guy. Tossing bouquets around willy-nilly is far, far removed from his style. Sutter, as everyone knows, is a pay-your-dues sort. An earn-your-keep man. Old-school, in the truest sense of the term, believing implicitly in hard work, subservience to the cause, and working your way up the ladder.

So when, on a visit by the L.A. Kings to the Scotiabank Saddledome in the spring of 2015, the dour Kings coach trotted out hefty praise for a 20-year-old kid finishing off only his second year in the big show, more than a few eyebrows shot up in disbelief. "I don't think [Sean] Monahan gets enough credit in the league," maintained Sutter, the former Flames uber-boss, that morning. "Everybody talks about the centermen in [the Western Conference], and they don't talk about Sean Monahan. They should. He's probably in that [Jonathan] Toews group in terms of all-around. Can play minutes, play in situations." Heady stuff, such comparisons.

Although fading toward the end of his rookie campaign—an affliction suffered by most kids his age entering a man's league— the sixth overall pick in the 2014 draft out of the Ottawa 67s still managed a commendable 22-goal, 34-point first-look season. Solid enough overall for the Flames to keep him rather than ship him back to junior when the cutoff deadline arrived.

"When I was his age," mused Calgary boss Bob Hartley, "I was working at PPG, the factory in my hometown. I got married at 19, bought my first house, and was playing Junior B hockey. I remember the house cost $49,500 and the mortgage was probably $44,000. So yeah, when you think about it, where he is at his age, what he's done, it's pretty amazing."

Usually acclimation to the hurly-burly world of pro hockey at the highest level is a gradual one. But in short order, despite his tender years, Monahan was being pitted head-to-head against the crème de la crème of centermen in the west—Ryan Getzlaf, Anze Kopitar, "Jumbo" Joe Thornton, Toews, etc. "If you're going to win the Masters," reasoned the coach, "you'd rather do it paired with Tiger on Sunday afternoon, right?"

Oh, there were the inevitable dips and sways, and a nondisplaced hairline fracture of the left foot slowed him down some, but by then it'd already become clear the kid was ready for prime time. The promise of year one gave way to a 2014–15 breakout season, particularly after Hartley paired off his promising sophomore with rookie whiz Johnny Gaudreau and the sublime yet erratic Jiri Hudler. Their chemistry proved immediate and prolific.

Interestingly, for a player still so young still, Monahan had to intermittently be reminded to take attacking chances. "I was talking to him a little bit about who as an organization we want him to be," explained Hartley. "I talked about his role since the start of the year. I reminded him that it's okay for him to go on the offense.

"He's been collecting points, but he's such a great young man, so committed to whatever a coach is gonna tell him that he follows it by the letter. The ultimate team guy. As we know, there's some independent contractors in this business. I told him, 'Monny, you need to explore a little bit the offensive side of the game.' I'm not trying to make a checker out of Sean Monahan, by no means. I just reminded him.

"Usually it's the other way around, it's all about offense. Since the start of the year I've given him a role to play against the Datsyuks and the Sedins and the Getzlafs, and Monny's so proud he wants to do it by the letter. He wants to shut them down, but at the same time my message was: 'I appreciate everything you do and I'm so proud of you, but at the same time, you can still take advantage of those players.'"

Additional responsibility seemed only to energize the teenager. "If I have to take a bigger role," Monahan reasoned, "so be it. Everyone wants to play more. Once you get on the ice more, you get more into the game. So I think this is going to be a big step for me."

In the final push to their first playoff berth in six seasons, the Monahan-Hudler-Gaudreau line sparkled, could arguably be labeled the league's best over the final two months of the regular campaign. Only heightening their importance, the trio finished 1-2-3 in club scoring: Hudler first (76 points), Gaudreau second (64 points), and Monahan third (62 points).

Not that other, outside forces weren't conspiring to build the Sean Monahan profile. A notoriously color-by-numbers quote (or maybe merely disinterested) for local media, Monahan's fake (yes, it is, actually) Twitter account often gets as much publicity as the man himself. The now-famous @boringmonahan has attracted 62,000 followers, a mountain of publicity, and includes such gems as: "Sam Bennett scored 4 goals tonight. I said Sam, you must have had lucky charms for breakfast but he said he didn't" or "Mason Raymond said everything on TV sucks. I said maybe we should watch the Oilers game and then we both started laughing. It was so funny." A one-joke affair, surely, but Flames fans seem never to tire of the gag. Or, obviously, its inspiration.

On August 18, 2016, after a career-high 63 point 2015–16 campaign, the Flames signed their star center, a pending restricted free agent, to a seven-year, $44.625 million contract. "Loyalty is key," said Monahan the day his signing was announced. "Obviously I want to be here. If you could play until you're 50, I would sign a 20-year contract. This is where I want to be."

90 Burke

Tie carefully askew, gray hair cascading backward in waves—that familiar look, but Brian Burke swore on a stack of Gideons that he'd changed, that he no longer felt the need to dictate or incite.

All the attending media in the Ed Whalen Media Lounge that day smirked while rubbing their hands raw with barely unrestrained glee that such a cauldron of controversy, such a dependable quote machine (This was the man, after all, legendary for such gems as: "*Sedin* is not Swedish for 'punch me' or 'headlock me in a scrum'" and, after a bitter salary arbitration with Brendan Morrison: 'After inviting us into the alley, you can't complain if you get kicked in the groin') had arrived to brighten up dull days.

During his years in Hartford, Vancouver, Anaheim, and Toronto, Burke morphed into one of the game's most fascinating personalities, a my-way-or-the-highway kinda guy. "I know people think I need to be driving the bus all the time," he protested, seated beside GM Jay Feaster, after being hired by the Calgary Flames as president of hockey operations back on September 3, 2013. "Well, I'm actually a pretty good teammate, too.

"The day-to-day guy, the guy that you talk to every day, is the coach. 'Played last night, day off today. What about line combinations? What about injuries?' That should be the coach. The transactional guy, if you make a trade, whether it's a big trade or a little trade, the guy that explains it is the guy that pulls the trigger, that's Jay. So I don't think there's any way this works unless the guy in my position takes a lesser role.

"To me it's not protecting Jay. Jay's a big boy. He's got as many rings as I do. It's more, 'This is how it has to work.' So no, I don't intend to be front and center. Actually, it'll be a nice break after being front and center."

No one, naturally, believed so much as one syllable of it. Everyone was convinced Burke, in typical fashion, would be stomping around the Saddledome soon enough, unable to resist his own worst instincts, like Godzilla trampling Tokyo underfoot, picking media fights, butting in on then-GM Feaster and coach Bob Hartley while generally entertaining the masses. Surprise, surprise.

Oh, he has not been immune to the occasional flare-up. Old habits, remember, die hard. The Bob Hartley–John Tortorella feud was retriggered by a bizarre corridor confrontation on January 18, 2014, with the Canucks boss—incensed over a line brawl that opened the game. During the intermission, the volatile Tortorella tried to storm the Flames' dressing room. Nearly four months later, during the season curtain-dropper, another incident—Paul Byron ramming Daniel Sedin into the woodwork from behind—was followed by a Tortorella postgame tantrum.

Burke felt the need to volley back. "John Tortorella was on my staff for the Olympics in 2010," he said. "He's a good guy. I don't know what's going on in his head, but you know what? Shut your mouth and worry about your team. Leave my coach alone." Ah, now *this* was more like it.

As quickly as the ember flared, it cooled again. Mostly, Brian Burke has been true to his word, content to work behind the scenes. A sort of grumpy-bear Wizard of Oz: the Man Behind the

Curtain. Not that his quieter, less public self had lost an iota of organizational ambition. The Flames missed the postseason (for the fifth straight year) in his first season. They'd shown improvement, bumped up expectations, but the disappointing finale was the same as people in Calgary had become all too accustomed to.

"This isn't a fun day for me today, missing the playoffs," said Burke, steely-eyed, in his exiting state-of-the-union address. "That means you failed. Your whole organization failed. It's that simple. I don't want to be up here again next year explaining a non-playoff season. So yes, the expectations go up. Yes, we expect the kids to do more. Yes, we expect to add personnel in the off-season to make us bigger and better. So yes, go ahead and raise the bar. That's fine with me."

That summer Burke was instrumental in the hire of current GM Brad Treliving from the Phoenix Coyotes organization to replace the fired Feaster. A bold, forward-thinking move, selecting a young up-and-comer for his first managerial stint instead of an old, familiar face.

Treliving certainly didn't seem the least concerned at the prospect of habitual interference from Burke. "The other reality of life is that we all have bosses," he joked. "I mean that's just how it works. When I leave here and go home, I've got a boss there; her name's Julie, and she scares the heck out of me a lot of nights. That's how it works. So this is not anything new. And I have zero— zero—reservation about how it's going to work."

It's worked out great having Burke on board. "He's a great resource, a great sounding board," said assistant GM Craig Conroy. "There isn't much Burkie hasn't seen over the course of his career. That kind of experience for the rest of us is invaluable."

Opinionated. In your face. Garrulous. That's Brian Burke. But largely content behind the scenes. That, shockingly, is him too.

91 Remembering Monty

A week removed from the one-year anniversary of that terrible, numbing day, Rhett Warrener found himself looking back. "A lot of those emotions," admitted the former Flames hard-rock defenseman, "the ones you felt at that time, come back. I've found myself thinking about Steve, about what happened, a lot these last couple of weeks."

On February 15, 2015, Steve Montador, one of those indispensible blue-collar linchpins of the compelling 2004 Stanley Cup fun, was found dead in his Mississauga, Ontario, home. He was 35 and had been battling post-concussion syndrome. Adding another tragic dimension to the loss, four days after Montador's death, his girlfriend gave birth to their son. "It takes a long time to get over the shock. Oh, yeah. A *long* time," said Warrener softly.

The memories of the man remain indelible. "His smile, his laugh," said Warrener. "Everyone always says that about people they've lost. But Monty really was a good-hearted, laugh-at-yourself kind of guy that didn't take things too seriously and just tried to enjoy himself. You miss that type of person."

From Phoenix, 2004 Flames assistant coach Jim Playfair recalled Montador's unique ability to relieve tension with a joke or some tomfoolery that helped deal with pressure-packed situations.

Tragedy is no stranger to professional sports, of course. And so through the passing years, the Calgary Flames have suffered their share of loss: "Badger" Bob Johnson succumbing to brain cancer. First-round pick George Pelawa dying in a car crash in 1986. Mickey Renaud, captain of the Ontario Hockey League's Windsor Spitfires, passing away at age 19 of hypertrophic cardiomyopathy, a rare heart disease.

The death of Montador, the funny, happy-go-lucky, blue-collar defenseman who in his way came to symbolize the improbable four-series run of 2004, struck an emotional chord. "Nobody had a bad word to say about Steve," said a somber Martin Gelinas, OT hero of the 2004 run and a Calgary assistant coach by the day the news broke.

Flames assistant GM Craig Conroy found himself in an airport when he heard the awful news. "My first reaction?" he said at the time. "I hoped it was a mistake. It had to be a mistake... I couldn't believe it.

"Jarome and Kipper aside, in 2004 we were just a bunch of lunch-pail players that came together, worked hard, and went farther than anyone could've imagined. The one thing about Monty, he was fun to be around.

"He just came every day, carrying his lunch pail, clocked in, and you appreciated him for it. Whatever you needed, Monty did. Big hit? Block a shot? Stick up for a teammate? Then he scores that huge OT goal in Game 1 against San Jose.

"Such a big influence on the team. Everybody had a part, played it to the hilt, and that's why we got as far as we did."

"Steve was a good friend off the ice," said Gelinas. "Someone who lived with my family for more than six months when I was in Florida. He was a family member. Someone that cared.

"He had a lot of good energy. He was sharp. A very intelligent guy. Obviously he had some demons that he had to deal with, but what I'll remember about Steve—he was just a caring guy for his teammates, a family member and friend. Everybody goes through dips and everybody deals with it differently. At the end of the day, I'm not too sure of the details, so I just want to leave it that he was a friend, a family member I care about."

In L.A., former Flames boss Darryl Sutter, a man who values effort and commitment and sacrifice above all else—all those Montador intangibles—paid tribute. "He was a real popular guy, a real smart guy," Sutter told the *Los Angeles Times*. "Obviously he had some demons. The last lockout, the 48-game lockout, he was in Chicago by then. He missed most of that season…he came into the lockout year with a concussion and missed most of that year and was hoping to get cleared. It was late in the year and they put him on waivers. He went to Rockford and never did play [with Chicago]. I spent some time with him in the conference finals because he was in Chicago. So that was good."

In the time that has elapsed since Montador's passing, Rhett Warrener has helped develop a program for players exiting the game that is hockey-specific but available, useful, to all. "When Steve passed away last year," he explained, "I was on the radio talking about what life is like after you leave the game and how you can get lost. I got a call from a guy, and in the last year we've spent a lot of time throwing around ideas, putting together a yearlong program, things to think about, available to players when they do finally leave the game.

"As players, we all think when we're finished that we've got it all figured out, but you quickly learn that life is different away from that environment you've known for so long."

In Calgary, for his role on a wondrous moment forever caught in time, Steve Montador will never be forgotten. "A lot of us on that team were a lot like Steve," said Warrener. "Mid-level players who worked their butts off to get to the NHL, and that hard work turned into a career. That's all we really were. Yeah, there were a couple of guys who stood out…Jarome [Iginla] and Miikka [Kiprusoff], having that breakout, 'Who is this new goaltender?' kind of year. But other than that, just a bunch of pluggers who came together, believed in each other, and went further than anyone could've imagined.

"Monty was a hardworking team guy. And that's no small thing. Friends with everyone. You couldn't not like Steve Montador. That was his personality. He epitomized what we all held dear, what we valued as a team. And as people."

92 Johnny Hockey

As the pint-sized prodigy made his first official appearance as an NHLer, having collected both his Hobey Baker Award and signed his first pro contract the day before in Philadelphia, a media wag slumped in the stands at Rogers Arena in Vancouver, mandatory Styrofoam coffee cup at the ready, strained for a better look at the focus of all the fuss. "Where," he joked, "is the rest of him?"

The situation and date: practice on April 12, 2014, the day before Game 82 of another playoff-deprived season for the Calgary Flames. Johnny Gaudreau would open his NHL goal-scoring account the night. Where was the rest of him? Well, that was it. But it was more than enough.

No one since Theo Fleury had created the kind of buzz at the Scotiabank Saddledome as the kid from Carney's Point, New Jersey, who learned to skate at the Hollydell Ice Arena in Sewell, New Jersey, where his dad, Guy, was (and is) hockey director. Guy would help improve his son's skating by running a trail of Skittles—a favorite candy—five feet apart along the ice as bait. That unorthodox ploy obviously worked and only added to the player's legend.

Sixty-four points, including a freshman-high 40 assists, to tie the late-charging Mark Stone of Ottawa for the rookie scoring lead of 2015. An All-Star Game appearance. A Calder Trophy finalist nod. An All-Rookie Team berth up front. Not that the path could be described as pothole-free. Without a point in the opening five games of his rookie season, struggling to find his niche at the pro level, Coach Bob Hartley sat Gaudreau for a game in Columbus in order to let him decompress a bit.

Two nights later, back in the lineup, he sniped a goal and added an assist in Winnipeg, and never looked back. On December 22 at the Staples Center in L.A., Gaudreau bagged his first career hat trick, becoming, at 21, the youngest Flame to do so since Joe Nieuwendyk on December 28, 1987.

Johnny Hockey, who signed a six-year extension keeping him in Calgary until 2022, has already made his mark on the franchise.

So much about him cried out for superlatives. His growing fame as Johnny Hockey, the point machine with the Boston College Eagles, a national champion. A World Junior showcase that saw him lead the tournament in scoring as the US claimed gold. All the mushrooming collegiate success for a 104th overall pick had Calgary fans unsettled. The unease grew as Gaudreau spurned initial Flames advances and returned to British Columbia and continued his schooling. People were convinced that was all nothing but a ploy in order to try and facilitate a trade away from the Flames and to a US market.

Then there was the unfounded speculation that the wee one would be splattered like a bug on a windshield when the pitiless carnivores who played defense in the NHL locked him into their sights. "He makes a move or throws a fake and two feet of space is suddenly five or 10 feet of space," marveled Hartley. "This you cannot teach. This is something you're born with."

After Gaudreau ghosted in to score twice against the Oilers in a 16-second span in late December, the customary 19,000-plus inside the Saddledome began a two-syllable chant: "John-NY! John-NY! John-NY!"

"That," said Gaudreau afterward, "was a first time for me. Definitely. Someone chanting my name. Pretty special. It took me a couple seconds there to realize they were saying my name. But it was pretty cool." That chant will be reverberating around the Saddledome for years to come.

In short order, as a result of Hartley's famous line tinkering, Gaudreau soon found kindred spirits in second-year center Sean Monahan and the crafty Jiri Hudler. During the second half of the campaign, they were as good a line as any in the league.

Meanwhile, the publicity machine was working overtime. Calgary's late-February swing through major US East Coast markets—Manhattan, Philly, Jersey, Boston—morphed into a media sideshow. The Johnny Hockey tagline that had taken hold during his college days was officially trademarked. "We were concerned," agent Lewis Gross explained, "that people were going to abuse the Johnny Hockey name."

It's a name already synonymous in Cowtown and across the league with sorcery, with speed and skill and audacity. In only three years, Johnny Gaudreau has—along with Monahan, defenseman T.J. Brodie, Dougie Hamilton, and Matthew Tkachuk—come to embody the Calgary Flames moving forward.

"Probably everybody says this now, but I saw how special he was right from the start," laughed assistant coach Martin Gelinas. "He's got a gift of knowing when to pass the puck, when to keep it, when to attract people, how to create separation. And that wow factor. I mean, even we're sitting there going 'Wow!' He's got that confidence, that gift. Creativity. Imagination. He's a mix of a lot of guys. At the end of the day, he has that wow factor because he has to. He's not a big guy. He isn't going to drive people through the boards or overpower them in front of the net. But he makes things happen. Incredible things."

Gaudreau followed those incredible things up with even more audacious achievements, hitting the 30-goal mark and finishing with 78 points, good for sixth in the league, in 2015–16, his second full season.

After prolonged negotiations, the 23-year-old restricted free agent signed a six-year, $40.5 million deal on October 10, 2016, just two days before the next season was set to open in Edmonton. Crisis averted.

93 Take the Tour

Rick Tulsie, it's perfectly safe to say, is a man passionate about his work. "I grew up in Calgary, in Inglewood, near the Saddledome," said Tulsie. "It was being built for the Olympics when I was going to school. So, in a way, I've really been there from the start. I'm a local boy. I'm a Flames fan. So this, for me, is…perfect."

For those keen on an insider's peek into the inner workings of the arena—whether you were an unabashed fan of Lanny McDonald or Al MacInnis back in the day or partial to today's stars such as Sean Monahan and Johnny Gaudreau—let Rick Tulsie be your guide through a tour of their home away from home.

In terms of flat-out energy and enthusiasm, Badger Bob Johnson has nothing on this guy. From such automatics the Flames' dressing room and the opponents room, you'll see it all. And uou're in good hands. In 2017, Tulsie received the Mayor's White Hat Award in recognition of his stellar contribution to tourism in the city.

"I've met Flames fans from all over the world," he reports. "From Switzerland, Germany, even Brazil. Last year, I met people from Hong Kong taking the tour.

"A lot of my enthusiasm comes from people that travel to different arenas all over the world and stadiums like the Bird's Nest in [Beijing] China and how they're struck by the Saddledome and the stories over the years. About the '89 Cup-winning team…. The fact that the Zamboni driver's been there since day one. There are only a handful of arenas in North America that can accommodate international ice, and the Saddledome is one of them.

"And some of the people who take our tour aren't even big hockey fans. They tell me they fell in love with the Flames' logo, they're here in Calgary and so…"

Tulsie's been shepherding devotees from near and far through the building's ins and outs, nooks and crannies, for five years now, three times a week, three times a day, an hour on average, though the summer months, starting June 1 until the end of September—except on event days, naturally. Best of all, the visit's absolutely free. (Longer private tours for groups are also available, through Flames customer service, for a donation to the Flames' charitable foundation).

Opened for business on September 24, 1983, the Dome, at the then-astronomical cost $97.7 million, is now the second-oldest building still housing an NHL team. Only the "new" Madison Square Garden, christened in 1968, has more stories to tell.

Tulsie, naturally, is a virtual encyclopedia of Dome facts, figures, and lore. For instance, he's quick to tell you, the roof on the building remains, 33 years after opening, the world's largest free-floating concrete structure. "Every time you're inside looking up," Tulsie reported, "it's actually moving 27 meters. You tell people that and they're like, 'Wow! Get outta here....'"

"Engineering-wise, it was one of the most advanced structures of its time. Think about it: construction started in '80–81. There were [rotary] phones then. No iPads, no computers. There's so much history there. So much has happened between then and now.

"And of course I talk about the flood [of 2013]. Due to the damage inflicted by the flood waters, most fans don't know this, but everything from Row 8 down is brand new. Everything."

The clock, cautions Tulsie, is ticking. A reminder of the relentless march of time is the old, 7,500-seat Corral, situated across the street from the Dome, which was home to the Flames for their first three seasons in Calgary. Nothing remains relevant forever.

"I tell all my friends, book a tour. Especially now that there's a time frame involved, with talks ongoing about a new arena. Come and see behind the scenes of an amazing architectural and engineering building.

"A new arena's going to be grand. That new house, that new car, right? But I always tell people the Saddledome is like the home you grew up in. You mention it or see it and it and those amazing kitchen stories of your family, the good Christmases, the bad Christmases. You'll always remember that old house won't you? Because it holds so many personal memories. So it'll always be special."

94 Bob Hartley: Populist

Even the general manager at the time, Jay Feaster, could not have predicted the eventual impact of May 31, 2012. That was the day the Flames hired Bob Hartley as coach. At the time, Hartley'd been out of the NHL for basically five seasons, since his Atlanta run, a recycled TV pundit who'd fled to Europe to reinvigorate his coaching career. He was an old pal of Feaster's from their days together in the Colorado Avalanche organization, assuming control of a floundering franchise. But the Stanley Cup–winning season in Denver, 2001, seemed an awfully long time ago. What was the best anyone could possibly hope for?

An escape clause provided Hartley an out from his ZSC Zurich contract should an NHL head coaching job arise. One did, with the dismissal of Brent Sutter. Hartley leapt at the chance. "I'm not looking back," he vowed at his unveiling. "I'm not here to run autopsies. To assign blame. To pick apart what went wrong. I'm not interested in the past. I'm looking forward. Every coach is like a new chef in a restaurant. You come in with your recipe book, and the players are the ingredients."

Mixing a blend of populist PR spinner in front of the company backdrop and tough taskmaster behind closed doors, Bob Hartley became a popular figure in the city. He wooed the media, spread the doctrine, wrangled the most out of his players, and pushed the collective to an improbable postseason appearance.

"You go to get gas," he marveled during the improbable 2015 playoff push, "and, gosh, you have to sprint to the nozzle because fans, they want to put the gas in the car for you."

That degree of adulation required some time to take hold. Hartley's first season behind the Calgary bench was a lockout-abbreviated 48-game campaign that finished six games below .500, at 19–25–4.

There was a 19–13 finish to 2013–14, buoying hopes. Sure, the Flames were all but mathematically eliminated when they made their run, but at long last there was something positive to draw on.

If those closing stages hinted at an upswing in possibilities, the next year short-circuited even the most avid fan's credulity. A whopping 20-point regular-season improvement. Calgary's first playoff berth in six seasons. Only the second time past the first round of postseason in a quarter century. The Flames came back from the dead more often than Bela Lugosi, fashioning numerous third-period renaissances. They overcame a potentially crippling eight-game losing streak at a critical part of the year and the loss of influential captain Mark Giordano down the stretch to a torn pectoral muscle.

In the midst of all the unexpected goodness, a new GM in charge, Brad Treliving, handed his commander in chief a richly deserved extension with his contract set to expire at season's close. "This," said Treliving, "should send a clear message to our dressing room that Bob is not only the coach for today but moving forward."

In retrospect, Hartley's hiring dovetailed nicely into the long-overdue rebuild (yes, he even used the word). Since he arrived, the franchise's twin titans for more than a decade departed:

Jarome Iginla dealt to Pittsburgh, Miikka Kiprusoff retired. Familiar faces were offloaded or allowed/encouraged to venture elsewhere—Michael Cammalleri, Lee Stempniak, Alex Tanguay, Curtis Glencross, Sven Baertschi, Chris Butler, Brian McGrattan, Jay Bouwmeester, Shane O'Brien.

The kids—Sean Monahan, T.J. Brodie, Joe Colborne, Kris Russell—all were handed increased responsibilities and made major developmental strides. With many skeptics expecting him to fold like a piece of origami, tiny Johnny Gaudreau exploded on the scene to great acclaim. Old campaigners Jiri Hudler (the Lady Byng Memorial Trophy winner) and D-man Dennis Wideman played way above expectations. Suddenly the Flames were fun again. Winning again. Relevant again.

A happy blend of many elements? Yes, indeed. But never underestimate Hartley's imprint on all this. "Details," said captain Mark Giordano. "It's No. 1 in his system. He's tough on guys but tough the right way. He's gotten a lot out of our group, and the reason is because he's hard but he's fair. He's demanding. There are definitely days where Bob's hard on some of our young guys, and they must be saying, 'Oh, man...' but years from now when they look back, being taught at the start of their careers to play the right way, especially in your own zone, they're going to appreciate it."

The tough-love approach paid off. "Bob has not wavered one inch from training camp," said assistant coach Martin Gelinas. "We're a team [that,] at the beginning of the season, nobody gave a chance to. And we're there. You have to know when to be hard and when to pull back. Some people have a gift for it, and I think Bob has that good feel in that area."

His longtime collaborator, assistant coach Jacques Cloutier, praised Hartley's mix of old-school and up-with-the-times attributes. "The biggest thing about Bob, he's really fair. We always tell our guys, 'It's not about "our" way, it's about playing the "right" way.' He makes everybody accountable. I wouldn't say he's mellowed, exactly. But as you get older, you get more mature. You have to adjust more to the players now than, say, 15 years ago. It's a big difference. The communication is so much better now."

For his contribution to an astounding season, Hartley was named one of three finalists for Coach of the Year. "If he doesn't win the Jack Adams Trophy," said Treliving with flat finality, "there should be an inquiry. "This one should be a layup." And sure enough, on June 24 Bob Hartley ambled up onstage at the NHL Awards to pick up his Jack Adams hardware, the only Calgary coach ever to do so.

In the follow-up season to their resurgence, though, the Flames stumbled out of the gate, never recovered, and finished a whopping 20 points behind their 97-point output of 2014–15. So on May 3, 2016, not yet a year after receiving the Jack Adams Trophy, Bob Hartley was fired. "This decision was not made with somebody in the on-deck circle," Treliving insisted at the media conference announcing the ouster. "This isn't about, 'Is there a prettier girl at the dance?' Bob has taken this team as far as I feel he can take it."

Hartley, in customary fashion, took the high ground a day following the decision. "There's no doubt in my mind this team is one or two years, a couple of players, away from being an excellent hockey club," he said, "and making a long push real deep in the playoffs. Obviously, it's going to be for somebody else. I fully understand the risks of our business, and I accept the responsibility."

95 The New Architect

No one else was officially interviewed. "I am *that* convinced," maintained the garrulous Brian Burke on the day of Brad Treliving's capture and public unveiling. "I've been at this a long time, so there's not a GM I can't call and say, 'Okay, if you were looking at a young guy, who'd you be looking at?' And it all kept coming back to Brad. I had one guy say to me, 'You're not going to interview anyone else, are you?' Like, incredulous.

"And everywhere I went, Brad was there. I kept bumping into Brad Treliving. Every rink I went into. I went to see [Aaron] Ekblad play, and they said, 'Oh, Tre was here.' Then I went in to see [Nick] Ritchie play, and they said, 'Tre was here the day before.' This guy, he works. And I don't think you can succeed if you don't work. So to me it was a very easy decision when we got permission."

Burke, Calgary's president of hockey operations, fully understood what he was getting. Treliving had played in the Vancouver organization when the big Irishman had control of the Canucks, and Burke knew the family well. Still, it was quite the assignment for a first-year man. As general manager, handed the keys to a decaying kingdom, entrusted with plotting the course to pull a decorated franchise back out of the mire.

Not that Treliving hadn't arrived prepared for the task. Growing up in the lap of luxury—Treliving's dad, Jim, is a former Royal Canadian Mounted Police officer who, along with partner George Melville, transformed a single Boston Pizza restaurant in Penticton into an empire. Now famous coast-to-coast for 11 seasons as a panelist on CBC TV's *Dragons' Den* (similar in format to *Shark Tank*), his net worth is estimated at $640 million.

But Brad Treliving bristled at the silver-spoon opportunity and set out on his own. A career minor-pro defenseman, he painstakingly absorbed the hockey business from the ground up. Even during his on-ice days, he'd help out in other aspects of the different organizations he played for—ticketing, marketing, etc.—broadening his scope, deepening his understanding.

The invaluable experience of starting up an entire circuit, the Western Professional Hockey League, dovetailed into seven informative years as right-hand man to Don Maloney in Phoenix with the Coyotes.

Treliving's old boss acknowledged that Calgary's gain was his loss. "Now," praised Maloney, "it's his turn in the driver's seat. Success creates opportunities, and for us to have survived our ownership saga and have some relative success on the ice, certainly people start looking at the organization and say, 'Okay, who's there, who's doing what and can they help us?' In Brad's case, he's done the work and been an important part in us surviving in the desert here, which certainly makes him attractive to other teams.

"Losing a confidant, a guy that's exposed to everything, doesn't exactly make my day, but on the other hand we're very proud and happy for him and his family. To work as hard as he did, he deserves an opportunity to run an NHL club."

Right off, Treliving displayed a cool-beyond-his-years approach. Rather than barge into a new situation, as many would, and make changes willy-nilly in an attempt to smudge his fingerprints all over the organization, he sat tight, took everything in, and made deductions. When his captain and competitive fulcrum, Mark Giordano, was lost for the year during a tense playoff run after suffering a torn bicep, he resisted the temptation to do the expedient thing, deal away young assets in order to fill a cavernous hole. And the Flames qualified for the playoffs anyway.

After taking the time to formulate his own read, he rewarded Bob Hartley by signing him to a contract extension (and Hartley rewarded Treliving by winning the Jack Adams Trophy months later). He got the indispensable Giordano signed to a contract extension. Then at the NHL draft in June, he made the biggest wave, signing blue-chip free-agent defenseman Dougie Hamilton, late of the Boston Bruins.

"How do you get better?" he repeated before his first camp in charge of the franchise began. "As an organization you get young players that push their way into the lineup. What that does, you've got players pushing, but it also puts people here on alert that there's somebody ready to grab that jersey.

"It's a process. But I can feel—whether by injury, whether directed by performance—it getting there. You're going to see more players here through the course of the season.

"Players are intelligent people. They look around and see there's competition. You don't have to be too intelligent to under-stand guys are pushing you."

The GM certainly isn't afraid to push. "We're excited about what's ahead," cautioned Brad Treliving, a nice mixture of shiny-surface optimism and cold, hard reality. "But let's also keep it in context. We have lots of work to do. And we need to get better in a lot of areas."

Those words, despite the upswing in fortune, are as true today as they were back then.

96 Renaissance

A new general manager scoping out territory. A coach entering the third and final year of his contract year with nary a whisper of an extension that would put him on more solid footing. Not a sniff of playoffs for five agonizing years. Their prized rookie as wide as a swizzle stick. A sub-.500 team in a perilous division, a crushing conference. The first full-on season of the—*shhhhhhh!*—"rebuild," and for the first time in more than a decade, no Iginla or Kiprusoff anywhere in sight to prop 'em up. "We just kept proving people wrong," said Coach Bob Hartley, with a helpless shrug.

A murderous six-game road swing in the wake of a curtain-raising loss to Vancouver at the Saddledome was supposed to spell doom. The Flames returned home in good health, 4–2 on their travels. A pitiless eight-game losing streak from December 6 through 20 had the naysayers prophesying disaster (the team accrued 54 points from then to the finish). The incalculable loss of captain Mark Giordano to a torn bicep in New Jersey on February 25 would surely be the end of them, skeptics said (they went 12–9 the rest of the way).

They were harder to kill than a salacious rumor and came back from the dead time after time. One insane night in Ottawa, in early March, they were on the final stop of a wearying seven-game trip necessitated by the Brier, Canada's men's curling championship, taking over the Saddledome. Down 4–0 in the third, apparently totally spent and the Senators on cruise control, the Flames rallied, as was becoming their custom, scoring four times in 11 minutes to send the game into OT and shock those congregated at the Canadian Tire Centre. The Senators eventually prevailed in the shootout, but out of nowhere, nothing, the Find-A-Way Flames, as they were being dubbed by that point, had conjured up a vital point. Astonishing stuff.

"Everywhere I go," said Hartley as a playoff berth loomed, "in movie theaters or on the street, restaurants, minor hockey practices, gas stations, there's a fire in town right now. A big fire. For myself, I'm just trying to feed as much wood into that big fire as possible.

"I know I keep bringing it up, but those two standing ovations we got after losses last year? You just don't see this. Anywhere. These people, they deserve a team to be excited about."

Added Giordano: "I feel like the entire city has our backs."

So much went so right in the season of renaissance for an ailing franchise. Freshman Johnny Gaudreau turned out to be every bit as magnetic, as elusive, as drop-dead fun to watch as any Flames-obsessed fan could've hoped for in his wildest dreams. Giordano was well on his way to a Norris Trophy before the bicep tear. In only his second season, Sean Monahan continued to blossom into a fine two-way center, tying Hudler for the team goal-scoring lead, at 31. The netminding, while not quite on a Kipper-esque level, nevertheless held up. Wiry Kris Russell set a record for blocked shots, 283, his total more than that of 25 NHL goalies listed in the final stats (including two full-time backups).

There were so many career seasons out of so many individuals. A franchise-high three end-of-season major trophy finalists: Gaudreau (Calder), Hudler (Lady Byng), and Hartley (Jack Adams). And, it played out, two winners. And there was a hard-to-wrap-your-head-around 20-point regular-season improvement, to 97. Most vitally, the Flames actually reached the playoffs, qualifying in Game 81—eliminating the reigning Stanley Cup champion L.A. Kings for good measure, 3–1, at a rapturous Saddledome.

And the good times weren't over yet, knocking off the Vancouver Canucks in six games to push past their opening round of the postseason for only the second time since the Cup-winning spring of 1989.

Hartley could be hard and demanding within the room, but he instinctively knew when to lay off too. After being thrashed and overmatched 6–1 by the Anaheim Ducks in Game 1 of their second-round series, rather than bag skate the troops, he popped in a DVD of winger Brandon Bollig, then seven years old, making his acting debut playing the son of former St. Louis tough guy Tony Twist in the long-forgotten 2002 western *Defiance*. "The boys had a good chuckle with this," reported Hartley gleefully.

The magic carpet ride had to end. And it did, in Game 5 of that Anaheim series on a Corey Perry OT goal at their personal chamber of horrors, the Honda Center. But the smiles, the chuckles, the achievements, were many. What an amazing ride it had been.

"This series against the Ducks was priceless," said Hartley the night the season ended. "Now they know how they have to suffer, how hard it is, how unbelievable the pace is. That's no guarantee of success, but it's another page in our book. We have a long way to go, but those playoffs are a great investment. We have a long way to go."

Maybe. But just think of how far they'd come.

97 The Big League Experience and Then Some

Want to feel like (or at least fantasize) you're Johnny Gaudreau, shedding a dithering defenseman at the blueline with the ease of a snake slipped out of its skin before wheeling in to leave the goalie floundering? Or come as close as possible to actually believing you're Miikka Kiprusoff or Mike Vernon flashing the leather to deny a gilt-edged scoring chance?

Been attending Calgary Flames tilts in person for years or watching them from afar on television? Ever wonder what a typical game situation for NHLers entails? Then the Big League Experience is right up your alley. For $5,000 your team and an opposition crew can live the way the pros do on a typical game day. At least, outside of the morning skate and obligatory afternoon nap.

The Big League Experience offers NHL atmosphere and one and a half hours on the Dome ice that since 1983 has hosted so many memorable playoff games, Canada Cup jousts, international competitions, the 1988 Olympic Hockey Tournament, and the 1985 NHL All-Star Game. In such an environment, scanning the upper bowl of seats while taking the whole thing in, you might even con yourself into believing you're capable of shooting the puck every bit as hard as Al MacInnis.

Participants are introduced and spotlighted pre–puck drop. There are nameplates in the dressing rooms for each player (the Flames' alumni room and sometimes the visiting NHL quarters, but no, sorry, not *that* dressing room) and jerseys hung up, waiting, adding to the big-league feel.

There won't be 19,000-plus fans roaring to cheer the teams on, but an in-game host and game-night-style music promise to keep the joint rockin'. And there's nothing like hearing that familiar goal horn go off after scoring a goal a la Jarome Iginla.

"We have our minor hockey Big League, which is our most popular, but we also accommodate corporate clients too," explains Carley Salive, assistant to the director of sales for the Flames. "We've received very good feedback from our customers; we have teams that come back every year.

"The corporate events can be quite elaborate. We just did one where they had their ice time, we rolled out the red carpet for their anthem singer and a big dinner reception afterwards. So the experience can be customized to whatever the client would like."

Added enticements for the minor-hockey outfits only too happy to live a dream: Hustle & Heart awards are presented to one player from each team at game's end along with 100 vouchers for each of the Western Hockey League's Calgary Hitmen, National Lacrosse League's Roughnecks, and Canadian Football League's Calgary Stampeders.

The sessions are based on arena availability, naturally, meaning space is extremely limited and the concept is a popular one. Interested parties should contact the club directly at 403-777-2177 to see which dates are available.

Short of signing a big-league contract, it's as close as you're likely to come to the real thing.

Meanwhile, for other flaming C–related options for the true supporter, either for homesteaders those or arriving in town for a short time, consider the following alternatives.

If it's licensed apparel you're after, Fan Attic has a wide variety of gear and knickknacks to please even the pickiest of partisans, from game-used pucks to game-worn jerseys to player bobbleheads to children's Harvey the Hound slippers. The other three sports properties owned by Calgary Sports and Entertainment Inc.—the Canadian Football League Stampeders, National Lacrosse League Roughnecks, and Western Hockey League Hitmen—are also widely featured. Visit online at www.flamesport.ca, or in person at any of the three Calgary locations: North Hill Mall, inside the Saddledome, and Calgary International Airport.

On the links, team captain Mark Giordano hosts the Italian Open every August in support of Team Giordano's involvement with high-needs children, and tee times are available. So if you're keen to rub shoulders with a Norris Trophy–caliber player and all-around good guy, this one might be for you.

Can't secure game tickets? If you're in town, there's no end of options to watch the game with like-minded fans. Schanks Sports Grill (both north and south locations), Hudson's Canadian Pub,

Canadian Brewhouse, National, the Pint, Cowboys, 1410, Bank and Baron, Shark Club, Jack Astor's, and Loco Lou's are all popular places to catch the game, a bite, and a drink. And for families, any one of the numerous Boston Pizza locations are a good bet.

One unique program for kids ages four through eight years who are totally new to the game is Learn to Play, a summer initiative spearheaded by the Flames and Hockey Alberta. Big-league alumni such as Curtis Glencross, Rhett Warrener, and Jamie Macoun from the '89 Stanley Cup–winning team are among the ex-players who've been involved. For $175, kids previously unregistered receive brand-new gear, head-to-toe, and a six-week camp introducing them to hockey. Locations may vary, but the 2017 camps were run in Lethbridge, Sylvan Lake, and Calgary. Registration details and more information is available through the team.

98 Red Mile Revived

On April 25, 2015, down a familiar stretch of 17th Ave. SW, in Calgary, they partied as if it were 2004. Or 1989. Or 1986. In fact, they partied harder. The Calgary Flames had overturned a 3–0 Game 6 deficit that night to eliminate the Vancouver Canucks and move on to the second round of the Stanley Cup playoffs for the first time in 11 years. The famous Red Mile was back in business.

More than 12,000 revelers gathered to party. Most of the fun was in good spirits. Giant cardboard cutout heads of current Flames stars—such as Johnny Gaudreau, T.J. Brodie, and Sean Monahan—were hung triumphantly from light poles. There was the usual spate of horn-honking and firecracker-lighting. One nervous suitor used the festivities to summon up his courage, get down on one knee, and ask his girlfriend to be his wife. (She said yes.)

But as so often happens, the antics escalated to a sometimes-regrettable level. The Red Mile quickly turned infamous worldwide for a few liberated females exposing their breasts and moronic chants such as "Flames in six! Show us your tits!" and "Show your cans for Monahan!" egging them on. Women were being targeted, reporters hassled.

One loser was arrested for wandering around wearing no pants. There were 13 stabbings, most on the "smaller scale" according to the Calgary constabulary, and the 11-game push that captured the city's imagination cost the police $850,000. Still and all…

"I'm putting it down as being highly successful in terms of public safety," police superintendent Ray Robitaille told reporters after the Flames' five-game elimination by the Anaheim Ducks in round two. "I wouldn't say I'm surprised. I've always been impressed with Calgarians and how they behave in sporting events and, in general, any kind of public gathering."

Still, the unfortunate side of "fandom"—using the term loosely—was enough to prompt the Flames organization to address the issue. "It's not negative behavior, it's stupid," spat Calgary Flames head coach Bob Hartley. "I'm sorry for my language, but there's a few jerks right there that are tarnishing the reputation of our organization and our city. That has no place. If you want to be part of the Red Mile, you are a Calgary Flame. We need all kinds of fans. We need babies, we need men, women. These are our real fans. We're better than this. I'm sure it's a very little group. I'd like someone to kick their asses for me."

Things were far less raucous 11 years earlier. Back then, given the destruction of many sporting "celebrations" over the years, the revelry was pretty tame, and Flames partisans were considered exceptionally well-behaved.

"I remember, in 2004, watching it on the news," recalled Hartley, who at the time was coach of the Atlanta Thrashers. "I had a friend working at Reebok at that time, telling me that every factory they had around the world, they were manufacturing one jersey—the flaming *C*—because they were going like hotcakes.

"Right now we feel the same [adoration]. You go to restaurants, you go to shopping malls, you go to put gas [in your car]—gosh, you've got to sprint to the nozzle because there are fans who want to put the gas in your car for you. That's how crazy it is right now. It's fun. We're a big part of the culture of this city."

The original handle Red Mile is credited to former Jack-FM radio host Mel Risdon. As more and more and more people began gathering in the bar/nightclub area of 17th Ave. as the Jarome Iginla / Miikka Kiprusoff–fueled Flames continued on their upset binge, she felt the stretch needed a tagline. So Risdon asked for her listeners to help out. A few of the other favored options? Iggy Way. Flaming Mile. Stanley Way.

The vote came down being between Red Mile—Risdon's contribution—or Red Avenue. A whopping majority of responders, 80 percent, sided with Red Mile. And the nickname stuck.

The Red Mile was, in essence, an updated offshoot of the Electric Avenue festivities that celebrated the Flames' earlier two runs to the Stanley Cup finals, in 1986 and 1989. Electric Avenue—closed in the 1990s—was a strip of nightclubs located on 11th Ave. SW and became party central for hockey fans. The night of the May 25, 1989, Cup-clinching win, an estimated 25,000—faces painted with flaming *C* motifs or adorned in bushy Lanny McDonald trademark mustaches—began to gather at 3:30 PM local time, two hours before puck drop of Game 6 at the Montreal Forum. "There is," Inspector Ray Wheppler told the *Calgary Herald*, from an overseeing rooftop vantage point, "an excessive amount of liquor down there."

When the Flames came back to win Game 6 4–2 and claim the series, becoming the only invading team to lift the Stanley Cup in the most venerated of hockey shrines, chants of "Lan-ny! Lan-ny!" and "We're No. 1!" could probably be heard as far north as Edmonton. The celebrations that night broke up around 2:30 AM, according to police.

99 CalgaryNEXT

When it was unveiled on October 15, 1983, at a cost of $97.7 million (roughly $214 million today), the Olympic Saddledome had been a wonder. Over the ensuing 32 years, the onetime belle of the ball has undergone a few facelifts. Functional still, but hardly the great beauty of past days.

For the better part of two years, rumors had been circulating that a blueprint/cost breakdown for a brand-spanking-new arena in Calgary were close at hand. With work on the $480 million Rogers Place in Edmonton—$604 million for the entire project—to replace Rexall Place already under way, the heat was on the Flames to keep up with their northern neighbors.

When finally brought to light, the mega-project turned out to be CalgaryNEXT, an ambitious, sprawling $890 million venture to include not only an all-the-bells-and-whistles 20,000-seat hockey arena, but a covered 30,000-seat stadium for the Canadian Football League's Calgary Stampeders—who have been playing in McMahon Stadium on the city's north side since 1960—and a long-overdue fieldhouse that would include a FIFA-sized soccer field and a 400-meter track. The location of the project has been blueprinted for the West Village area of downtown Calgary, adjacent to the Bow River.

Under the initial proposal, Calgary Sports and Entertainment—which owns the Flames, Stampeders, National Lacrosse League Calgary Roughnecks, and Western Hockey League Calgary Hitmen—would pony up $200 million, the remaining $690 million generated through a $250 million ticket tax, $200 million from the city for the fieldhouse, and $240 million from a community revitalization levy.

What was left unaccounted for was the remediation of an estimated two million liters of toxic creosote in the land slated for the project, and who exactly would foot the bill for that. Some estimates adding the cleanup into the package had the total cost rising to $1.5 billion.

The timing of the announcement didn't help matters. A change in provincial power—from longstanding Conservative rule to the NDP, and the freefalling price of oil—only added to the controversy.

The proposal sparked instant debate, its supporters outlining the importance of the Flames and the benefits to the community as a whole, its detractors pointing to the cost and those weighty questions still to be answered regarding the creosote cleanup.

"CalgaryNEXT is a bold new vision for Calgary," said Calgary Sports and Entertainment Corp. president and CEO Ken King in announcing the blueprint. "The question is simple: 'Is this good for Calgary, and is this good for Calgarians?' If we can come to an affirmative answer, we'll get to the starting line of a very difficult, a very arduous process to bring this home and to bring it to fruition."

One of the staunchest skeptics of the bid happens to be Calgary mayor Naheed Nenshi, outspoken in his caution at spending public tax dollars for professional sports teams, particularly during such a delicate economic time for his city. The battle lines were quickly drawn.

In mid-January, NHL commissioner Gary Bettman paid a visit to Cowtown and spoke at a chamber of commerce breakfast, using the forum to throw his clout behind the project. "It is not an overstatement," Bettman declared, "to say the future stability, viability, and continuity of the Calgary Flames, and perhaps the city of Calgary, rests on the achievement of CalgaryNEXT. If this project is going to happen, the mayor needs to embrace it, the city needs to embrace it. If he's not prepared to embrace it, then the people will have to deal with that.

"I'm having trouble understanding why there hasn't been further progress on CalgaryNEXT. No matter what anyone thinks of the proposed CalgaryNEXT project or the cost of the project, the cost is never going to be lower than it is today."

A plan B involving an event center in Victoria Park on the Stampede Grounds was discussed by the city, with the original CalgaryNEXT concept put "on pause" by the hockey club.

During a March 2017 visit to Calgary, the commissioner and the mayor sat down for discussions. In a media conference later that same day, Bettman later referred to the Saddledome as an "old, antiquated, inefficient building."

He went on, "In terms of amenities, in terms of facilities, in terms of egress and the like, for all the events that go here, this building was built in the 1980s. They don't build buildings like this anymore. It's a grand old building, it's got a great roofline, it's historic in many ways, but...these aren't the facilities our hockey teams typically have."

The game of hockey goes on. The game of politicking continues, too.

100 Where Are They Now?

They remain the standard for all who followed. The Class of 1989. The individuals who made up the lone Stanley Cup–winning team in Calgary Flames franchise history. A little thinner and grayer up top now in some cases, a little thicker around the waistline in others—some remain in hockey while others embarked on business careers after their playing days were done.

Here's what the best team in hockey in 1989 is doing today:

Goaltenders
- 30. Mike Vernon: Sales rep for Triumph Tubular
- 31. Rick Wamsley: Until recently, goaltending coach for the Ottawa Senators

Defense
- 2. Al MacInnis: Vice president of hockey operations for the St. Louis Blues
- 4. Brad McCrimmon—Died at 52 in a plane crash that took the lives of 37 members of the KHL Lokomotiv Yaroslavl team on September 7, 2011
- 5. Dana Murzyn: Owner of Diamond Wood Products, Calgary
- 6. Ric Nattress: Public speaking, emcee work, charity fundraising, Toronto
- 20. Gary Suter: Retired, enjoying life in the wilds of Minnesota
- 23. Ken Sabourin: Owner of Sabourin Insurance, color analyst on Washington Capitals Radio Network
- 34. Jamie Macoun: Macoun Real Estate

- 55. Rob Ramage: Development coach for the Montreal Canadiens

Forwards
- 7. RW Joe Mullen: Most recently an assistant coach for the Philadelphia Flyers
- 9. RW Lanny McDonald: Works for Flint Energy and owns Tamarack Brewing Company in Lakeside, Montana
- 10. LW Gary Roberts: Owner of Gary Roberts High Performance Center and Fitness Institute
- 11. LW Colin Patterson: Works for Strad Energy
- 12. RW Hakan Loob: Retired as president of hockey operations for Färjestad, Swedish Elite League, following the 2016–17 season
- 14. C/RW Theoren Fleury: Motivational speaker, sexual abuse advocate, country singer
- 16. LW Sergei Pryakhin: Formerly a coach in the KHL
- 17. C Jiri Hrdina: Scout for the Dallas Stars
- 19. RW Tim Hunter: Head coach for the WHL Moose Jaw Warriors
- 22. RW Mark Hunter: Director of player personnel for the Toronto Maple Leafs
- 24. LW Jim Peplinski: Vice president of business development for the Calgary Flames
- 25. C Joe Nieuwendyk: Pro scout and advisor for the Carolina Hurricanes
- 27. LW Brian MacLellan: Senior vice present / general manager for the Washington Capitals
- 29. C Joel Otto: Assistant coach for the WHL Calgary Hitmen
- 39. C Doug Gilmour: General manager for the Ontario Hockey League Kingston Frontenacs

Coaches/Management/Staff

- General Manager Cliff Fletcher: Senior adviser for the Toronto Maple Leafs
- Assistant GM Al MacNeil: Retired, living in Calgary
- Assistant to the President Al Coates: Senior adviser of special projects for Hockey Canada
- Head Coach Terry Crisp: broadcaster for the Nashville Predators
- Tom Watt: Pro scout for the Toronto Maple Leafs
- Goaltending Consultant Glenn Hall: Retired in Stony Plain, Alberta, and still pondering painting the barn
- Trainer Jim "Bearcat" Murray: Flames ambassador
- Assistant Trainer Al Murray: Works for environmental and energy services company Tervita
- Equipment Manager Bobby Stewart: Retired, living in Florida

Acknowledgments

It's been more than three decades of traipsing along, hanging out in airports and rinks and hotels. A sometimes maddening, often exhausting, and always wildly fulfilling existence.

I'm old enough, lucky enough, to have profound memories of the grandeur of the regal Montreal Forum, the anthem reverberating around the foundations of the old Chicago Stadium, the unbeatable press-box view inside Boston Garden, and munching on the unbeatable *chien chauds* (hot dogs) at le Colisée in Quebec City. Of life before charters when everybody flew commercial (and usually in a middle seat, somewhere in the vicinity of the rear washrooms) and players were only too happy to chat. When you could land a one-on-one, 45-minute post–morning skate interview with, say, a Marcel Dionne for a takeout that had to be done prior to game time. Great days.

I owe a large debt to so many fantastic people whom I've worked with over the years who have encouraged me. From the Flames: "Badger" Bob Johnson, Pierre Page, Al Coates, Dave King, Terry Crisp, Cliff Fletcher, Bob Hartley, Brad Treliving, and Glen Gulutzan, and others. My friendly rival at the *Calgary Herald* during those beat years, Eric Duhatschek, a Hall of Famer in everything, and Scott Cruickshank, the talented beat writer after I jumped ship, changed papers, and was bumped up to columnist. The lovely folks at Calgary Sports and Entertainment, who let me continue to write when I was at unexpected loose ends. Sports editors such as Jack Matheson, Bill Davidson, Pat Doyle, Peter Menzies, Larry Wood, and the rest. The copy-reading deskers patient enough to fix my infamous "dangling Johnsons" and somehow make me look good. Thanks to the media-relations crews in Winnipeg, Edmonton, and Calgary—my three ports of call—and all the players, too exhaustive to mention, who put up with my questions and took the time to answer them; but a special thanks to Theoren Fleury, a very busy fellow, who nonetheless agreed to pen the foreword for this book. Best. Quote. Ever.

To my Winnipeg family: my mom, Ruth; dad, Jerry—who instilled in me a love of the games people play—and brother, Dan.

And naturally, to my beautiful wife, Rita Mingo, who understands the business because she's in the business, and to my two understanding, supportive daughters, Michela and Sabrina. A No. 1 line on anyone's team. They're all a big part of this book, a big part of this career, and are owed debts that can never be repaid.

Sources

Having spent more than half a lifetime chasing around the Calgary Flames hither and yon, much of the material for this book centers around articles and interviews done firsthand. I thoroughly researched the two newspapers I used to work for, the *Calgary Sun* and *Calgary Herald*. In addition, the following old friends and acquaintances updated several chapters, filling in blanks and otherwise prodding an often wobbly memory: Theo Fleury, Jim Peplinski, Perry Berezan, Neil Sheehy, Joe Nieuwendyk, Bearcat Murray, Bob Murdoch, Doug Risebrough, Grant Kelba, Dave Elston, Martin Gelinas, Candice Goudie, Tim Hunter, Colin Patterson, Paul Reinhart, Joel Otto, Max Offenberger, Terry Crisp, Al MacNeil, Lanny McDonald, Al Coates, Kim "Santa" Thomas, Gary Suter, Dave King, John Garrett, Craig Conroy, Denis Gauthier, Scott Nichol, Gus Thorson, Grant Pollock, and Rhett Warrener. Hockey folk are notoriously generous with their time.

About the Author

George Johnson has spent the last 33 years covering the Calgary Flames. He began his association with the team as a beat reporter for the *Calgary Sun* back in 1984 before moving on to the *Calgary Herald* as columnist in 2000 for an additional 16 years and now on to Calgary Sports and Entertainment, writing for the team's website. He has traveled with the Flames to Japan, the then–Soviet Union, and the Czech Republic, as well as across North America and throughout their three Stanley Cup Finals appearances. He has also covered seven Olympic Games, four men's soccer World Cups, and three women's World Cups. In 2006 he received Sports Media Canada's Outstanding Sportswriting Award and is a proud inductee into the media wing of the Manitoba Sports Hall of Fame. He is married to Rita, also a sportswriter, and they're the lucky parents of two beautiful daughters, Michela and Sabrina.